JAPANESE CAPITALISM SINCE 1945

CRITICAL PERSPECTIVES

T. MORRIS-SUZUKI
SEIYAMA TAKURŌ
TERUOKA SHUZŌ
SUMIYA TOSHIO
KUROKAWA TOSHIO
FUJIWARA SADAO

**Edited by
T.Morris-Suzuki
T.Seiyama**

An East Gate Book

M. E. Sharpe, Inc.
Armonk, New York
London, England

An East Gate Book

Copyright © 1989 by M. E. Sharpe, Inc.

Available in the United Kingdom and Europe from M. E. Sharpe,
Publishers, 3 Henrietta Street, London WC2E 8LU.

Library of Congress Cataloging-in-Publication Data

Japanese capitalism since 1945 : critical perspectives / edited by Tessa
   Morris-Suzuki and Seiyama Takuro.
     p. cm.
  ISBN 0-87332-551-6
  1. Japan—Economic conditions—1945- 2. Capitalism—Japan—
History—20th century. I. Morris-Suzuki, Tessa. II. Seiyama,
Takuro, 1933-
HC462.9.J328   1989   89-4297
330.952'04—dc19   CIP

Printed in the United States of America

BB 10 9 8 7 6 5 4 3 2 1

Contents

Tables

Figures

Contributors

Fujiwara Sadao is professor of economics at Yamaguchi University. He has researched and published on U.S.-Japan trade relations and on Japanese investment in Southeast Asia and is joint author of *Gendai sekai keizai o toraeru* (Understanding the contemporary world economy).

Kurokawa Toshio is professor of economics at Keio Gijuku University, Tokyo. His publications include *Gendai rōdō mondai no riron* (The theory of contemporary labor problems) and *Gendai Nihon no keizai kōzō* (The structure of the contemporary Japanese economy).

Tessa Morris-Suzuki is senior lecturer in economic history at the University of New England, Australia, and has researched and published on Japan's economic relations with the Pacific region and on the social history of modern Japan. Her books include *Showa, Beyond Computopia: Automation, Information and Democracy in Japan*, and *A History of Japanese Economic Thought* (forthcoming).

Seiyama Takurō is professor of economics at Ōita University, Kyūshū, and author of numerous works on the Japanese economy, including *Nihon keizai no kōzō to hatten* (The structure and development of the Japanese economy) and (with K. Michimata) *Sengo Nihon no rōdō mondai* (Labor problems in postwar Japan).

Sumiya Toshio is professor in the department of management at Ritsumeikan University, Kyoto. He has published widely on problems relating to the structure of business in modern Japan, including *Marukushugi keiei-gaku ronsō* (Debates on the Marxist study of management), *Nihon keizai to roku dai kigyō shūdan* (The Japanese economy and the six great industrial groups) and *Sengo Nihon no kigyō keiei* (The management of enterprise in postwar Japan).

Teruoka Shuzō is professor of economics at Utsunomiya University and an expert on the development of Japanese agriculture. His works include *Nihon nōgyō mondai no tenkai* (The development of agricultural problems in Japan) and *Nihon nōgyō-shi* (A history of Japanese agriculture).

JAPANESE CAPITALISM SINCE 1945

1
Introduction:
Japanese Economic Growth,
Images and Ideologies

TESSA MORRIS-SUZUKI

For almost a century the study of economics in the West has been
dominated by the Neoclassical paradigm. Within this paradigm, the
economy is seen as a system whose operation may be objectively
analyzed using scientific principles: just as Newtonian science
seeks to discover immutable natural laws in the mechanisms of the
physical world, so Neoclassicism aims to disclose the immutable
laws hidden in the mechanisms of the economic world. The student
of the economy, therefore, is not concerned with opinion or ideology, but "solely with what is."[1]

This perspective has inevitably framed the perception of many
of the most influential English-language studies of Japanese economic development. Ohkawa Kazushi and Shinohara Miyohei,
whose painstaking reconstructions of statistical data provide the
basis for much recent research on Japanese growth, emphasize the
importance of the "historical laboratory" within which the ex-
periments performed should be "as neutral as possible to avoid
injecting one's own biases."[2] The 1960s' debates on Japanese modernization took place within the framework of an "attempt to devise a unified and objective conception of modernization,"[3] while a
more recent overview of postwar growth, noting that "history does
not belong either to the establishment or to those who fancy themselves to be antiestablishment," attempts "to grasp the flow of

postwar economic history from an objective, neutral position."[4]

In recent years, however, the limitations of Newtonian positivism have become increasingly apparent even within the traditional hard sciences themselves. As the physicist Werner Heisenberg wrote in 1958, "What we observe is not nature itself, but nature exposed to our method of questioning."[5]

In the study of a complex and controversial social system like the Japanese economy, it seems all the more certain that what is observed will be reality exposed to a specific method of questioning, and that the method of questioning itself will be defined by the social and political position of the observer in the changing relationship between Japan and the outside world.

By way of introduction to the essays that follow, I shall explore some of the influences that have molded the "method of questioning" (or, as Japanese writers would call it, the *mondai ishiki*, or "problem consciousness") within postwar studies of Japanese economic development. In particular, it is important to examine the reasons for a peculiar gap that has long existed between English-language and Japanese-language studies of Japan's economic history—a gap that many Western writers have commented on, but few have attempted to fill. This gap arises from the fact that, while a large proportion of Japanese-language works are written from a Marxian perspective, their English-language counterparts generally ignore the Japanese Marxian tradition,[6] or at most dismiss it in a few paragraphs heavily laced with words such as "dogmatic," "deterministic," and "unrealistic."[7]

Western Studies of Japanese Development: The Background

Roland Barthes begins the opening chapter of his *Empire of Signs* with the following passage:

> If I want to imagine a fictive nation, I can give it an invented name, treat it declaratively as a novelistic object, create a new Garabagne, so as to compromise no real country by my fantasy. . . . I can also—though in no way claiming to represent or analyse reality itself (these being the major gestures of Western discourse)—isolate somewhere in the world (far away) a certain number of features . . . , and out of these features deliberately form a system. It is this system which I shall call Japan.[8]

What Barthes does explicitly and consciously in *Empire of Signs* is also done, implicitly and unconsciously, in many texts on Japanese economy and society.

Postwar Japan was the first non-Western country to attain a high level of industrialization. Certain universal problems inherent in the industrialization process are therefore clearly apparent in Japanese development. At the same time, however, Japan differs from earlier industrialized nations in terms of many of its cultural traditions. Japan, moreover (in spite of a high degree of ethnic homogeneity), is a large and diverse society in which regional differences, differences between urban and rural society, differences between large and small enterprises, and so forth create kaleidoscopic patterns far too complex to be comprehended in any simple social or economic model. By selecting certain elements from this complexity, though, many scholars have found it possible to use Japan as the source of a particular type of construct: an image of a society in which the universal goals of contemporary capitalism (rapid growth, high levels of consumption) have been achieved by distinctive and unusual means.

Postwar Western writing on Japan—both academic and popular—has been dominated by this use of Japan as an alternative model of capitalism, which may be held up against the more familiar European and American models for purposes of contrast. In some cases, the contrast is favorable to Japan, and Japan is thus used to demonstrate that problems inherent in the Western industrializing process can be avoided; in others, it is unfavorable and is used to reassure Western readers of the inherent superiority of their system. This process of creating a mental construct built from selected features of Japanese society is not, in itself, invalid. It may reveal important disparities between the historical experiences of Japan and those of other industrialized countries, or illuminate interesting common threads in the worldwide process of development. Problems arise, however, when one mistakes models for comprehensive pictures of reality. For the images projected by any study of Japan usually tell as much about the economic and political problems of the country in which the study originated as they do about Japan itself.

A recent sociological study of Japan observes that "the emergence of a fairly intelligible and coherent image of Japanese society in the English-language literature is largely a postwar phenomenon."[9] The same is true of coherent theories on the Japanese economy. Western scholarship on Japan was profoundly influenced by the fact that Japan was one of the few Asian countries to escape colonization. If, as Said and others suggest,[10] Western knowledge of and prejudice about "the East" were molded by the need to sustain and justify colonial rule, then the paucity of Japanese studies in prewar Europe and America surely reflects Japan's noncolonial status. This academic neglect of Japan was aggravated during the 1930s by increasing international tensions and the growing xenophobia of the Japanese political establishment.

Before 1945 a number of pioneering scholars had, of course, published works related to Japanese economic development, the outstanding example being E. H. Norman's *Japan's Emergence as a Modern State* (1940),[11] in which economic, social, and political history is interwoven into a persuasive thesis on the origins and consequences of Japanese industrialization. Norman, however, remained a unique and isolated figure in Japanese studies: indeed, until writers such as John Dower and Jon Halliday inspired a "Norman revival" in the 1970s, his works were far more widely read and appreciated in Japan than they were in the English-speaking world.

The status of Japanese studies was dramatically altered, however, by the Pacific War and subsequent Allied occupation of Japan. During the war, the United States in particular (and Britain to a lesser extent) experienced a desperate shortage of Japanese speakers who could be used for intelligence purposes. The response was to institute crash courses in Japanese language within the armed forces. After August 1945, when the occupation authorities (like colonial rulers elsewhere) required knowledge of the language, culture, history, and institutions of their foreign subjects, it was the graduates of these courses who supplied the necessary expertise. Though few were appointed to significant policy-making positions, a substantial number served in interpreting, advising, and research positions during the occupation, and some later went on to academic positions in which they laid the foundations for postwar English-language scholarship on Japan.

The "wartime generation" of Japan scholars was drawn largely from the American liberal tradition that had flourished in U.S. academia in the immediate prewar years: the years of New Deal economics and Chicago sociology. They brought to Japanese studies memories of the Pacific War, but also an almost possessive sense of commitment to and responsibility for Japan.[12] The experiences of the occupation period gave rise to some seminal studies on various aspects of Japanese economy and society, including R. P. Dore's *Land Reform in Japan* (1950) and T. A. Bisson's *Zaibatsu Dissolution in Japan* (1954).[13] Most of these studies, however, are relatively specialized, concerned with the prewar nature and postwar transformation of specific social structures or institutions. They provided the basis for the subsequent emergence of theories of Japanese development, but the formulation of these theories and the creation of coherent schools of thought within Japanese studies was yet to come.

Models of Japanese Growth During the Economic Miracle

It was during the late 1950s and particularly the 1960s that English-language studies of the Japanese economy came to be structured by a dominant paradigm (in Thomas Kuhn's sense of the word).[14] The timing is significant, for there were three features of Japan's world role in this period that were of critical importance in the creation of the paradigm. First, this was the era of the so-called economic miracle, when Japan was experiencing unprecedentedly high rates of growth. Second, it was the period that saw the highly controversial renewal of the Mutual Security Treaty with the United States in 1960. Japan therefore became even more firmly embedded in the structures of postwar U.S. world strategy. Third, in the 1960s the United States was steadily drawn into the vortex of the Vietnam War, and the superpower rivalry was increasingly focused upon the struggle for influence over the newly independent nations of the Third World.

The nature of Japanese studies, as they evolved within this international environment, has been succinctly delineated by the U.S. historian John Dower: "Much American scholarship on Japan has tended to be congruent with the objectives of the American government. . . . Postwar American objectives internationally have been rested on the twin pillars of counter-revolution and support of a capitalist mode of development, and in that scheme Japan plays a key role both materially and as an alleged Asian model of the advantages of gradual, non-revolutionary development along capitalist lines."[15]

This comment is particularly applicable to scholarship on the Japanese economy. It needs to be remembered, of course, that at this time the scope of academic, business, and social contact between Japan and other industrialized nations was quite narrow. U.S. academics and researchers with a knowledge of Japanese language were certainly less rare than they had been before the war, but they still did not number more than a few hundred. (The numbers in Britain and other English-speaking countries were much smaller.) Expertise on Japan, moreover, was heavily concentrated in a handful of academic institutions, including Harvard, Yale, Columbia, Michigan, and California (Berkeley). Major groups of "Japan experts" consisted of specialists in language, literature, history, or sociology, and only a small percentage combined knowledge of Japanese with an interest in economic issues. Those who did for the most part derived their inspiration from the new ideas in development economics that flourished in the United States during the 1960s, and they naturally sought out and cooperated with Japanese economists who shared their enthusiasm for these ideas.

The consequence can be likened to the creation of a very narrow funnel through which the flow of economic ideas between Japan and the West was filtered. On one side of the funnel were development theorists such as Arthur Lewis and Gustav Ranis, and quantitative analysts of growth such as Simon Kuznets. On the other were their Japanese counterparts: economists such as Ohkawa Kazushi, Shinohara Miyohei, Ichimura Shinichi, and Okita Saburo. In between, a handful of Japanese-speaking U.S. economists such as Henry Rosovsky helped to facilitate contact between the two sides, while at the same time applying the theories of development economics in their own studies of Japanese growth.[16] The funnel was also maintained by the activities of a number of scholarly bodies such as the U.S. Social Science Research Council's Committee on Economic Growth (of which Kuznets was chairman) and the privately funded Japan Economic Research Center.[17]

The paradigm created through this exchange of ideas can be described as the "lessons of growth" approach.[18] From the perspective of this approach, the main object of studying the Japanese economy was to define, as precisely as possible, the factors contributing to Japan's unusually rapid growth in the twentieth century, and, where possible, to derive from this analysis lessons that might be applicable to less developed countries in their drive toward industrialization. The methods used were mostly quantitative, involving the painstaking compilation of data on the supply of capital and labor, the level of foreign trade, and so forth, and the outcome was an assessment of the relative importance of these factors in various historical phases of Japanese growth.

Perhaps predictably, the lessons drawn from Japan's experience were generally positive ones. In particular, the concept of dualistic development was frequently extended to Japan to suggest that abundant supplies of labor (a characteristic of most underdeveloped countries) could be an asset in promoting rapid industrial growth.[19] Japan's development was often juxtaposed with the industrialization of the Soviet Union, because these countries are the two latecomers among the major nations that have entered the phase of industrialization and modern economic growth.[20]

Here again the contrast favored Japan. Simon Kuznets's contribution to a collection of essays on Soviet development, which abounds with phrases such as "repression of freedom," "heavy human costs" of growth, and "misery and failure," may be compared with his contribution to a similar volume on Japan, in which discussion of the negative effects of growth is conspicuous by its absence.[21] Angus Maddison, though less harsh in his condemnation of the Soviet Union, presented Japan as offering many positive object lessons for less developed nations. He derived a quite different type of lesson from his analysis of the Soviet economy, however: "Soviet experience has shown that the economic and human costs of transition to a completely socialist economy are very heavy, that it is extraordinarily difficult to organize the government agricultural sector efficiently, that there are major difficulties in providing high quality consumer goods, and that the investment cost of growth is rather high."[22]

This is not to deny achievements of the "lessons of growth" school. The interchange of ideas between Japanese, U.S., and other development economists, and the publication during the 1960s of a number of English-language studies of Japanese growth, unquestionably led to greater international knowledge of and interest in the Japanese economy. The search for lessons from

Japan's experience also illuminated some interesting features of Japanese development and contributed to wider debates on issues such as economic dualism, technology transfer, and the role of education in development.

The problem, however, is the overwhelming influence of the "lessons of growth" school on English-language studies of the Japanese economy during the 1960s and 1970s. Because of their virtual monopoly of the field, it was easy to assume that the writings produced by this school represented an objective and comprehensive picture of the realities of the Japanese economy. The questions they posed—Why has the Japanese economy grown so fast? What are the lessons of Japanese growth?—structured thinking on Japanese development to such a degree that it became almost inconceivable that different questions could be posed. As a result, even texts written in a less quantitative, more eclectic style than those of Rosovsky, Kuznets, and Ohkawa et al. tended to concentrate upon the same fundamental issues.[23]

Meanwhile, the free exchange of ideas between prominent development economists in Japan and the United States coexisted with a remarkable absence of communication between scholars of other intellectual persuasions. In particular, Marxist economists in Japan and the West were almost wholly isolated from one another. To be more precise, while the works of Western Marxists like Maurice Dobb and Paul Sweezy were read and debated in Japan, Japanese Marxist writers such as Yamada Moritarō, Uno Kōzō, and Ōuchi Hyōe continued to be virtually unknown in the West.

Japanese Studies Since the Early 1970s:
Japan as Model or Menace?

Since the early 1970s, several factors have broadened the scope and altered the emphasis of Western studies of Japanese development. In the first place, although the speed of Japanese growth decreased, Japan achieved the status of a major economic power and moved toward the forefront in a growing number of technologically advanced industries. Not only did Japanese exports come to exert a substantial influence on the economies of the nation's major trading partners, but also (as discussed in chapter 4) the Japanese economy became increasingly international. Both Japanese investment overseas and foreign investment in Japan expanded. Western enterprises therefore experienced increasing contact with Japanese firms and discovered a growing need for knowledge of Japanese economic institutions and business practices.

Partly in response to this need, the number of courses on Japan offered by educational institutions in English-speaking countries grew. At the same time, the Japanese government and private corporations, aware of their country's new-found status in the international economic and political order, devoted larger and larger sums of money to promoting educational and cultural exchange between Japan and other countries. Moreover, several Japanese scholars, many of them trained in U.S. universities under Fulbright scholarships during the 1960s, took up teaching posts in universities outside Japan. All of these factors helped to broaden and diversify the nature of intellectual and social contact between Japan and the outside world. This diversification was also encouraged by the growth of international tourism, both to and from Japan, and by the increasing number of young foreigners spending periods of time in Japan as exchange students, teachers of English, and so forth.

These trends are reflected not only in an expansion in the number of English-language publications on the Japanese economy, but also in the increasing variety of their content. If 1960s' scholarship could be seen as being dominated by a single paradigm, studies of the Japanese economy in the 1970s and 1980s fall into a number of distinct categories.

The most thriving and successful area of study has probably been the "Japan as managerial model" approach. This approach undoubtedly evolved from the growth of contacts between Japanese and Western managers that accompanied the internationalization of the Japanese economy. But at the same time it also reflects a search by Western enterprises for new managerial formulas to combat the effects of recession and of rising competition from Japan and its "newly industrializing" Asian neighbors. An early enthusiast for this approach was the U.S. management theorist Peter Drucker, whose writings on Japan were influential during the 1970s, but the genre reached its apogee in 1981 with the publication of two popular best-sellers on Japanese managerial techniques, William Ouchi's *Theory Z* and R. T. Pascale and A. G. Athos's *The Art of Japanese Management*.[24]

The concept of Japan as a model for emulation by industrialized European and American countries (as opposed to less developed Asian countries) has not been confined to the management theorists. During the 1970s and early 1980s a wide range of books and articles, some by "Japan experts," others by economists, journalists, public servants, or government-sponsored research bodies, popularized the notion of the Japanese model.[25] These writings not only share an extremely positive assessment of Japan's economic progress but also express a good deal of unanimity on the lessons of its success. Most emphasize the active participation of the government in long-term industrial planning, the "lifetime employment" system, company unionism, the consensus decision-making process, the high quality of Japanese education and skill-formation, and the concept of the corporation as a community with an all-embracing concern for the social welfare of its members.[26] These features are presented as being characteristically (indeed, often uniquely) Japanese, and as being characteristics whose emulation might revive flagging economic growth and improve competitive performance in other industrialized nations. The fundamental message of the "Japan as model" approach, in short, is that by making certain adjustments to their management and planning procedures, other countries can achieve rapid technological progress without undertaking radical economic restructuring or painful social change. Just as the 1960s' "lessons of growth" school extracted from Japan's experience a message congruent with the international needs of U.S. business and government, so the 1970s–1980s' "Japan as model" school extracts a message congruent with their domestic needs.

But, unlike the dominant paradigm of the 1960s, the concept of Japan as a model for other industrialized nations was almost immediately subjected to critical scrutiny from a number of directions. On the one hand, increasing Western paranoia at Japan's industrial success prompted the publication of popular works depicting Japan not as a model but rather as a sinister menace.[27] In these, the "unique" characteristics praised by the "Japan as model" school are transformed into symptoms of moral and cultural inferiority: loyalty to the company becomes subservience, group cooperation becomes lack of individual initiative, long-term planning becomes a conspiracy for world determination.[28]

On another level, however, the response has been more serious.

Historians and sociologists, in particular, have questioned the popular Western stereotype of Japan as a society in which harmony, consensus, and loyalty reign supreme.[29] Their explorations of conflict in Japanese history have cast doubt on many features of the Japanese managerial model as portrayed by writers such as Drucker, Ouchi, and Pascale and Athos, and they have led to the emergence of a new picture in which aspects of the system appear as well-planned means to subvert worker radicalism rather than as natural outgrowths of a harmonious social order. The general expansion of English-language research in the long-neglected field of Japanese social history has also helped to focus attention on the social costs of economic growth. The works of writers like Hane Mikiso[30] force students of Japanese economic development to confront the fact that the fruits of growth were not evenly distributed throughout Japanese society, and indeed that many individuals lost more than they gained in the race toward industrialization.

These studies have inevitably influenced Western scholarship on the Japanese economy. It is interesting to compare the collections of essays on Japanese economic growth published during the 1960s with the collection edited by Hugh Patrick and published in 1976 under the title *Japanese Industrialization and Its Social Consequences*.[31] The latter work was, in Patrick's own words, "The first book in Western languages treating Japanese industrialization which provides extensive emphasis on the social dimensions" (p. 2). It was indicative of a general trend, apparent in many subsequent writings on Japanese development, toward a greater concern with the social costs and benefits of growth.

Despite the growing diversity within Japanese studies, however, English-language presentations of Japanese Marxian thought remain limited. This reflects the continued neglect of Marxian theory by the economics faculties of English-speaking universities. It is common for Marx's ideas, if they are taught at all, to be confined to "special interest" courses offered to the handful of students who volunteer for the subject. As a result, the chances of a student combining a knowledge of Marxian economics with the study of Japan are remote indeed. It is indicative of this state of affairs that the only serious attempt at an English-language presentation of Japanese development from a Marxist perspective—Jon Halliday's *Political History of Japanese Capitalism*—was written by someone outside the "Japanese studies" establishment.

Likewise, although interest in Japanese Marxian scholarship has increased a little in recent years, the works of Japanese Marxists that have been translated into English are those dealing with general questions of economic theory rather than with the Japanese economy itself. The most important of these is Uno Kōzō's *Keizai genron* (Principles of political economy), which was published in English in 1980 and has since received some attention from Marxist economists in the West.[32] A few Japanese contributions to debates on the labor theory of value have also become available.[33] But the great range of Japanese works that apply Marxist theoretical concepts to the realities of Japanese development have continued to be inaccessible to overseas readers, and this is unfortunate, for (whatever the merits or demerits of individual works) they expose those realities to a method of questioning quite different from that of the "lessons of growth" or "Japan as model" schools. In this way, they illuminate issues that lie outside the range of the dominant paradigms in Western studies of Japan.

Marxian Economics in Japan

Foreign scholars have often expressed bewilderment at the extensive influence of Marxism on Japanese thought. For example, Edwin Reischauer writes:

> Japanese Marxism has proved an extremely hardy plant. Its failure to correspond to the facts of twentieth-century history, even as these unfold within Japan itself, has not blighted it. The true believers and even many conservative Japanese, who are unaware of how much they remain influenced by their Marxist education, seem hardly to have noticed that so-called capitalism has turned into something far different from what Marx assumed it would become and that the supposedly socialist societies have approximated Marx's dream only in words and superficial details. Marxism has flourished even despite a most infertile emotional soil.[34]

Closer examination of the environment of Japanese economic thought, though, makes the appeal of Marxism in this area of study much less mysterious. (In fact, one could quite well reverse the problem and ponder the reason why such a significant and influential body of thought as Marxism has been so widely neglected by economists in the English-speaking world.) In the first place, although economics as a distinct discipline was not introduced into Japanese education until after the Meiji Restoration of 1868, Japan already had a tradition of inquiry into economic issues. In this tradition, however, economics problems were integrally connected to questions of power, justice and morality.[35] It is not surprising, then, that early twentieth-century Japanese students of Western economics should have felt uncomfortable with the Neoclassical claim to ethical neutrality and scientific objectivity and should have been attracted instead to the clear ideological and moral commitment of Marxist political economy.[36]

Second, university education in general, and economic education in particular, was strongly influenced by continental European models. Several of the leading Japanese economists of the Meiji period, especially those associated with Tokyo Imperial University, studied in Germany, and from the 1890s to the First World War the study of economics in Japan was powerfully influenced by the "social policy" approach of German economists such as Gustav von Schmoler, Ernst Engel, and Lujo Brentano. Marxist ideas were much more readily integrated into the discourse of economics on the European continent than they were in Britain or America, and it was therefore inevitable that Japanese adherents of the social policy school should have come into contact with these ideas. Fukuda Tokuzō, a prominent member of this school, was responsible for writing what is probably the first Japanese-language critique of Marxist thought.[37] Though the adherents of the social policy approach were critical of Marxism, some of their students proved more sympathetic. Among them was Kawakami Hajime, who, by 1920 had emerged as one of the founders of the Japanese Marxist tradition.[38]

A third (and most important) reason for the willingness of Japanese scholars to espouse Marxism undoubtedly lay in the structure and development of the Japanese economy from the First World War to the early 1930s. If Japanese realities did not always fit neatly into Marxist categories, they also most certainly failed to fit the theoretical constructs of Western Neoclassicism, with its assumption of perfect competition, freely moving capital and labor, and rational, utility-maximizing consumers. During the 1920s, approximately half the Japanese work force consisted of farmers, a large share of whom were tenants laboring under the burdens of very high rents, tiny and fragmented holdings, and the decaying remnants of complex traditional obligations to their landlords. Industrial production was dominated by a handful of giant enterprises (the zaibatsu) whose owners and senior management had close links with the Japanese political elite. In the mid-1930s, for example, three companies (Asano, Mitsubishi, and Mitsui) produced 69.9 percent of Japan's cement, three (Mitsui, Mitsubishi, and Yasuda) produced 88.4 percent of its paper, two (Mitsubishi and Mitsui) produced 87.2 percent of its flour, and six (Mitsubishi, Sumitomo, Mitsui, Asano, Yamashita, and Ishihara) controlled more than half its shipping.[39] At the same time, more than half the manufacturing work force was employed in tiny workshops with less than five employees, in which pay and working conditions were often determined more by the power of family relationships than by normal market forces.

It was against this background that Marxism came to play a dominant role in Japanese economic studies, and that the major Marxist debates of prewar Japan took shape. The central debate was the famous Rōnō-ha/Kōza-ha controversy, which has been outlined in a number of English-language works and therefore need only be briefly summarized here.[40] There has been a tendency for Western writers on Japan to treat the Rōnō-ha and Kōza-ha schools of thought as obscurantist attempts to force Japanese history into the straitjacket of Marxist terminology, but it is important to observe that the adherents of these schools in the 1920s and 1930s had intellectual objectives that were fundamentally different from those of postwar U.S. development economists. The ultimate objective of scholarship for prewar Marxist economists in Japan was to promote the transformation of Japan into a socialist society. In this respect they were no mere *Kathedersozialisten*. Many participated actively in political movements and went to jail for their beliefs. Some, like the economist and historian Noro Eitarō, died for them.

The essential question addressed by the Rōnō-ha/Kōza-ha debate was whether or not Japan had reached a stage of development where a socialist revolution was possible. The Rōnō-ha, named after their periodical *Rōnō* (Workers and farmers) and including such figures as Kushida Tamizō, Inomata Tsunao, Sakisaka Itsurō, and Tsuchiya Takao, argued that it had. In their view, the emergence of Japanese capitalism had its roots in the Tokugawa period. Although they recognized that the survival of feudal elements, together with Japan's status as a latecomer to industrialization, created differences between Japanese and European capitalism, they were at pains to emphasize the essentially capitalist nature of Japan in the 1920s and 1930s.

By contrast, the Kōza-ha, with the approval of the Comintern and the Japanese Communist Party, argued that the peculiarities of Japanese economic development had prevented the full-fledged emergence of capitalism and liberal democracy in their country. This group, which takes its name from the publication *Nihon shihonshugi hattatsu-shi kōza* (Lectures on the development of Japanese capitalism), included scholars such as Noro Eitarō, Yamada Moritarō, and Hani Gorō. Yamada, drawing parallels between the economic structure of Japan and that of other late industrializers such as Russia, argued that the Japanese economy was characterized by semifeudalism and militarism. A liberal-democratic revolution would therefore be necessary before the nation could begin its transformation to socialism.

The debates reached their peak during the early 1930s, before being gradually stifled by the growth of militarism and intellectual repression from 1937 onward. They left a legacy, however, of both empirical research and theoretical inquiry which was to provide the foundations for the development of Marxist thought in postwar Japan.

In the years immediately following Japan's defeat in the Pacific War, the authority of Marxist scholarship in Japanese academia was reinforced by the fact that a number of prominent Marxists had been among the few who actively opposed Japanese militarism. At Tokyo University, for example, the Marxist economist Ōuchi Hyōe, who had been dismissed and imprisoned for his political views in 1938, emerged as an influential force in the immediate postwar years.

As the Allied occupation transformed the structure of agriculture, big business, labor relations, and political life, and as economic recovery flowed into the beginnings of rapid industrial expansion, so the arena of Marxian economic debate altered. The issue of whether or not the Meiji Restoration was a bourgeois revolution continued to be of great interest to economic historians but was obviously of declining relevance to contemporary Japan. Although some fundamental divisions between former members of the Rōnō-ha and Kōza-ha survived, postwar Marxist economics in Japan has been marked less by a single sharp dichotomy than by a multiplicity of approaches, and it has incidentally displayed far greater flexibility and innovation than Reischauer gives it credit for. Here I shall simply provide some impression of its diversity by sketching a few of the main areas of debate.

During the late 1940s and early 1950s, debate continued as to whether Japan could be seen as a wholly capitalist society. Some followers of the prewar Kōza-ha maintained their emphasis on the survival of semifeudal elements in Japanese society—pointing, for example, to the retention of the emperor and to the fact that postwar land reform had failed to redistribute large tracts of forest land.[41] They suggested that the occupation reforms of the political, landholding, and labor systems and the dissolution of the zaibatsu had failed to democratize Japanese society but had resulted in its subordination to the power of the United States. As time went on, however, the lasting effects of the occupation reforms became increasingly difficult to ignore, and alternative interpretations became more widely accepted. One significant reinterpretation came from the prominent Kōza-ha economist Yamada Moritarō, who from 1949 onward put forward the view that the occupation reforms—and land reform in particular—marked a turning point in the establishment of bourgeois liberal democracy in Japan.[42]

New ideas were also creating intellectual ferment among survivors and heirs of the Rōnō-ha. A particularly significant influence, from the mid-1950s onward, was the work of Uno Kōzō. Although Uno did not identify himself as a member of the Rōnō-ha, his theories decisively shaped the debates of Marxists outside the Japanese Communist Party in the postwar period. The main innovation in Uno's work was the distinction he drew between the "pure theory" of capitalism and the application of this theory to the real world. On the one hand, he reworked Marx's *Capital* to extract from it a purely theoretical logic of capitalism, while on the other hand he argued that the history of capitalism in the real world was marked by various stages of development, to which the pure theory would apply in differing ways.[43] Furthermore, Uno recognized that the actual working of capitalism in various contemporary societies was influenced by a wide range of social, political, and economic factors that could only be analyzed by means of empirical observation. Pure theory, stage theory, and empirical study therefore constituted three distinct but interdependent conceptual levels in the study of capitalism.

In the late 1950s and early 1960s this approach was taken up by economists like Ōuchi Tsutomu, who sought to develop an empirical analysis of the evolution of Japanese capitalism since the First World War. A crucial concept in this analysis, and one that is used not only by the Uno school but very widely by Marxist writers in Japan, is the notion of "state monopoly capitalism." This phase refers to the stage of capitalist development in which the economy comes to be dominated by large oligopolistic firms, whose productive power induces chronic tendencies to underconsumption and economic depression. To combat these tendencies, the state takes on an increasingly active role in the maintenance of demand and of general conditions for the survival and growth of the capitalist system. Like Paul Baran and Paul Sweezy in the United States,[44] many Japanese economists have traced the worldwide formation of state monopoly capitalism to the interwar period, and particularly to the depression of the 1930s. Ōuchi Tsutomu and other scholars who followed his approach suggested that the democratization measures introduced by the postwar occupation forces should be seen as having removed existing barriers to the mature emergence of state monopoly capitalism in Japan.[45]

Debates over the nature of postwar Japanese capitalism could not be divorced from the issue of Japan's role in the world economic system. Although Marxist scholars generally agree that the Mutual Security Treaty subordinates Japan to the political and military interests of the United States, the nature of the economic relationship with the United States has been a source of recurring controversy. Like the prewar Rōnō-ha/Kōza-ha debate, this question has implications for practical politics: Can Japanese socialists, in other words, begin to achieve their objectives without first severing the complex links that tie the country to a U.S.-controlled international order? There has been a general tendency for descendants of the Kōza-ha tradition to emphasize Japan's subordination to the United States, and for Rōnō-ha scholars to emphasize Japan's relative economic independence, but the debate has by no means proceeded along simple or clear-cut lines. In the second half of the 1950s, for example, there was considerable dissension within the Japanese Communist Party over the "subordination thesis" according to which big business in Japan was seen as comprising a sort of "comprador" sector, similar to the dependent capitalist sectors of less developed countries. A number of prominent economists entered into both sides of the debate, with figures such as Ono Yoshihiko arguing forcefully both for the relative independence of Japanese capitalism and for the need to pay greater attention to Japan's own economic impact on the outside world.[46] A somewhat similar debate resurfaced in the late 1960s, with the emphasis now being not so much on Japan's industrial subordination to the United States, but rather on its dependence in the fields of finance and raw materials. An issue highlighted by this debate was the growing reliance of the Japanese economy on sources of raw materials controlled by U.S. multinational enterprises. By this time, however, the undesirable impact of Japan's exports and foreign investment on the outside world was shifting the focus of attention to Japan's own role in postwar neo-imperialism—a role that was recognized even by those who continued to emphasize the overall dominance of "Pax Americana." As one recent work puts it: "In terms of GNP and industrial production, we may say that Japan has grown to be 'the second economic superpower in the capitalist world.' As a result of this economic development Japan, while retaining its political and military subordination to the United States, has itself acquired greater economic influence than it had before the war and has reemerged as a member of the world imperialist camp."[47]

The years of high economic growth from 1956 to 1973 created new intellectual challenges for Japanese Marxists. The analyses that emerged from the application of Marxian theories to the so-called economic miracle at some points seemed to converge toward the debates that were simultaneously occurring among non-Marxian development economists, and it is unfortunate that there was not greater cross-fertilization of ideas between the two groups. To Marxist economists, Japan's high growth had to be viewed in the context of state monopoly capitalism, a stage of capitalist development that was bringing high rates of industrial expansion to many advanced nations. Japan's exceptionally high growth rates, however, were clearly associated with special features of the Japanese economy. Ōuchi Tsutomu, for example, defined these features as being "postwar recovery" and "late development," under which two headings he included such factors as land and labor reform, the intense competition resulting from the restriction of monopolistic enterprises, the potential for imports of foreign technology, and Japan's dual industrial structure.[48] It is interesting to observe that the latter two factors were also emphasized, in a quite different theoretical context, by Ohkawa and Rosovsky's analysis of Japanese growth.[49]

Contemporary Marxist economics in Japan is much concerned with analyzing the causes and effects of the collapse of high growth since the early 1970s, and with defining appropriate responses to the severe "rationalization" measures that are currently being undertaken by large Japanese enterprises. Among the outcomes of this analysis are some useful contributions to debates on the impact of mechanization and automation on the working class. As Japan has emerged as a world leader in robotics, Japanese Marxists have taken up themes similar to those debated by Serge Mallet, Harry Braverman, and others in the West.[50] Yamaguchi Masayuki, for example, expresses a view quite similar to that of French writers such as Mallet when he argues that the socialization of production and increasing levels of mechanization are drawing supervisory, technical, and even managerial workers into the realms of the proletariat and so creating new foundations for working class organization and action.[51] Japanese Marxists, however, do not universally accept this view. Tokita Yoshihisa points out that although many technicians and supervisors may be wage laborers, their role as intermediaries between the ruling classes and manual work force is likely to induce a divided consciousness, so that their political sympathies will be equivocal at best.[52]

There can be little doubt that Marxist thought no longer occupies the dominant position in Japanese economics that it held in the immediate postwar period. The period of high growth from the 1950s to 1970s saw the dissemination and development of Keynesian economics, quantitative growth analysis, and other non-Marxian schools of thought in Japanese academia. More recently, in Japan as elsewhere, monetarist ideas have enjoyed considerable vogue. The interaction of Marxist and non-Marxist thought in the 1960s and 1970s had a number of positive results. On the one hand, non-Marxist economists such as Morishima Michio demonstrated how modern mathematical methods could be used to clarify the logic of Marxian theory.[53] On the other, writers such as Miyazaki Yoshikazu used eclectic theoretical approaches to develop a critical analysis of contemporary Japanese capitalism.[54]

The waning intellectual dominance of Marxism in recent years, however, has been associated with a resurgence—so far small-scale but nonetheless alarming—of extreme right-wing nationalism in Japanese academic life. The publicity given to these right-wing ideas makes it all the more important that Western readers should have access to the large and diverse corpus of left-wing writings that continue to be produced by Japanese economists, historians, and social scientists.

This book is not designed to present a uniform theoretical perspective on modern Japan, but rather to introduce readers to some aspects of recent Japanese economic development which are widely discussed by contemporary left-wing writers in Japan but which create startling contrasts to the image of Japanese growth commonly presented in English-language texts. In chapter 2, Seiyama Takurō examines the role of economic policy in Japan's "miraculous" postwar growth. As Seiyama emphasizes, postwar policies cannot be seen in isolation but need to be analyzed within the context of the special characteristics of the development of Japanese capitalism. A particularly central feature of this development process has been the holding down of labor costs to promote unusually high levels of capital accumulation.

In the 1930s and in the early postwar period it was common for outside observers to attribute Japan's industrial success to its "cheap labor." As this rather simplistic view of Japanese growth was abandoned, however, there has been a tendency for many writers on Japan to go to the opposite extreme, explaining Japan's rapid industrialization almost entirely in terms of superior policy or management practices, while ignoring the importance of high levels of exploitation. Seiyama's essay helps to correct the balance. As he points out, Japan's competitive power in the contemporary world is no longer merely a matter of low labor costs but is a reflection of the increasing technological sophistication of Japanese products. Yet it remains true that although Japanese labor is no longer "cheap" in international terms, it is poorly rewarded in terms of the great productive capacity of the Japanese economy. Besides, in Japan as in other major industrial economies, labor is at present facing an erosion of the gains achieved over the past three decades. As Seiyama cogently argues, this weakening of the economic and political position of labor can only be understood and confronted on an international basis.

The ability of Japanese business and government to hold down the living standards of the work force, and so to promote high levels of profit and growth, was inseparably connected to Japan's status as a latecomer to industrialization, and to the important role that agriculture continued to play in the Japanese economy during the early postwar period. As Teruoka Shuzō shows in chapter 3, a central and in many ways paradoxical factor in Japanese growth was the land reform carried out under the Allied occupation immediately after Japan's defeat in the Pacific War. Although this reform undoubtedly raised the status and living standards of Japan's agrarian population, it converted the countryside into a "reserve army" of relatively cheap and flexible labor power. At the same time, by turning peasant farmers into miniature landowners, it also helped to build a solid basis of support for the conservative governments whose growth policies Seiyama analyzes in chapter 2.

The other crucial component of the process of rapid capital accumulation was the structure of big business itself. Writers like Baran and Sweezy, in their analysis of U.S. monopoly capitalism, have concentrated upon the role of the giant, vertically integrated enterprises that dominated the U.S. economy in the twentieth century. In Japan, however, big business, for a variety of historical reasons, has developed along distinctive lines. The most significant characteristic of big business in the post–World War II period has been its tendency to form federations or groups that enable a number of large but relatively specialized firms to pool their strengths and resources. In chapter 4, Sumiya Toshio analyzes the structure and evolution of these groups and shows how their dominant role in the Japanese economy acted as a positive factor in rapid postwar growth and accumulation, while simultaneously resulting in distortions of the economic social and political system—distortions that are most vividly illustrated by recurrent political scandals like the Lockheed Affair.

The nature of the agrarian sector and the unusual structure of big business help to explain the relative weakness of organized labor in postwar Japan. As Kurokawa Toshio shows in his analysis of the contemporary weakness of working class movements (chapter 5), Japanese labor has not always been passive and obedient to the wishes of management. In place of the traditional stereotype of the loyal workers and harmonious labor relations, Kurokawa offers a picture of a society in which repeated upsurges of union activism have been undermined by the policies of management and by peculiarities inherent in the structure of the Japanese work force. A particularly interesting section of this discussion focuses upon the development of quality control circles and similar "small group" management techniques. These techniques, which have been widely popularized as outstanding examples of Japan's harmonious industrial relations, are shown to have evolved as a calculated counterattack on the organizational strength that unionized labor had acquired during the late 1940s and 1950s.

In the final chapter of this collection, Fujiwara Sadao places Japan's postwar growth in its international context. Although he analyzes Japan's development within the framework of "Pax Americana," Fujiwara's emphasis is less upon Japan's subordination to the United States than upon the emergence of Japan as an economic power in its own right. Just as the United States succeeded nineteenth-century colonial powers as the dominant force in the world economy—and in the process altered the structure of international economic relations—so Japan is now imposing its own distinctive pattern of vertical economic ties upon the Asia-Pacific region. Fujiwara describes this pattern as "industrial imperialism," an international order that differs in significant respects from the neo-imperialism of "Pax Americana," while at the same time retaining the fundamental characteristics of dominance and dependence.

Although these essays contain differing emphases and perspectives, two themes recur throughout. The first is an emphasis on the possibility of change. Japan's economic structure is not seen as being immutably determined by culture or history, but rather as being a changing system, constantly open to reshaping and redirection through the activity of organized social forces. The second theme is a desire for a freer and fuller exchange of ideas between those who are critical of the economic and political structures of Japanese capitalism. As long as the only Japanese voices heard abroad are those of writers sympathetic to management and government, there is little hope that the problems of labor relations, trade friction, and technological competition discussed in this volume will be fully understood, let alone resolved.

Notes

1. John Neville Keynes, quoted in Phyliss Deane, *The Evolution of Economic Ideas* (Cambridge: Cambridge University Press, 1978), p. 102.

2. K. Ohkawa and M. Shinohara, *Patterns of Japanese Economic Development: A Quantitative Appraisal* (New Haven: Yale University Press, 1979), p. 6.

3. John Whitney Hall, "Changing Conceptions of the Modernization of Japan," in *Changing Japanese Attitudes Toward Modernization*, ed. Marius Jansen (Princeton: Princeton University Press, 1965), p. 14.

4. Tatsuro Uchino, *Japan's Postwar Economy: An Insider's View of Its History and Future* (Tokyo: Kodansha International, 1978), p. 11.

5. Werner Heisenberg, *Physics and Philosophy* (New York: Harper and Row, 1958), p. 58.

6. Rare exceptions to this rule have been the works of E. H. Norman. See J. W. Dower, ed., *Origins of the Modern Japanese State: Selected Writings of E. H. Norman* (New York, Pantheon Books, 1975), and J. Halliday, *A Political History of Japanese Capitalism* (New York: Monthly Review Press, 1975) (though the latter relies entirely on translated sources).

7. E.g., Edwin O. Reischauer, *Japan Past and Present* (London: Duckworth, 1964), p. 258; Hall, "Changing Conceptions of Modernization," p. 14.

8. Roland Barthes, *Empire of Signs*, trans. R. Howard (London: Jonathan Cape, 1982), p. 3.

9. R. Mouer and J. Sugimoto, *Images of Japanese Society* (London: Routledge and Kegan Paul, 1986), p. 23.

10. Edward W. Said, *Orientalism* (New York: Pantheon Books, 1978).

11. E. H. Norman, *Japan's Emergence as a Modern State* (New York: Institute of Pacific Relations, 1940).

12. Herbert Passin, himself a member of the "wartime generation," evokes this mood when he recalls: "those of us who held responsible positions in the Occupation—even if they were somewhat less than of cabinet rank—found ourselves extremely attentive to everything that was happening in the country. I used to have the feeling that I could not rest in the morning until I read all the news available, or heard it on the radio, or picked up the information reports that were constantly circulating around our offices. We had a sense that we were involved in, or connected with, everything that was going on in Japan." Passin, *Encounter with Japan* (Tokyo: Kodansha International, 1982), p. 189.

13. R. P. Dore, *Land Reform in Japan* (Oxford: Oxford University Press, 1950); T. A. Bisson, *Zaibatsu Dissolution in Japan* (Berkeley: University of California Press, 1954).

14. Thomas S. Kuhn, *The Structure of Scientific Revolutions* (Chicago: University of Chicago Press, 1962).

15. Dower, *Origins of the Modern Japanese State*, p. 33.

16. E.g., K. Ohkawa and H. Rosovsky, *Japanese Economic Growth: Trend Acceleration in the Twentieth Century* (Stanford: Stanford University Press, 1973).

17. See L. Klein and K. Ohkawa, eds., *Economic Growth: The Japanese Experience Since the Meiji Era* (Homewood, Ill.: Richard D. Irwin, 1968).

18. I have discussed this approach more fully in an article entitled "Gyappu ōkii Ō-Bei no Nihon keizai kenkyū—'Seichō no kyokun-teki' apurochi o koete," *Ekonomisuto*, April 10, 1984.

19. See J. C. Fei and G. Ranis, *Development of the Labor Surplus Economy: Theory and Policy* (Homewood, Ill.: Richard D. Irwin, 1964); Allen C. Kelly, Jef-

frey G. Williamson, and Russell J. Cheetham, *Dualistic Economic Development: Theory and History* (Chicago, University of Chicago Press, 1972).

20. A. Bergson and S. Kuznets, eds., *Economic Trends in the Soviet Union* (Cambridge: Harvard University Press, 1963), p. 371.

21. Ibid. See also S. Kuznets, "Notes on Japan's Economic Growth," in *Economic Growth*, ed. Klein and Ohkawa.

22. Angus Maddison, *Economic Growth in Japan and the USSR* (London: George Allen & Unwin, 1969), p. 132.

23. See, for example, G. C. Allen, *A Short Economic History of Modern Japan* (London: Macmillan, 1946); K. Yoshihara, *Japanese Economic Development—A Short Introduction* (Oxford: Oxford University Press, 1979).

24. Peter Drucker, "What We Can Learn from Japanese Management," *Harvard Business Review* (March–April 1971): 110–22; W. G. Ouchi, *Theory Z: How American Business Can Meet the Japanese Challenge* (Philippines: Addison-Wesley, 1981); R. T. Pascale and A. G. Athos, *The Art of Japanese Management* (Harmondsworth: Penguin Books, 1981).

25. E.g., E. F. Vogel, *Japan as Number One: Lesson for America* (Cambridge: Harvard University Press, 1979); Roy Hofheinz and Kent E. Calder, *The East Asia Edge* (New York: Basic Books, 1982); P. Marsh, "Japan's Recipe for Industrial Success," *New Scientist*, November 15, 1980; Jerry Fox, "Japan's Electronic Lesson," *New Scientist*, November 20, 1980; A. Weiss, "Simple Truths of Japanese Manufacturing," *Harvard Business Review* (July–August 1984); B. Boatwright and J. Sleigh, "New Technology: The Japanese Approach," *Department of Employment Gazette*, July 7, 1979.

26. Vogel, *Japan and Number One*, pp. 70–78, 134–35, 142, 144, 153–54; Marsh, "Japan's Recipe"; Fox, "Japan's Electronic Lesson"; Weiss, "Simple Truths"; Drucker, "Japanese Management"; Ouchi, *Theory Z*, pp. 15–22, 25–32, 36–40, 44–47; Boatwright and Sleigh, "New Technology."

27. See M. J. Wolf, *The Japanese Conspiracy* (Sevenoaks: New English Library, 1984); Russell Braddon, *The Other Hundred Years War: Japan's Bid for Supremacy 1941–2041* (London: Collins, 1983).

28. Wolf, *The Japanese Conspiracy*. Similar, though more carefully reasoned, criticisms are made in F. Herschede and R. Wiltgen, "Japan's Alternative Road to Serfdom: J. M. Clark and the Japanese Experience," *Review of Social Economy* (December 1981).

29. See Mouer and Sugimoto, *Images of Japanese Society*; T. Najita and J. Victor Koschmann, eds., *Conflict in Modern Japanese History: The Neglected Tradition* (Princeton: Princeton University Press, 1982); Ellis S. Krauss, Thomas P. Rohlen, and Patricia G. Steinhoff, eds., *Conflict in Japan* (Honolulu: University of Hawaii Press, 1984); Gavan McCormack and Yoshio Sugimoto, eds., *Democracy in Contemporary Japan* (Sydney: Hale and Iremonger, 1986).

30. Hane Mikiso, *Peasants, Rebels and Outcasts: The Underside of Modern Japan* (New York: Pantheon Books, 1982).

31. Hugh Patrick, ed., *Japanese Industrialization and Its Social Consequences* (Berkeley: University of California Press, 1976).

32. Kozo Uno, *Principles of Political Economy: Theory of a Purely Capitalist Society*, trans. Thomas T. Sekine (Sussex: Harvester Press, 1980). See, for exam-

ple, Brian Maclean, "Kozo Uno's Principles of Political Economy," *Science and Society* (Summer 1981).

33. For example, Makoto Itoh, *Value and Crisis: Essays on Marxian Economics in Japan* (London: Pluto Press, 1980); Shinzaburo Koshimura, *Theory of Capital Reproduction and Accumulation* (Kitchener, Ontario: DPG Publishing Co., 1975).

34. Reischauer, *Japan Past and Present*, p. 225.

35. See Eijiro Honjo, *Economic Thought and History of Japan in the Tokugawa Period* (New York: Russell and Russell, 1965).

36. See Gail Bernstein, *Japanese Marxist: A Portrait of Kawakami Hajime* (Cambridge: Harvard University Press, 1976), pp. 36–40.

37. Nahada Haruo, *Kindai Nihon shakai keizai shisō-shi* (Tokyo: Maeno Shoten, 1973), pp. 110–11.

38. Bernstein, *Japanese Marxist*.

39. Tamaki Hajime, *Nihon zaibatsu-shi* (Tokyo: Shakai Shisō-Sha, 1976), p. 49.

40. See Itoh, *Value and Crisis*, pp. 22–26; Mikio Sumiya and Koji Taira, eds., *An Outline of Japanese Economic History 1603–1940* (Tokyo: University of Tokyo Press), pp. 5–11; Germaine A. Hoston, *Marxism and the Crisis of Development in Prewar Japan* (Princeton: Princeton University Press, 1986).

41. See *Nihon shihonshugi kōza* (Tokyo: Iwanami Shoten, 1953).

42. Yamada Moritarō, "Nōchi kaikaku no rekishikeki igi," in *Sengo Nihon keizai no sho-mondai*, ed. Tokyo Daigaku Keizaigaku-Bu (Tokyo: Yūzankaku, 1949).

43. Uno, *Principles of Political Economy*.

44. Paul A. Baran and Paul M. Sweezy, *Monopoly Capital* (New York: Monthly Review Press, 1966).

45. Kajinishi Mitsuhaya, Ōshima Kiyoshi, Katō Toshihiko, and Ōuchi Tsutomu, *Nihon shihonshugi no daraku*, vol. 5 (Tokyo: Tokyo Daigaku Shuppankai, 1965); Ōuchi Tsutomu, "Sengo kaikaku e no futatsu no apurōchi," *Shakai kagaku kenkyū* 21, 5–6 (1970). See also Ōuchi Tsutomu, *Kokka dokusen shihonshugi* (Tokyo: Tokyo Daigaku Shuppankai, 1970).

46. Ono Yoshihiko, *Sengo Nihon shihonshugi-ron* (Tokyo: Aoki Shoten, 1963). For a discussion of these debates see Baba Hiroji, "Taigai kankei," in *Nihon keizai kenkyū nyūmon*, ed. Saeki Naomi and Shibagaki Kazuo (Tokyo: Tokyo Daigaku Shuppankai, 1972).

47. *Gendai teikokushugi taisei to Nihon shihonshugi*, vol. 1 of *Konnichi no Nihon shihonshugi* (Tokyo: Ōtsuki Shoten, 1981), p. 267.

48. See Ōuchi Tsutomu, ed., *Gendai Nihon keizai-ron* (Tokyo: Tokyo Daigaku Shuppankai, 1971).

49. Ohkawa and Rosovsky, *Japanese Economic Growth*.

50. Serge Mallet, *La Nouvelle Classe Ouvriere* (Paris: Editions du Seuil, 1963); Harry Braverman, *Labor and Monopoly Capital* (New York: Monthly Review Press, 1975).

51. Yamaguchi Masayuki, *Keizai to kagaku* (Tokyo: Aoki Shoten, 1975).

52. Tokita Yoshihisa, *Gendai shihonshugi to rōdōsha kaikakū*, vol. 5 of *Gendai shihonshugi bunseki* (Tokyo: Iwanami Shoten, 1982).

53. Michio Morishima, *Marx's Economics: A Dual Theory of Value and Growth* (Cambridge: Cambridge University Press, 1973).

54. Miyazaki Yoshikazu, *Kasen* (Tokyo: Iwanami Shinsho, 1972).

2

A Radical Interpretation
of Postwar Economic Policies

SEIYAMA TAKURŌ

Japanese Economic Development:
The Nature of Rapid Growth

Japanese capitalism came into existence in the latter half of the nineteenth century, far behind the advanced capitalist countries of Europe and America.[1] In the short space of one hundred years, however, the Japanese economy passed through the stages of primitive accumulation, industrial revolution, the formation and development of monopoly capital, and the shift of its industrial structure into the heavy and chemical sectors. More recently, Japanese capitalism has undergone further transformations essential to its continued development. These include the introduction of new technologies and the emergence of advanced industries. Japan is now the second largest capitalist economy after the United States,[2] and in terms of international competitive power it may be said to be the strongest economy in the capitalist world.

As these facts indicate, Japanese capitalism, having emerged relatively late, has been characterized by the high speed of its development. It may be recalled that remarkable growth rates achieved in the period 1955 to 1973 were termed "miraculous," and that Japan's economic performance in that period was held up as a model for emulation, not only by less developed countries but also by the advanced capitalist nations of Europe and North America. Even in the 1970s and 1980s, when the world economy entered a period of low growth, Japan's growth rate remained relatively high.

In Japan, too, economic development was affected by the deepening global economic crises of the 1970s and 1980s. As in the West, growth fell sharply, from an average of 11.0 percent in the period 1964–1968 to an average of 4.1 percent in 1979–1983. However, these figures compare favorably with the statistics for other industrialized countries (see table 2.1). In relative terms, then, Japan's performance continued to appear impressive. In other words, even after Japan had caught up with the earlier industrializing nations of the West and entered the ranks of the developed nations, its growth rate remained high by international standards. It is important to bear this in mind when considering the issues to be examined in this chapter.

Developed Economy, Underdeveloped Welfare

It is also important to note that, during the 1970s and 1980s, the relatively strong growth of the Japanese economy has been supported by the shift toward high technology industries. From the 1970s onward, the development and application of semiconductors, computers, office automation equipment, robots, and mechatronics have been occurring at a high speed in Japan. The remarkable progress in high technology and advanced industries means that Japan now clearly leads Western industrialized countries in the transformation of its industrial structure toward the new high-tech sectors. In terms of the present situation of the three major developed regions—North America, Europe, and Japan—Japan is characterized by a strong competitive position based upon the quality and technological sophistication of its products, while Europe is characterized by its relative competitive weakness.

This situation is the result of two trends that have emerged as Japan and other countries have responded to the deepening economic crisis and worsening trade friction of the 1970s and 1980s by seeking to develop and apply advanced technologies. On the one hand, there has been an overall strategic shift toward advanced industries and high-tech products, while on the other, efforts have

Table 2.1

Growth Rates of Major Countries (real annual average, percent)

	1964–1968	1969–1973	1974–1978	1979–1983	1983	1984
Japan	11.0	8.9	3.4	4.1	3.0	5.8
United States	5.1	3.5	2.8	1.3	3.7	6.8
West Germany	4.4	4.9	2.1	1.2	1.3	2.6
United Kingdom	2.9	3.5	1.0	0.8	3.4	1.7
France	5.2	5.9	3.1	1.5	0.7	1.6
Italy	4.9	4.5	2.1	1.6	−0.4	2.6

Source: Bank of Japan, "Comparative Economic and Financial Statistics, Japan and Major Countries."

been made to rationalize production and raise labor productivity within existing industries by the introduction of technologically sophisticated equipment designed to save labor and energy. Nowadays, when one speaks of the competitive advantage of Japanese products, one is not only referring (as in the past) to their low prices but also to their superiority in terms of quality and technological sophistication. This is particularly conspicuous in the case of high-tech industries.

At present, trade and economic friction among North America, Europe, and Japan primarily takes the form of criticism from the former two regions directed at the one-way, concentrated flow of high-tech exports from Japan to Western industrialized nations. To solve this friction, there are growing demands for local production facilities to be set up by Japanese enterprises in Europe and North America. Needless to say, technologically sophisticated industries are experiencing relatively high growth when compared to other industrial sectors, and, as the scientific and technological revolution progresses, the further expansion of these industries may be expected. Moreover, since high levels of technology (and, in many cases, of capital) are needed to enter these industries, and since there is relatively little competition from other nations and enterprises, profits are usually great. For these reasons, advanced industrialized nations attach considerable strategic importance to technologically advanced industries and their products and have taken active steps to promote their development.

In assessing a nation's degree of economic development, it is common to consider the importance of certain advanced or strategic industries in its economic structure. If one takes the competitive power of technologically advanced industries as the standard of measurement, one may argue that Japan is economically the most developed of the three advanced capitalist regions under consideration. In terms of the productive power of its domestic economy, Japan is catching up with or even overtaking the United States.[3]

During the 1970s and 1980s, simultaneously with this advance in Japan's international economic status, large Japanese enterprises have been extending the multinational spread of their activities. Here again, enterprises engaged in technologically advanced industries have been especially conspicuous. Moreover, since the 1970s Japan has also been placing increasing emphasis upon independent technological research and development, with attention in recent years directed particularly toward basic research.

Yet it must be noted, in comparing the economic and social conditions of Japan and two other advanced capitalist regions, that Japan is characterized by the underdeveloped state of its welfare provisions. As I stressed earlier, Japanese products have a clear competitive advantage over those of the other regions in terms of quality, technology, and labor productivity (and therefore also production costs). However, insofar as wages, labor conditions, social security, and public welfare services are concerned, Japan lags behind North America and Europe. Japan's record is particularly poor when compared with those of the United States and the Federal Republic of Germany. These problems are of great relevance to the issues to be considered in this chapter.

The underdeveloped living conditions and welfare of the Japanese working classes result from the tactics of Japanese monopoly capital, which still retains its traditional methods of accumulation, using low wages and poor working conditions as weapons in its competitive struggle. Within our "economic superpower" this self-centered approach to capital accumulation is supported by the economic policies of the government. The analysis of these problems constitutes the central focus of the present chapter and will be developed in more detail below. Here I should simply like to draw attention to the fact that, in comparing the current status of the three main advanced capitalist regions, Japan is characterized by a developed economy and underdeveloped welfare, while North America and Europe are characterized by stagnating economy and developed welfare. If this characteristic of Japanese economy and society could be overcome, not only would the contradictions inherent in the living standards of Japanese workers be resolved, but the way would be paved to a resolution of the trade and economic conflicts between Japan and Western industrialized nations.

Historical Characteristics of Japanese Capitalism

In relation to the rapid development of the Japanese economy, three aspects of Japanese capitalism may be singled out for particular comment.

First, the structure and periodization of capitalist development in Japan differ from those of Western industrialized nations. In Japan, for example, the primitive accumulation of capital and the industrial revolution both occurred in a relatively short space of time, and the two stages partially coincided with one another. Furthermore, the stage of classical industrial capitalism within Japanese development was extremely contracted. This phase of development was completed within a single decade, between the Russo-Japanese War (1904–1905) and the First World War (1914–1918). These years are particularly crucial to the historical analysis of Japanese capitalism.

Second, political intervention in various areas of the economy has always been strongly marked in Japan, and the role and influence of economic and other policies have been especially significant. The development of such policies was made possible by the existence of specific power structures and institutions. By way of example, one might consider the policies, pursued under the prewar emperor system, of promoting a "prosperous country and strong army" (fukoku kyōhei), of fostering the development of specific industries (shokusan kōgyō), and of creating government-controlled enterprises such as the Yawata Iron Works. Similar examples from the postwar period include the inflationary policies and the priority production system introduced by the U.S. occupation authorities, the Dodge Line, and so forth. A further illustration of this system is to be found at present in the pro-U.S. political bureaucratic and big business power structure, which has provided the breeding ground for incidents such as the Lockheed Affair.

Third, because of the incomplete nature of the bourgeois revolution in Japan, the civil rights of the working classes have always been restricted. Social security and other welfare policies were neglected, and traditional economic and social structures were retained and utilized to maximize the accumulation of capital. The Meiji government, for example, used the land tax to strengthen the power of absentee landlords, and the police and public order laws to suppress the formation of trade unions. Factory legislation remained extremely weak, while minimum wage and unemployment insurance systems were nonexistent. Even after the Second World War, the denial of public employees' right to strike caused problems with the International Labour Organization (ILO), while the level of pensions and insurance remained low. On the one hand, the implementation of democratization measures required by the Potsdam Declaration of 1945 and by the postwar constitution resulted in sweeping improvements in civil liberties. On the other, however, the early stages of the cold war undermined the implementation of many democratization measures. Consequently, civil rights in Japan remained underdeveloped, a situation that continues to the present day.

Developmental Structure of Japanese Capitalism and Implications for Economic Policy

Fundamental problems have arisen from Japan's status as a late-developing capitalist nation. Japan has pursued a path, often regarded as typical of late-developing economies, of capitalist development "from above," with all resources being mobilized for the purpose of capital accumulation, and particularly for high levels of accumulation by monopolistic enterprises. The consequence has been a peculiar and distorted system of accumulation that has structured the directions of economic development. This system has not only survived to the present day, but is currently being reinforced by the activities of ad hoc committees on expenditure reduction and by the policy of administrative reform introduced in the face of the economic crises of the 1970s and 1980s. Here, however, I should like to examine two aspects of the distorted structures of accumulation and development, and of the economic policies that support these structures.

First, to promote high accumulation by monopoly capital and increase the international competitiveness of Japanese enterprises, the economic and political establishment has placed priority on solving the various potential bottlenecks faced by large companies. These include the areas of capital, technology, equipment, markets, and raw materials. At the same time, wage policies have been enacted to preserve, strengthen, and re-create Japan's low wage base. By comparison with Europe and North America, and taking levels of productivity into consideration, wages have remained low and working conditions poor. This developmental structure has depended upon the existence of modernization and growth policies that emphasized the promotion of productivity.

Although these modernization and growth policies have resulted in the precocious development of Japanese monopoly capital, they have not encouraged the balanced growth of Japanese economy and society as a whole. Monopoly capital has experienced phenomenal expansion, but the living standards and welfare of the working classes have fallen behind, and outmoded social structures have been retained to serve the interests of big business. An example of this situation is provided by the extensive bottom segment of the famous Japanese "dual industrial structure." This segment consists of a mass of small subcontractors who surround large enterprises. It also includes contract and part-time employees (whose working conditions are particularly bad).

Of course, if one considers real wages in absolute terms, it is apparent that Japanese wage levels rose considerably in the high-growth period from 1955 to 1973. Moreover, even though wage levels have stagnated since then, they are now comparable with those of Western industrialized countries. However, wage costs per unit of production are exceptionally low in Japan. In other words, the rate of exploitation is unusually high, and the share of labor in the value of output is unusually low. In addition, working hours are long and provisions for paid holidays, social security, and public welfare services are poor. As productivity rises, it is inevitable that the range of goods and services that workers require to maintain their labor power will expand. In Japan, however, the inadequate provision of services creates severe contradictions between various aspects of life and labor.

Second, the nature of capital accumulation in Japan has restricted advances in living standards and thus limited the expansion of the domestic market. To solve this problem, the Japanese enterprises have been obliged to turn to overseas markets. Japanese capitalism has therefore acquired aggressive, militaristic, and dominating characteristics, and these characteristics have been reinforced by government policy.

In describing Japanese capitalism as "aggressive," I refer not merely to the prewar military invasion of neighboring countries, but also to foreign economic penetration by Japanese goods and capital. This penetration often occurs so rapidly and on such a large scale as to undermine the domestic industries of trading partners and drive domestic enterprises into bankruptcy. In this case, equal international exchange is transformed into economic aggression, which evokes a strong reaction from Japan's trading partners. Economic and military aggression, moreover, are almost invariably accompanied by increasing cooperation with, reliance on, and subordination to other major powers, as in the Anglo-Japanese Alliance of the Meiji period or the Japan-Germany-Italy Axis during World War II. A further example is provided by the postwar alliance between Japan and the United States, discussed below.

It should also be emphasized that, in speaking of the "militaristic" nature of Japanese capitalism, I am referring not only to the prewar history of brutal military aggression, but also to recent trends toward increasing military power and militaristic behavior within Japan. Some additional comments are perhaps necessary if such references to militarism are not to be misunderstood. Since the Second World War, overseas military activity by Japan has been prevented by the constitution and by the peace movement, both of which firmly reject the maintenance of military forces or involvement in acts of war. Postwar overseas economic penetration by Japanese capital has therefore taken place under the U.S. "nuclear umbrella," and such penetration cannot be explained without reference to Japan's subordinate relationship with the United States, and specifically to the Japan-U.S. Security Treaty. In this connection it is important to note that the relatively low burden of Japanese military expenditure since the high-growth period may well be one factor in the speed of Japanese economic development and in the recent expansion of the Japanese economy.

Postwar Starting Point of Capitalist Development

In the 1930s and 1940s Japan became the most recent in a series of

invaders of mainland Asia. Together with Germany, it was responsible for the outbreak, expansion, and continuation of the Second
World War. By the second half of 1944, however, Japan was reel-
ing under the impact of destructive attacks and had lost the organizational ability to prosecute the war effectively. In August 1945
Japan accepted the Allies' fundamental demands as set out in the
Potsdam Declaration of the preceding month and surrendered unconditionally. The Potsdam Declaration was the outcome of the
trilateral summit conference between the United States, Great
Britain, and the Soviet Union but also reflected the wishes of the
fifty-odd other countries then at war with Japan. It imposed the
following conditions upon Japan: the Japanese armed forces were
to surrender unconditionally and be disbanded; militarism was to
be abandoned and armaments industries dismantled; all territory
occupied by Japan was to be returned; war criminals were to be
prosecuted; provisions for freedom of speech, religion, and
thought were to be enacted within Japan; and, to ensure the
realization of these objectives, Japan was to be occupied by Allied
forces.

The beginning of the postwar development of Japanese capitalism and the various policies of the postwar period must therefore be seen against the background not only of the restoration of
war damage but also of the following circumstances: (1) The need
for the state to implement policies to create the democratic, non-
military economic and social structures required by the Potsdam
Declaration. (2) The termination of military production and the
loss of Japan's overseas colonies. These two developments caused
the collapse of the old structures of capitalist accumulation and
reproduction, which had been based upon the militarization of the
economy, overseas invasion, and the expansion of the colonial
market. The consequent fall in the levels of production across all
industries made it increasingly essential to introduce policies
that would set the Japanese economy on the path toward recovery.
(3) Japan's loss, albeit temporary, of national sovereignty. The
country was obliged to adapt to the circumstances of occupation by
the Allies. (In practice, this virtually amounted to occupation by
the United States alone.) The occupation, which ended in 1952
with the restoration of Japan's independence under the Treaty of
San Francisco, had a great influence upon political, economic, and
social life.

War Damage

In general, the war damage sustained by Japan was characterized by its great extent and uneven distribution. The total number of people killed or missing in action during the war with China and the Pacific War amounted to some 2 million, and (according to war pension data) a further 300,000 were seriously injured. Civilian casualties totaled 320,000 killed or missing and 340,000 injured. In terms of material damage, besides the inevitable destruction of military hardware and installations, serious damage was inflicted on factories and productive equipment, housing and social amenities, shipping (including fishing boats), and so on. The war years had also witnessed the massive devastation and deterioration of agricultural land, mines, and machinery. Large amounts of equipment used to produce light industrial and consumer goods had also been scrapped and converted to military uses. As a result, there had been a sharp fall in productive capacity. The loss to shipping, including fishing vessels converted for military use, was severe. This factor, together with the poor harvest of 1944, caused serious food shortages and soaring food prices. There was also a serious lack of trade organizations able to handle the import of foodstuffs and raw materials. Overall, the fact that manufacturing equipment had suffered relatively little damage by comparison with other sections of Japanese economy and society was to be of great importance in relation to the problems of postwar economic recovery.

Another factor that affected living standards immediately after the war was the return to Japan of military personnel and civilian emigrants from former colonies or areas invaded by Japan. At the same time, the suspension of military production resulted in the dismissal of large numbers of workers and students who had been recruited as labor for armaments factories. These developments were major causes of mass unemployment. The number of unemployed people at the end of 1945 has been estimated at 13 million, an enormous figure when compared with a 1935 population of 73 million and employed work force of 32 million.

Economic Policy in the Second Half of the 1940s

Democratization Policies

Immediately after the war, as often seems to happen in such periods of economic and social transformation, two contrasting types of economic policy were pursued simultaneously. The first involved production-related policies, which were essentially aimed at the democratization of the economy, while the second involved output-related policies—in the earlier stages, inflationary policies, and later, the Dodge Line.

During the occupation, politics and administration were conducted through a system of indirect rule by the Allied powers (in effect, by the United States). Policy developments, therefore, strongly reflected U.S. objectives. There was, however, some scope for the Japanese people and government to influence policy directions, and it is important to note that, with the reconstruction of the political, economic, and social order within Japan, this influence became stronger. "Democratization policies" were of course designed to fulfill the Potsdam Declaration's demands for the democratization and demilitarization of Japanese economy and society. They therefore extended far beyond the realm of economic policy to include the implementation of such measures as the disbanding of the armed forces and the dismantling of the absolutist and fascist political, administrative, legal, and law enforcement structures. A new constitution, drawn up in 1946, defined the emperor's position as a purely symbolic one, enshrined the principles of respect for human rights, and renounced the use of war and the maintenance of armed forces. A variety of laws were also enacted to support these objectives. Meanwhile, at an individual level, war criminals were prosecuted, and many leading wartime figures from the political, financial, administrative, educational, and media arenas were purged from public office.

Democratization policies were also carried out in the economic sphere. Land reform abolished the absentee landowner system and created an agricultural structure based on small farmers (see chapter 3). The dissolution of the zaibatsu (big business combines) resulted in the breaking up of the holding companies whose shares were privately owned by the zaibatsu families. The use of zaibatsu trademarks and the system of interlocking directorships were prohibited, and eighteen major business groups were disbanded. Labor reforms were implemented by means of the "Three Labor Laws": the Trade Union Law (1945), Labor Relations Adjustment Law (1946), and Labor Standards Law (1947).

The first point to be made about these reforms is that they constituted the achievement of a bourgeois revolution in Japan. On the one hand, this revolution increased the rights and improved the status of the workers, while on the other hand it weakened the control and the economic power of the ruling class. As a result, the power structures and regulatory framework within which postwar Japanese capitalism operated were very different from those of the prewar period. Democratization policies brought about the destruction of the absolutist emperor system and, most importantly, eliminated absentee landlords from the ruling class.

Democratization, which was carried out under the strong leadership of the United States, was in another sense, however, a part of the process of subjecting Japan to the imperialist hegemony of the United States. Thus, while the power of the Japanese ruling class was eroded, Japanese monopoly capital came to be subordinated to U.S. monopoly capital, and an unequal but cooperative relationship was established between the two sides. The result of this process was the sabotaging or reversal of democratization policies: in particular, of zaibatsu dissolution, demilitarization, and protection of the fundamental rights of the working class. Although land reform was carried out in a thorough and radical fashion, the newly expanded class of small independent farmers was then used to create a conservative agricultural bloc, and so to split the increasingly active working class movement. Zaibatsu dissolution did not touch the zaibatsu-related financial institutions, but permitted interlocking shareholdings by large firms. As the result of these omissions, it left the door open to the re-creation of business groups based upon the supply of finance and the interconnected ownership of shares. Thus the foundations were laid for the revival and reorganization of monopoly capital, and for the undermining and weakening of the zaibatsu dissolution measures. Many aspects of postwar democracy, in other words, were soon reduced to mere empty shells.

These developments are generally known as the "reverse course." As a consequence of the reverse course the United States was transformed, in the eyes of the Japanese working classes, from a liberator to an oppressor. These trends in U.S. policy toward Japan and Asia as a whole must be viewed in the context of the emergence of U.S.-Soviet confrontation, civil war and revolution in China, and the outbreak of the Korean War.[4]

Inflationary Policies

The second strand during the occupation period consisted of measures related to manufacturing output. These were designed to deal with the extremely low levels of production caused by the destruction of capacity during World War II. In the initial stages, an inflationary policy was pursued. In other words, recovery was stimulated by means of market and demand expansion based on deficit spending and inflation.

The main features and characteristics of this inflationary policy were as follows:

Budget deficits ran at levels exceeding even those of wartime, financed by bonds issued through the Bank of Japan.

Important basic industries, such as coal, steel, and fertilizers, were supported by government subsidies designed to offset the gap between costs and prices. The products of these industries were then sold at low prices to related strategic industries. As a result, the markets and profits of the coal, steel, chemicals, and other industries were guaranteed. Through this system—known as the priority production system (*keisha seisan hōshiki*)[5]—the government hoped to use the major basic industries as an "engine" to raise the overall level of production.

Since long-term financing is difficult in times of inflation, the government established a Reconstruction Finance Bank, which provided long-term capital to the various major industries. Because this fund was also financed by the issuing of bonds through the Bank of Japan, it acted as a further spur to inflation. To prevent this inflation from causing mass withdrawals of savings deposits and the collapse of the private banking system, the government was forced to introduce an Emergency Financial Measures Ordinance (February 1946). This provided for the issue of new paper money and limited individual holdings of the new notes. Old currency was to be deposited in financial institutions, and restrictions were placed upon the withdrawal of savings. In this way further private savings were demanded at a time when deposits were being frozen and financial institutions were protected by the government.

A policy of tight wage restriction was enforced. For example, when wages for public servants were fixed in July 1947, they were calculated on the basis of a food consumption level of 1,550 calories per day. The objective was clearly to base postwar economic recovery upon wage levels even lower than those that had existed in the prewar period (see chapter 5).

To prevent economic disruption caused by an influx of foreign goods, special trade controls were introduced. A system of protection for domestic industries was created by means of multiple exchange rates, and by direct government control of all foreign trade activities.

Under these policies, the ratio of subsidies to the unit cost of products in many industries was extraordinarily high. For example, in fiscal year 1948 the level of subsidies was 70 percent in the iron industry, 40–45 percent in rolled steel production, and 40 percent in ammonium sulfate production. As industrial production recovered, the amount of public spending absorbed by such subsidies became increasingly burdensome, and fiscally induced inflation reached levels higher than those experienced during the war years. The proportion of public spending devoted to the various production subsidies rose from 10.1 percent in 1946 to between 20 percent and 30 percent in 1947–1949.

As the United States turned its attention from occupation policies aimed at the democratization and demilitarization of Japan to policies (consistent with its new Asian strategy) of building military bases and deploying its forces in Japan, the Japanese government was obliged to contribute large sums of money to the maintenance of American forces and the construction of U.S. bases. These payments, which were officially termed "charges associated with organizing the termination of hostilities," amounted to U.S. $5.06 billion in 1945–1949.[6] Expressed as a percentage of total government spending, they stood at 33 percent in 1946, 31 percent in 1947, 25 percent in 1948, and 19 percent in 1949.

From these comments it will be clear that the immediate postwar period saw the enactment of democratization measures that liberated the Japanese working classes and raised their social status, but it also saw the development of an increasingly parasitic and predatory relationship between heavy industrial monopoly capital and the state. At the same time, the Japanese people had to shoulder the substantial expenses of the construction of U.S. military bases. In terms of their economic situation, it could be said of the Japanese working classes that "the real war was not yet over." It is therefore essential to bear in mind that postwar economic reconstruction in Japan was made possible above all by the sacrifices and privations of working people.

The Dodge Line and the Dodge Recession

The inflationary policy pursued immediately after the war imposed disproportionate sacrifices on the lives of working people and threw the political and economic system into a state of disorder. It was, therefore, a policy that could not be continued indefinitely. Moreover, it is significant that during the period in which the inflationary policy was in force, U.S. economic aid to Japan was running at a level equivalent to 60–70 percent of total Japanese imports, or roughly equal to Japan's total trade deficit.[7] As production recovered, there was growing recognition, both within Japan and overseas, that, given the dependence of the postwar Japanese economy upon imports of foodstuffs, raw materials, and energy sources, it was essential to hasten the reestablishment of the country's economic independence by expanding exports and achieving a balanced trade situation.

It was against this background that the occupation authority's financial adviser Joseph Dodge (then president of the Bank of Detroit) put forward a proposal for the creation of an "independent and stable" Japanese economy, a policy that came to be known as the "Dodge Line." The main principles of the Dodge Line, which was implemented at the beginning of fiscal year 1949, were as follows:

In the sphere of financial policy, budgets were to be balanced and there was to be a trend toward budget surplus. This was to be achieved by increasing tax revenue through the imposition of heavy taxes on the general population, and through reductions in price differential subsidies. Budget surpluses would be used to commence repayment of the nation's accumulated debts and would also serve the purpose of placing a monetary restraint upon inflation.

In association with these financial policies, the existing priority production system was to be replaced by a new "concentrated production system" (*shūchū seisan hōshiki*). This system, which aimed to increase the efficiency of production and to raise the level of labor productivity, focused on protecting and nurturing large enterprises in the heavy industry sector and excluded small enterprises from its scope.[8]

The Reconstruction Finance Bank, which had contributed to high levels of inflation, was phased out. In its place an Aid Counterpart Fund Special Account was established. This account channeled money raised by the sale of U.S. aid commodities into industrial investment.

To deal with the problem of reestablishing Japan's economic independence, a first step was taken toward freeing the economy from its current state of extreme isolation from the world market. This involved the fixing of a single exchange rate of 360 yen to the dollar, and the abolition of export subsidies. Subsequently, in 1950, the occupation authorities permitted the reopening of foreign trade by private enterprise. However, the Foreign Exchange and Foreign Trade Control Laws of 1949 imposed a strict quota system on the allocation of foreign currency for import purposes, and so in effect offered continued protection to domestic industries.

To promote balanced financial and trade recovery, the Dodge Line encouraged widespread reductions in the size of the work force. The new policy may therefore be seen as marking the starting point of the postwar "rationalization" movement.

The Dodge Line thus attempted, on the one hand, to resolve the problem of inflation and, on the other, to reestablish Japan's independence through the expansion of exports. In effect, however, it achieved neither of its proclaimed objectives of "independence and stability" and instead resulted in a severe phase of economic recession—the "Dodge Recession." The expectation behind the Dodge Line had been that, by reorganizing and reducing price subsidies and thus reducing the domestic market, it would impel Japanese enterprises to rationalize production and thus expand exports. However, given Japan's low international competitive power and the contemporary international economic climate, such expectations could not be realized.

In the first place, many of the Japanese production facilities then in operation had been constructed before or during the war, often with little regard to cost, and the technology they embodied was already obsolete. Second, the Dodge Line was carried out when the world economy was experiencing the first postwar recession, and many countries (including Great Britain) were devaluing their currencies. Under these circumstances, a rate of 360 yen to the dollar somewhat overvalued the Japanese currency. Furthermore, because of the success of the Chinese revolution, Japan's trade links with China were effectively severed, in conformity to the United States's new China policy. Since Japan had relied heavily upon China both as a source of raw materials and as a market, this change in policy weakened the international competitiveness of the Japanese economy by reducing its raw materials base, while at the same time restricting Japan's export markets. An additional consequence of this postwar interruption of Japan's trade with China was a decline in the economic status of western Japan, which is geographically close to China, and an increase in the economic power of the Pacific coastal belt, which faces the United States.

The results of the Dodge Line were not only reductions in government spending (which had until then helped to prop up the domestic market), sluggish export growth, and worsening of the economic recession. A growing mass of accumulated stocks were also financed by capital pumped into the private banking system and private industry by the Bank of Japan, which felt obliged to use expansionary financing to prevent the effects of the recession from spreading. As a consequence, the Dodge Line was unsuccessful even in its other proclaimed objective of halting inflation.

The Japanese economy under the Dodge Line experienced simultaneous severe recession and accumulating underutilized stocks and capital. Yet a means of escaping this trap and initiating economic recovery was not easy to find. The government could not continue indefinitely to pump money into the economy, and indeed a year after the initiation of the Dodge Line, in May 1950, the administration changed its policy to one of tightening the money market. The Japanese economy at that stage had not yet recovered from the damage inflicted by the war and thus continued to face a prolonged and structural crisis of reduced production. To overcome this crisis, desperate efforts were made to cut back on employment and to lower the levels of employees' wages and working conditions. In the postwar period, however, heavy industry was emerging as the basis of the Japanese economy. As is evident from the course of subsequent Japanese development, international competitiveness in heavy industry cannot be created merely by reducing wages and imposing poorer working conditions while ignoring the need for new equipment and technology.

Economic Policy in the Early 1950s

Updating Technology

The processes of development at work in the Japanese economy and Japanese economic policy during the first half of the 1950s are rather simple when compared with the developments of the previous five years. In looking at the early 1950s it is enough to focus on two major points. The first point to be considered is the emergence of a policy of technological modernization, which resulted in a wave of rationalization based upon capital investment and the introduction of new know-how. This rationalization movement must be viewed against the background of an economic boom caused by the Korean War (June 1950–July 1953).

As is well known, the Korean War was the first modern localized war to be fought after World War II. It involved the use of Japan as a base for United Nations forces. The early phases of the war in particular took the form of a war of attrition, and this situation resulted in a large quantity of goods and services being ordered from Japanese enterprises (so-called Korean War procurements). Consequently, the Japanese economy, which only a short while before had been facing the Dodge Recession and severe monetary restrictions, was able to dispose of its accumulated stocks and enter into an unprecedented boom: the "Korean War boom."

The importance of the Korean War boom's impact on the Japanese economy can be appreciated if one considers a few statistics. By June 1951, one year after the outbreak of the war, the index of manufacturing production (in real terms) was 50 percent higher than it had been in June 1950. In the same period the index of manufacturing productivity increased by 30 percent, and the wholesale commodity price index by 52 percent. Between 1950 and 1957 the total value of special procurements amounted to U.S. $1.57 billion. By comparison the value of normal exports was $0.51 billion in 1949 and $0.96 billion in 1950. When considering the Korean War boom in the Japanese context, it is also important to remember that the boom affected the world economy as a whole, and that, in these circumstances, ordinary exports increased by 89 percent from 1949 to 1950 and by 40 percent from 1950 to 1951.

Given this economic environment, technological modernization was able to proceed, particularly in large heavy industrial enterprises, without imposing the sorts of pressures upon wages and working conditions that had characterized the rationalization movements of the Dodge Line era. Rather, the aim was now to rationalize industry by capital investment and the introduction of new productive techniques.

To achieve this objective, long-term plans for investment and technological modernization in each industry were drawn up, and incentives were offered to promote the realization of these plans. On the basis of reports compiled by the Industrial Rationalization Council, a number of ordinances and laws, including Outline Measures for the Rationalization of the Steel and Coal Industries (1950), an Enterprise Rationalization Promotion Law (1952), and an Electricity Development Promotion Law (1952), were enacted. These provided legal and administrative mechanisms for control over long-term rationalization plans in each industry. A variety of other arrangements were also made to encourage the introduction of more productive equipment. These included accelerated depreciation arrangements, a partial exemption from property taxes, the channeling of public finances into the development of infrastructure (roads, ports, etc.), access to low-interest-rate loans from government-controlled financial institutions, priority access to foreign currency for those wishing to import equipment and technology, and measures to promote the inflow of foreign capital.

Two points need to be made about these technological modernization policies. First, the policies were presented as constituting a long-term plan for rationalization of all industries. In practice, however, they focused mainly on large monopoly enterprises in the existing heavy industrial sectors, including the energy sector. Second, these heavy industrial sectors, which had expanded in response to military demand during the war period, still had considerable excess capacity and were using equipment that was obsolete by Western standards. The process of rationalization through capital investment and technological upgrading, however, did not encompass all production processes within heavy industry, but concentrated on those parts of the production process where the problems of obsolescence were particularly evident.

In this sense, the policy operated only on a small scale. The Korean War boom rationalization measures are significant, however, because they provided the prototype for the heavy industrialization policies that were later to serve as the driving force behind the period of high economic growth.

Political Independence and Rearmament

A further factor to be emphasized in an analysis of economic developments in the first half of the 1950s is the trend toward rearmament that accompanied the restoration of Japan's political independence. After the Korean War and the concurrent economic boom, there was a shift away from adherence to the postwar constitution, which had prohibited Japan from possessing military forces. Japanese monopoly capital sought to propel the economy in the direction of a military-based structure similar to that which had existed in the prewar era by strengthening the Japan-U.S. relationship and accentuating Japan's political and economic subordination to the United States. This attempt, however, was frustrated by popular movements that developed to defend the constitution and promote the cause of peace.

Japanese rearmament began immediately after the outbreak of the Korean War, when the occupation authorities ordered the establishment of the 75,000-member Police Reserve and the strengthening of the 8,000-member Maritime Safety Agency. Then, in March 1952, immediately before Japan regained its independence, the authorities officially recognized the establishment of an air force. Thus, by the time independence was restored, Japan had already reestablished a military capability including army, navy, and air force. These were subsequently reinforced and were successively renamed the Security Forces in October 1952 and the Self-Defense Forces in July 1954. Moreover, at the time of the Korean War Japan was granted the right to manufacture military hardware, and this area of manufacturing has been expanding ever since.

The wave of rearmament that commenced from the Korean War reflects the efforts of Japanese big business to avert the structural depression that was anticipated when Korean War procurements ceased. It was also an attempt to re-create the structures of capital accumulation that had existed prior to the Pacific War. In fact, during fiscal 1952 (the first year of independence) government military expenditure amounted to 182 billion yen, or more than 20 percent of total public spending. In May 1953 the Defense

Production Committee of the big business lobby group Keidanren published an "Eight Year Plan for Defense Spending" in which they demanded an acceleration of rearmament and proposed a 2.9 trillion yen long-term military expenditure plan. In addition to these developments, under the U.S.-Japan Mutual Security Agreement of 1954, the Japanese government promised to strengthen Japan's arms capability in return for U.S. military assistance. This further supported the efforts of big business to promote rearmament.

These efforts were also accompanied by the passing of the 1952 Anti-Subversive Activities Law, and of the 1953 Strike Restriction Law, which placed limitations on strike activity in the electrical power and coal industries. Attempts to promote rearmament, however, evoked such a powerful reaction from the working class that it proved impossible for business to reestablish the structures of accumulation that had prevailed before the Second World War. Later, during the high-growth era, guidelines were established according to which military spending was to be kept below 10 percent of government expenditure and 1 percent of GNP (quite low levels compared with the military expenditure of other major capitalist nations). The establishment of these guidelines, which came to be a significant feature of the postwar Japanese economy, can be largely attributed to the activities of the popular peace movement.

Finally, it should be noted that, with the restoration of Japanese independence, a number of treaties and agreements were concluded between Japan and the United States. These treaties, which included the Mutual Security Treaty and a Commerce and Navigation Treaty, among others, provided formal recognition of the political, economic, and military privileges already acquired by Americans during the Allied occupation of Japan. These developments indicate the extent to which the postwar reorganization of Japanese capitalism took place within a framework of subordination to the United States.

Of course, the subordinate relationship with the United States cannot be regarded as an unchanging one. With the development of Japanese capitalism, Japan-U.S. relations, and the problems inherent in these relations, have also altered. It is a fact, however, that the development of Japanese capitalism in the high-growth era was based upon access to the raw materials, energy resources, technology, and markets of the United States, and that even today the relationship between the two countries is a close one.

Fundamental Characteristics of High-Growth Policy

In 1953–1955 production levels in Japanese heavy industry regained the peak achieved during the Second World War, and thereafter the speed of economic development accelerated. As a result, particularly in the heavy industrial area, Japan was soon to attain levels of production second only to those of the United States, and by about 1970 it had succeeded in creating the most competitive heavy industrial sector in the world. The period of postwar high economic growth in Japan may be defined as lasting for nineteen years: from 1955 to 1973. Following the post-Korean War recession of 1954, the so-called Jimmu Boom of 1955 heralded the start of a full-fledged upturn in the Japanese economy. (The Jimmu Boom was named after the Emperor Jimmu, who according to legend was the first emperor of Japan—the implication being that this was the greatest boom since the reign of Jimmu. The later "Iwato Boom" of 1958–1961 likewise derived its name from ancient legend.) With the first oil crisis of 1973, the Japanese economy was plunged into a structural "oil crisis recession" from 1974 to 1975. The problem of structurally depressed industries (in cluding a number of areas of heavy industry) emerged, and GNP growth also fell to low levels. Levels of production in manufacturing were not to regain their 1973 level for five years.

If one looks in concrete terms at production in various industries in 1973 and compares these figures with the figures for 1955, it is apparent that high growth was particularly conspicuous in the heavy industrial sector. The 1973 volume of crude steel production (199 million tons) was 12.7 times the figure for 1955, while the automobile production in 1973 (at 7.1 million vehicles) was 102 times as high as it had been in 1955. The output of electrical power also increased 7.2-fold to a level of 470.1 billion kwh by 1973.

During the high growth era, as in other phases of Japanese economic development, government policy played an important role. During the period under consideration the policies pursued can aptly be characterized as "high-growth policies." The essential features of these policies were as follows. First, a concerted attempt was made to foster heavy industrialization, and thus to achieve high growth and high rates of accumulation in the monopoly capital sector. For the most part the focus was on the reorganization and strengthening of traditional areas of heavy industry, though from the end of the 1960s the emphasis shifted toward the promotion of technologically sophisticated industries and products. Second, the strategy of maintaining the standard of living of the working class at relatively low levels was perpetuated. As has been seen, this strategy played an important part in the historical process of capital accumulation in Japan. A characteristic feature of the strategy was that efforts were made to contain the demands of the working classes so that improvements in their employment and living conditions were more gradual than increases in the size of the national product. All the power of state monopoly capital was mobilized to achieve this aim.

Industrial financing, science and technology, resources, energy, industrial structure, wages, the labor force, prices, distribution, trade, and overseas economic relations were all structured, within the framework of economic and other policies, with a view to increasing the competitive power of heavy industry and restricting rises in the living standards of working people. At the same time, energetic ideological campaigns were conducted to obtain a public consensus on the desirability of high economic growth. In this context, it is interesting to observe how the image of Japan's economic backwardness, the dangers of resource and energy shortages, and the threat of economic crisis were used as propaganda weapons whenever appropriate.

To provide a more detailed understanding of high-growth policies, it is useful to divide the era of rapid economic growth into a number of shorter phases and to analyze each separately. Such divisions are necessary because, as Japanese capitalism developed throughout this period, so changes occurred in the practical problems of capital accumulation and in the demands placed upon government policy. As a consequence, the content and focus of policy itself underwent considerable alteration.

Phase One—Technological Upgrading and Capital Investment

In the year in which high economic growth began, the Economic White Paper for 1956 included the now famous statement that "the period of postwar recovery is over." By that time, the overall level of heavy industrial output had recovered to its pre-1945 peak. Ammonium sulfate production overtook its previous peak in 1950, cement production in 1951, automobile and steel production in 1953, shipping in 1957, and machinery in 1960. On the other hand, however, in the export-oriented light-industrial sector, although production of rayon yarn had recovered by 1954, cotton yarn, cotton fabrics, and silk had all failed to regain their prewar peak. While the center of gravity of the economy was shifting toward heavy industry, the international competitiveness of Japanese goods was still weak, as can be seen by the fact that in 1955 exports (on a volume basis) were still at a mere 71.6 percent of their highest prewar level. As is well known, at that period the Japanese economy struggled to survive by export methods that were often little more than dumping. Exports were firmly based in the light industrial sector, where wages were still lower than they had been before the war.

Under these circumstances it is hardly surprising that the main objective of monopoly capital should have been to transform traditional heavy industries such as steel, shipbuilding, automobiles, electrical machinery, and petrochemicals into the key sectors of the economy and to foster their international competitiveness. This objective, which needs to be viewed in the context of a world where newly independent less developed countries were emerging as rivals to Japan in light industrial production, was to be achieved by large-scale investment in more technologically sophisticated equipment. Such investment was clearly going to need something more far-reaching than the rather half-hearted technological modernization measures of the early 1950s. New factories and industrial zones, all equipped with the most up-to-date plants and machinery, would be required. For the full-scale development of heavy industry, it was also necessary to have a highly evolved division of labor. Not only must the costs of the major heavy industrial producers and parts and components makers be reduced; it was also essential to develop a host of other related industries. In addition, there was a need to provide industrial infrastructure such as roads, ports, and water supply.

Large-scale capital investment in heavy industry tends to promote investment in a wide range of other industrial areas, and so to create a widespread and prolonged boom, whose length will vary according to the gestation period of the investment. It also raises, however, a number of important economic problems. These include the question of access to capital and technology, the problems of a long gestation period before returns on investment can be generated, and the issue of ensuring the existence of markets for output once the investment boom has ended. For Japan in the mid-1950s, with little experience in solving such issues, the drive toward heavy industrialization represented a life or death gamble.

High-growth policies in this first period were addressed to the problems of capital accumulation by big business. Their central concern was the widespread introduction of new technologies by means of capital investment, and they were characterized by particular emphasis on a number of specific measures. First, the exchange control system created by the Dodge Line was used as a means of maintaining a protected domestic market for the products of heavy industrial monopoly capital. Second, efforts were made to promote the import of foreign capital and technology, particularly from the United States. Third, enterprises were encouraged to reinvest their profits. Such reinvestment was supported by a variety of tax measures, including accelerated depreciation on technologically advanced equipment. Finally, the credit facilities of the Bank of Japan were used to promote investment in modern technology by large monopoly enterprises. The mechanism by which this latter policy was put into effect was as follows: the Bank of Japan injected a flow of credit into the private city banks, and the city banks in turn provided long-term low interest rate loans to large enterprises associated with their particular business group. (For details of the business groups, see chapter 4.)

Other, less significant policy measures included the concentration of government spending in the area of public works and industrial infrastructure investment. This served to expand the market for heavy industrial goods and to offer further incentive to investment in the technological modernization of plants and equipment. At the same time, efforts were made to maintain secure overseas supplies of raw materials, while reparations negotiations with Southeast Asia were used to guarantee both a resource base and a market for the products of heavy industry.

During the first phase of high growth, with support of the policies listed above, large enterprises in Japan were essentially successful in dealing with the issue of capital accumulation and in placing the traditional heavy industrial sector on an internationally competitive footing. Indeed, it is conspicuous that in this period, by contrast with other phases of growth, the expansion of mining and manufacturing output was more rapid than the expansion of government expenditure or exports (see table 2.2). The characteristics of this first phase, then, are the explosive growth of private investment, centered on heavy industry, and the fact that this investment initiated a ripple effect resulting in the continuing expansion of investment throughout Japanese industry. Between 1955 and 1961 mining and manufacturing output increased 2.5-fold.

Particularly rapid increases were recorded in machinery production and, to a lesser extent, in other areas of heavy industry. Output of electrical equipment increased 7.8-fold; transport machinery 3.9-fold; steel 2.9-fold; and chemicals 2.3-fold. It was also characteristic of this period that, because of the prolonged nature of the investment boom, heavy industry did not face serious problems in finding markets for its ever-expanding output.

Liberalization Policies and the National Income Doubling Plan

In 1960 the Japanese economy was in the midst of the so-called Iwato Boom, but the first phase of high economic growth was soon to draw to a close: for it was in this year that two of the central elements of a new growth phase emerged. The first was the policy of economic liberalization, which was put forward simultaneously with the revision of the Japan-U.S. Mutual Security Treaty; second was the National Income Doubling Plan, which indicated the outlines of government economic policy for the next period of growth.

It was inevitable that the capital investment boom stimulated by the economic policies of the late 1950s would ultimately run up against the barrier of limits to consumer demand, and that the characteristic contradiction of capitalism—a gap between production and consumption—would appear. This contradiction tends to be particularly acute in countries like Japan, where domestic resources are few, wages and working conditions poor, and the scale of the rural market small. To resolve these market-related problems, Japanese monopoly capital developed a new strategy of expanding into overseas markets. To carry out this strategy, however, it was not only necessary to invest in new technology, in-

Table 2.2

Annual Average Rate of Increase of Major Economic Indicators, 1955–1977 (percent)

	1955–1961	1961–1965	1965–1970	1970–1973	1973–1977
Real GNP	10.7	8.1	12.1	8.8	3.1
Production (mining and manufacturing)	17.2	10.1	16.2	8.5	0.1
Export (customs, dollar)	13.6	19.0	18.2	24.2	22.8
Financial expenses (general accounts)	12.6	16.1	17.1	23.0	17.9
Regular employment (manufacturing)	11.0	4.6	3.1	−0.3	−2.5
Real wages (manufacturing)	5.0	3.2	8.8	9.5	1.4
Consumer prices	2.2	6.5	5.5	7.4	13.5

crease productivity, and strengthen the international competitiveness of Japanese industry; it was also necessary to shift toward a policy of liberalization and to begin to open Japan's doors to foreign trade. At the same time, in the late 1950s, the United States was beginning to experience the economic problems associated with the so-called dollar crisis. Demands therefore grew for Japan to shoulder part of the burden of aid to Southeast Asia, and to open its markets to U.S. monopoly capital.

It was against this economic background that policies for the freeing of trade and investment were put into effect. These were based on the government's so-called Fundamental Principles for the Liberalization of Trade and Exchange and involved, first, a commitment to increase the trade liberalization ratio[9] from 41 percent in April 1960 to 80 percent in 1963, and to continue liberalization thereafter. Capital movements were also to be liberalized, smoothing the way for U.S. direct investment in Japan. As a result of these policies, trade restrictions were rapidly reduced, and the liberalization ratios achieved (89 percent by April 1963 and 92 percent by April 1964) actually exceeded anticipation. Moreover, 1965 saw the removal of controls on imports of fully manufactured passenger vehicles, a long-standing issue of contention between Japan and the United States.

The National Income Doubling Plan announced by the cabinet

in December 1960 was in part a means of allaying public concern at the drift toward liberalization. The plan set a target of 7.2 percent annual economic growth from 1960 to 1970, with a growth rate of 9.0 percent in the first three years. To achieve this target, which would double the size of the national income in a decade, an attempt was made to secure a popular consensus on two points: the further promotion of rationalization in heavy industry and other areas of manufacturing, and a large-scale shift of labor power out of the more backward sections of the Japanese economy, particularly the agricultural sector, where a large number of people were employed on small family farms. This latter process was essential to secure the additional labor required for high economic growth. It was estimated that an increase in the nonagricultural work force of 13 million (or some 71 percent) would be required to meet the government's growth targets. To achieve this figure it would be necessary to reduce the number of self-employed and family workers by 6 million (27 percent). In the primary sector alone a reduction of 4.9 million (32 percent) would be required. The Income Doubling Plan was important in reassuring Japanese monopoly capital that liberalization measures would be accompanied by the promotion of high growth, particularly in heavy industry. It also led to the publication of a wide range of reports and articles emphasizing the necessity of flexibility, adjustment, and restructuring in the areas of labor, enterprise, and large-scale industry.

Finally, the new Japan-U.S. Security Treaty, which became effective in June 1960, provided the conditions for the beginning of overseas economic expansion by Japanese capital. The scope of the alliance went beyond the boundaries of Japan, extending the sphere of U.S. and Japanese mutual defense responsibilities to Asia, while at the same time offering the protection of the U.S. nuclear umbrella. It was also agreed that Japan should support U.S. economic security objectives by liberalization of its trade policies and by the provision of overseas economic aid. This military treaty between Japan and the United States not only provided the basis for the imperialistic expansion of Japan, which continues to the present day; its influence also extended into the economic sphere, since it strengthened economic ties between the two countries and provided a basis for the resolution of economic policy conflicts.

The year 1960 also saw the simultaneous emergence of several areas of social conflict. The most important were the "Ampō Campaign," in which the working classes joined in concerted opposition to the new Japan-U.S. Security Treaty, and the Miike Strike, directed against energy and industrial rationalization policies that involved reductions in the size of the coal industry. The first of these movements in particular succeeded in placing a brake on the revival of Japanese militarism and resulted in limitations on the expansion of rearmament and military spending.

Phase Two—Effective Demand Expansion and Structural Change

In the second phase of high growth, which began with the end of the Iwato Boom, Japan's economic structure started to suffer from endemic problems of excess capacity in heavy industry. In response, the emphasis of high-growth policies was shifted from investment promotion to demand expansion. At the same time, the implementation of liberalization policies was extended and brought about a wholesale restructuring of the economic system.

As seen, the high productivity of the new technologically advanced factories and industrial zones encouraged Japanese monopoly capital to develop a long-term strategy of expanding exports of heavy industrial products, and this strategy in turn necessitated the liberalization of the trading system. At this time, however, many problems relating to the international competitiveness of heavy industry remained to be solved. Alongside the new factories that had been built during the first phase of high growth, many enterprises still suffered from problems of scale and capital structure. Older factories that survived from the prewar years were now uncompetitive in cost terms, while small firms and subcontractors faced difficulties arising from the low productivity of their equipment. Consequently, to justify continuing support for capital investment at a time of excess capacity, heavy industrialization policies moved toward a "scrap-and-build" model. At the same time a policy of supporting increased capital concentration—a so-called new industrial order—was put into effect. This encouraged large-scale mergers of major enterprises, the creation of vertically integrated enterprise groups (kigyō keiretsu), and the adjustment and restructuring of subcontracting relationships between large and small firms. The effect of these policies was to turn the existing structure of competing oligopolies into a new system of collaborating oligopolies.

The main elements of this phase of high-growth policy can thus be defined as follows: (1) Liberalization measures, resulting in the opening up of the Japanese economy. (2) The strengthening of budgetary and financial measures designed to stimulate demand in a period of excess capacity. To meet this objective a "Comprehensive National Development Plan" was put into effect, based upon the 1962 Law for the Creation of New Industrial Cities. The plan provided the framework for widening the scope of infrastructure-related public works projects. (3) Concerted efforts to promote overseas economic expansion. (4) Comprehensive economic restructuring measures designed to counteract the effects of liberalization. While, on the one hand, these involved support for increased accumulation and concentration within the monopoly capital sector, on the other, they implied reorganization, retrenchment, and selective closures in the areas of agriculture, mining, and small business, which were less well-equipped to resist the pressures of liberalization. Such restructuring policies were supported by a number of new pieces of legislation, including the 1961 Basic Agricultural Law and the 1963 Basic Law on Small Enterprises.

In short, therefore, the second phase of high economic growth can be seen as a period in which the liberalization of the economy was accompanied by the reshaping of the structure of monopoly capital and of the economy as a whole. Consequently, economic growth in this period fell to the relatively lower annual average rate of 8.1 percent. It is particularly interesting to observe that, by comparison with the first phase of high growth, while the rate of growth of productivity fell sharply (from 17.2 percent to 10.1 percent), the growth rate of government expenditure and exports rose sharply (government expenditure from 12.6 percent to 16.1 percent; exports from 13.6 percent to 19.0 percent). It is also significant that, during the second phase, the rate of growth of government spending and exports exceeded the growth rate of industrial productivity (see table 2.2). This indicates that budgetary measures aimed at expanding effective demand played a leading part in stimulating growth during this period. It also suggests that, as the competitive power of Japanese heavy industry increased, so export expansion became a more important source of growth.

Phase Three—Intensification of High-Growth Policies

The most striking characteristic of the third phase of high growth was the continuation of remarkably rapid rates of economic expansion, exceeding even those of phase one. A major factor in this rapid growth was the contribution of exports. By now, at least in traditional heavy industrial areas, the products of Japanese manufacturing were able to compete with the best in the world, and heavy industrial exports therefore continued to expand rapidly. A further element—emphasized in the 1969 Economic White Paper—was the disappearance of the constraint on growth which had previously been imposed by balance-of-payments problems. In the past, prolonged periods of economic expansion had resulted in the overheating of the economy: imports had increased, balance-of-payments deficits had risen, and the government had been forced to take measures to restrain growth. With the expansion of Japanese exports, however, the threat of such crises receded. The taboo on budget deficits, imposed under the Dodge Line, was now freely ignored, and, with the strengthening of demand-expanding budgetary measures, policies for the promotion of high growth were further intensified.

A milestone in the process of economic growth was passed in 1968, when Japanese GNP overtook that of West Germany, and Japan became the second largest economic power in the capitalist world. A further sign of the growing competitive power of Japanese heavy industry was the fact that, in 1965, Japan's balance of trade with the United States went into surplus, and from then on the surplus steadily expanded. It is also significant that, while Japan's exports to the United States consisted of manufactured, and particularly heavy industrial, products, U.S. exports to Japan consisted mainly of raw materials and foodstuffs. A pattern was thus established that resembled the structure of trade between a developed and less developed country. As shown in table 2.3, by 1970 Japan's per capita level of production in most traditional areas of heavy industry had already overtaken that of West Germany and the United States.

This phase therefore saw Japanese heavy industry enter a new stage in which its competitive position in the world economy was assured. As Japan increasingly assumed the role of the world's "heavy industrial manufacturing zone," so the speed of monopoly

Table 2.3

Per Capita Production Levels in Heavy Industry, 1970

	United States	West Germany	Japan
Synthetic fabrics	100	64[a]	249
Newsprint	100	47	125
Plastic[b]	100	190	127
Cement	100	191	163
Rough steel	100	132	155
Aluminum	100	47	49
Synthetic gum	100	50	62
Automobiles	100	188	96
Trucks	100	64	249
Ships[c]	100[d]	1,073[d]	3,869[d]
Televisions	100[d]	87[d]	181[d]
Electric power	100	52	44

[a]1969.
[b]Total of PVC, polyethylene, polystyrene, and polypropylene.
[c]Steel ships.
[d]1968.

capital accumulation accelerated. The nature of the high-growth policy, too, became more assertive and more systematic. The first major feature of policy in this period was the further strengthening of liberalization policies and their extension to the area of capital movement. This helped to improve the environment for expanded exports of heavy industrial products. Second, the growth of exports was accompanied by a general thrust toward increased overseas economic expansion. Third, large-scale government spending and deficit financing were used to upgrade the quality of industrial infrastructure, and this helped to create a growing domestic market for heavy industrial products. Fourth, further incentives were offered to heavy industry to undertake large-scale, labor-saving investment. These incentives included low levels of corporate taxation and the provision of low-interest finance. At the same time enterprises were encouraged to merge or form price cartels, while controls on the work force and on wages were further strengthened. Finally, preparations were undertaken to enable the Japanese economy to move forward to a new stage of development. With this in mind, overseas investment by Japanese enterprises was encouraged, and efforts were made to secure reliable sources of raw materials. On the technological front, domestic research and development activities were promoted in areas such as micro-electronics, nuclear energy, and space science. Meanwhile, the New Comprehensive National Development Plan of 1969 envisaged the transformation of the entire Japanese archipelago into one vast industrial zone.[10] At the same time, proposals were put forward for overcoming growing labor shortages by recruiting larger numbers of women and older people into the work force.

It should also be observed at this point that, throughout the first three phases of high economic growth, the working conditions and living environment of the working classes had been growing increasingly precarious, and that the situation was by now approaching the crisis point. Wage rises had failed to keep up with increases in productivity, while social security and welfare provisions had also fallen behind. Since the beginning of the second phase of high growth, inflation had worsened, and the buying up of land by monopoly capital had led to sharp rises in land prices. Pollution problems were also proliferating, while the movement of labor and population into cities was resulting in problems of urban over-crowding and rural depopulation. As a result of these trends, dissatisfaction among the working classes was growing, expressed in an increase and diversification in the nature of economic conflict. On the political level, electoral support for the ruling Liberal Democratic Party declined, and from 1969 on there was a left-wing trend in local government, as a variety of opposition parties obtained control of the major cities.

The Collapse of the International Framework of High Growth

The first years of the 1970s witnessed the end of the "growth era," which had lasted throughout the 1950s and 1960s, and the onset of worldwide stagflation. The worsening world crisis was heralded by the U.S. recession of 1969–1970. It was against this background that, in 1971, U.S. President Nixon announced the suspension of the dollar's convertibility to gold and the imposition of a 10 percent import surtax. Despite two devaluations, in 1971 and 1973, the value of the U.S. dollar failed to stabilize, and one country after another found itself forced to adopt a floating exchange rate. These years also saw the emergence of international trade and economic friction, and a tendency for nations once more to seek refuge in the formation of regional economic blocs. Even in the United States—the main upholder of free-trade principles in the postwar era—a strong current of protectionism was resurfacing.

As the collapse of the dollar-based system and the development of competitive devaluations transformed the world economic system during the 1970s, it became clear that only a handful of advanced industrialized countries retained their belief in the strategy of protecting growth by the mutual liberalization of domestic markets. The remaining countries had little alternative but to reverse the liberalization policies of the 1950s and 1960s in order to protect their own economic and industrial base. This new trend in the world economy was given further impetus in 1973 by the first oil crisis and the associated rise in oil prices.

Here two points should be made about the new world economic environment. First, it must be borne in mind that the structures of monopoly capitalism and the policies of high economic growth established on a worldwide scale under the tutelage of U.S. imperialism had never solved the basic capitalist contradiction of imbalances between production and consumption. It was therefore inevitable that world capitalism should sooner or later be plunged into a state of prolonged structural stagnation. Also, in the new international economic climate, the competitive strength of a nation's economy was not necessarily directly proportionate to its economic growth. This latter factor helps to explain the growth of international economic friction, exchange-rate instabilities, and resurgent protectionism that took place against the background of world economic stagflation.

Phase Four—Growth Policy as a Defense Against Recession

In examining the Japanese economy, the fourth phase of growth can be divided into two subperiods. The first covers the one-year recession, beginning in August 1970, provoked by a slump in domestic demand for cars, television sets, and other consumer durables and by U.S. restriction on imports of Japanese goods. (The latter includes U.S. restrictions on Japanese textile imports, measures against the dumping of Japanese color televisions, and voluntary restrictions by Japan on exports of steel to the United

States.) The second subperiod lasted from the Nixon Declaration of August 1971 to the first oil crisis of October 1973. In other words, just as the Japanese economy began to recover from the recession that followed the third phase of high growth, it was assailed by the problems of the falling dollar and the rising yen.

Between 1971 and 1973 the revaluation of the yen against the dollar took place in a number of stages. Immediately after the Nixon Declaration the yen was allowed to float, and by December 1971 it had risen in value from 360 yen to 330 yen to the dollar. The Smithsonian Agreement of December 1971 marked a return to fixed rates, but the yen was soon straining at the upper limit of 301 to the dollar imposed at the Smithsonian. By March 1973, the agreement had collapsed and the yen was again allowed to float, reaching a level of 260 to the dollar by October. During this period, which came to be known as the "first yen revaluation," the real value of the yen against the dollar rose by 35.9 percent.

The first yen revaluation had a major impact on the increasingly export-dependent Japanese economy and resulted in a period of instability and uncertainty. On the other hand, however, the situation helped to highlight the strong international and domestic competitiveness of Japanese heavy industry. Since Japan relies very heavily on imported raw materials, revaluation lowered the cost of such resources and helped to offset any rise in prices of exported manufactured goods. Between 1971 and 1973 exports (in dollar terms) rose at an annual average rate of 24.2 percent, and the output of heavy industry increased at a similar rate.

While the world economic crisis was deepening and the external environment was unfavorable to growth, the Japanese government in this period intensified its growth-promoting policies. To prevent a "yen revaluation recession," deficit spending was expanded and further infrastructure-related public works programs undertaken. The 1972 election for leadership of the ruling Liberal Democratic Party was unusual in that all four candidates (Tanaka Kakuei, Miki Takeo, Fukuda Takeo, and Ohira Masayoshi) made public pledges to combat recession by increasing the national debt. It is no coincidence that the most ardent proponent of this policy, Tanaka Kakuei, was elected and became prime minister. Tanaka's "Plan for Remodeling the Japanese Archipelago" (later published as a book of the same name) was produced at this time. The plan, which emphasized both economic expansion and welfare, put forward proposals to strengthen growth policies by means of an accelerated "comprehensive national development" program. Under the 1972–1973 Tanaka administration, the partial implementation of these proposals resulted in the relocation of manufacturing facilities and construction of large new industrial zones, but it also gave rise to economic overheating, inflation, and shortages of consumer goods, all of which were aggravated by hoarding and land speculation by monopoly capital.

The fall in the price of imported consumer goods and raw materials induced by the rising yen might have been expected to encourage competitive price reductions by domestic producers. As a result of the government's antirecessionary measures, however, yen revaluation and inflation proceeded side by side. This period therefore saw the onset of "price madness" (as it was popularly named): by September 1973, the month before the beginning of the first oil crisis, Japanese inflation was running at an annual rate of 14.6 percent, the highest level of any developed nation at that time. It is significant that, in these circumstances, government policy was utilized in a frantic attempt to protect high levels of accumulation by monopoly capital. Recessionary cartels to prevent price falls were permitted in a number of industries, while the prices of many public services were raised to provide revenue for the government's demand-expansionary policies.

The fourth phase of high growth was therefore characterized by policies that were quite unusual in the context of Japan's economic history. With the support of expansionary policies, the Japanese economy managed to sustain relatively high rates of growth, and its experience was in this sense unlike that of the advanced capitalist countries of Europe and America, which were already experiencing severe stagnation by the early years of the 1970s. In Japan's case, by contrast, these years can be regarded as marking the closing chapter of high economic growth.

The First Oil Crisis and the Mid-1970s' Recession

The first oil crisis was the clearest and most dramatic manifestation of the general rise in raw material prices which played a major role in the worldwide spread of stagflation during the 1970s. This price rise marked the end of an era in which cheap and stable supplies of resources from less developed countries had supported high growth in the developed world. It also made it increasingly difficult for governments like Japan's to pursue high-growth policies. The rising cost of energy and raw materials not only raised the price of commodities, thus provoking worsening inflation and falling consumption, but also made it necessary for governments to alleviate inflation by pursuing policies that reduced effective demand.

The increase in oil prices had a decisive impact upon economic trends and policies throughout the world. The official OPEC price of Arabian light crude, which had stood at U.S. $3.07 immediately before the first oil crisis, had risen 3.8-fold, to $11.65, by 1974. The effects of the oil crisis on Japan were particularly severe, and in the ensuing inflation and recession Japan fared worse than many other developed nations. It was particularly vulnerable because its high growth had been based upon imported energy resources (of which Middle Eastern oil was the most important), and because of the concerted growth-promoting policies pursued during the first years of the 1970s. Consumer prices in 1974 recorded a 24.5 percent rise over the previous year, and wholesale prices a 31.3 percent rise. Between the peak attained in the fourth quarter of 1973 and the nadir reached in the first quarter of 1975, output of mining and manufacturing fell 21.1 percent. The 1973 peak, moreover, was not regained until the final quarter of 1978. The fall in industrial output caused by the oil crisis was considerably smaller in Japan's major industrial competitors: 14.4 percent in the United States, 8.2 percent in Britain, 11.3 percent in West Germany, and 13.2 percent in France.

The so-called oil crisis recession was at its most severe in 1974-1975. The government responded, on the one hand, with major antirecessionary measures which included cuts in the official discount rate and further increases in the budget deficit. On the other hand, however, it argued that wage-rises were in large measure responsible for the high levels of inflation, and that wage restraint was therefore an essential prerequisite for price restraint. The defeat of the 1975 "spring offensive"—the annual coordinated round of wage demands put forward by labor—signaled an end to the upward trend in real wages that had been occurring since the initiation of the spring offensive twenty years earlier. As will be seen, a new policy that combined wage cuts with redundancies began to take shape.

The particular severity of the oil crisis recession in Japan can be attributed to the government's eagerness to promote high levels of accumulation by monopoly capital, and to its determination to press ahead with high-growth policies regardless of the circumstances. The government, however, not only failed to admit its responsibility but placed the burdens imposed by the recession squarely upon the shoulders of the working classes. As had been the case with earlier policies, the oil crisis antirecessionary measures were designed in such a way as to give maximum benefit to monopoly capital. Although the "Plan for Remodeling the Japanese Archipelago" had emphasized welfare as well as growth, and the government itself had proposed 1973 as the year for launching a reform of Japan's underdeveloped welfare system, such intentions quickly wilted before the onslaught of the oil crisis.

Economic Trends and Policies in the Second Half of the 1970s

As a consequence of the first oil crisis, the value of the yen against the dollar fell by 11.79 percent (to 300 yen to the dollar). On the other hand, between September 1973 and the end of 1974, the value of Japan's exports rose by 35 percent, and Japan's balance of trade moved from a deficit of U.S. $2.7 billion in the first half of 1974 to a surplus of $4.3 billion in the second half of the year. In this sense, it can be argued that the oil crisis did not in the long run undermine Japan's international competitiveness. Rather, the policies pursued by monopoly capital to reduce the size of the labor force and costs of production resulted in a rapid recovery and strengthening of competitive power.

In response to the oil crisis, monopoly capital widely adopted the strategy of "slim-line management" (genryō keiei). This strategy involved rationalization and cost-cutting measures designed to restore competitiveness in a time of recession. Investment in energy- and labor-saving equipment was promoted, while at the same time widespread redundancies, including some dismissals of so-called permanent employees, were carried out.[11] As a result, the share of manufacturing in total employment declined by 1977 to a level 5–10 percent lower than it had been in 1973. It is also significant that, although production levels did not return to their 1973 peak until 1978, productivity had already recovered to its 1973 level by 1976: indeed, after the first oil crisis, increases in productivity were

Table 2.4

Production, Employment, and Productivity Levels in Manufacturing, 1973–1977

Year	Production (A)	Employment (B)	Productivity (A/B)
1973	100.0	100.0	100.0
1974	96.1	99.5	96.5
1975	85.5	94.2	90.8
1976	95.0	91.6	103.7
1977	98.9	90.1	109.7

consistently higher than increases in production (see table 2.4).

In the context of decreases in employment it is particularly important to note that reductions in the work force occurred even in the industries that were quickest to recover from the recession, indicating that these industries were able to achieve an increase in output with a smaller labor force. Between 1973 and 1977, for example, output in the precision instruments industry increased by 68.8 percent, while employment in the industry fell by 6.8 percent; in electrical machinery, output increased by 11.2 percent and employment fell by 6.8 percent. It is also significant that particularly large work-force reductions took place in many of the major companies that were known for their competitive strength: Matsushita Electric reduced its labor force by 27.7 percent, Hitachi by 16.37 percent, and Dai Nippon Printing by 25.8 percent. The process of employment reduction, however, tended to spread from the larger, more efficient enterprises to their less competitive counterparts. As large firms responded to the oil crisis by strengthening their competitiveness and introducing "slim-line management" policies, so the Japanese labor movement lost its power to resist dismissals, and the renowned Japanese "lifetime employment" system began to crumble.[12]

A further important feature of this period was the worsening problem of structural depression which engulfed a number of areas of heavy industry. At the time of the first yen revaluation, industrial sectors that had a large labor-intensive element had lost domestic and foreign markets. Now, with the oil crisis recession, other areas such as highly energy-consuming heavy industries and manufacturers of nonessential consumer goods faced stagnant or falling demand at home and abroad. By the end of 1977, twelve industries with a total of four million workers (including textiles, chemical fertilizers, nonferrous metals, and shipbuilding) had been officially declared to be in a state of structural depression.

Meanwhile, as the productivity of the Japanese economy revived and expanded, exports also increased, despite restrictions imposed by some of Japan's trading partners. As early as January 1977, the yen entered a second phase of revaluation, which lasted until October 1978. During this twenty-two-month period the value of the yen in dollar terms rose 63.9 percent, from 295 yen to a new high of 180 yen to the dollar. In the prevailing environment of worldwide stagflation and increasingly institutionalized trade and economic friction, Japan's growing competitive power was directly translated into rises in the value of the yen.

As discussed previously, in April 1975 the government responded to the drastic drop in demand that followed the oil crisis by introducing a number of expansionary policies. During the second half of the 1970s the demand-creating approach continued to be emphasized in both monetary and fiscal policy. Of course, stagnation in the international economy, and the consequent sluggishness of worldwide demand, exerted a downward pressure on Japanese growth rates, and this pressure was further intensified by the second crisis, which began early in 1979. The government's debt dependency ratio (the ratio of new government borrowings to annual general account expenditure) rose rapidly, however, to 33.4 percent in 1977, 32.0 percent in 1978, and 39.6 percent in 1979. By the end of the 1970s, therefore, the debt ratio was reaching dangerous proportions. As a result, a plan was put forward that would involve increasing government revenue by the imposition of heavy sales taxes. This met with strenuous working class opposition and was therefore temporarily abandoned in favor of the policies of "expenditure reduction and administrative reform."

Economic Strategy in the 1980s

During the 1970s Japanese monopoly capital had continuously confronted limitations on accumulation imposed not only by low growth but also by international trade friction, recurrent currency and oil crises, budget deficit blow-outs, and so forth. By the end of the decade, however, a new strategy for maintaining the process of capital accumulation was becoming apparent. The main elements of this strategy were as follows.

1. New strategic industries and products were singled out for development. The new growth areas were to be technologically sophisticated industries and the production of goods that embodied the application of advanced technology.

2. In response to structural trade surpluses and growing trade friction, the industries whose products lay at the heart of this friction were encouraged to relocate overseas.

3. Comprehensive policies to promote the import of goods and the export of capital were developed.

4. Economic penetration of less developed countries was encouraged. This was aimed particularly at utilizing Third World countries' supplies of resources and labor power and can be regarded in effect as an internationalization of Japan's dual economic structure.

5. Particular efforts were directed at raising levels of labor productivity through the extensive use of microelectronics and automated equipment. At the same time, wage costs were controlled or reduced by a variety of means including the rejection of pay claims, introduction of small group and meritocratic management systems, and the use of low-wage contract, casual, and part-time labor (see chapter 5).

6. It was accepted that the current circumstances made demand-expansionary policies undesirable. Government finances were therefore to be tightly controlled and tax rises prevented, while the burden of tax paying was to be shifted increasingly to the working classes. Economic activity was also to be stimulated by reducing the size of government assets and privatizing state-owned enterprises.

7. In association with the growing multinationalization of Japanese capital, the military alliance between Japan and the United States was to be strengthened and plans were made to extend Japan's imperialist role, particularly in the Pacific Rim area.

Using the opportunity afforded by the budget blow-out of 1979-1980, the government, in the following financial year, launched its new policy of expenditure reduction and administrative reform. This policy may be seen as an extension into the political sphere of the strategy Japanese business had devised for the new decade. In practical terms the measures to be carried out were detailed in a report compiled between 1981 and 1983 by the Second Ad Hoc Committee on Administrative Reform. The new policy had two major features. First, to achieve the objective of "small government," the level of welfare and other public services was to be reduced, while at the same time, military expenditures were to be expanded and the competitiveness and economic power of monopoly capital were to be defended. These latter aspects were justified by references to the exigencies of economic growth and technological progress, and to the need for international economic cooperation and effective defense. Second, it was proposed not only that the Japanese government should respond positively to U.S. demands for an increased defense commitment, but that the U.S.-Japan alliance should be used as a basis for the extension of Japan's imperialist influence in the Pacific.

A variety of propaganda campaigns were launched, emphasizing Japan's new status as a nation whose social and economic development was as advanced as that of Europe and America, and pursuing a conservative line very similar to the ideologies of Reaganomics and Thatcherism. The working class, it was argued, should be encouraged to be "independent and self-reliant," while the increasing cost of public services was directly attributed to the growing burdens imposed by "welfare scroungers." On the other hand, the interests of monopoly capital were served by the popularization of slogans such as "tax reform not tax rises," "simpler and more efficient administration," and "the creation of a vigorous free-market economy." It is hardly necessary to emphasize that this new policy approach served to aggravate a number of economic problems, including the expansion of Japan's trade surplus, rises in the value of the yen, and the problems associated with industrial "rationalization." It can also be seen as having contributed to rising international military tension.

Essentially, the policy of administrative reform and expenditure reduction aims to strengthen Japan's competitive power by reducing wages, lowering the level of working conditions, and cutting social security and welfare provisions. From the point of view of fair competition, such an approach is, of course, unacceptable to other industrialized countries. The policies of the "new Right," which are typified by the administrative reform, threaten to initiate a vicious circle of falling living standards for the working class throughout the world. It is therefore vital that, in defending their standards of living and welfare, working people should begin by attacking these policies. It will also be increasingly important to develop international labor standards, particularly in heavy industry, whose coverage includes newly industrializing countries (NICs). Without such international arrangements, involving Japan and the NICs as well as the older industrialized countries, it will be very difficult for European and North American workers to hold onto the economic and social gains achieved in earlier phases of development. Overall, the administrative reform policy must be seen as ill-conceived, inappropriate to contemporary circumstances, and acceptable only to Japanese big business and government.

Although the first three-year phase of administrative reconstruction was completed by fiscal year 1984, the state of government finances in Japan has continued to deteriorate. One can therefore anticipate no early end to the policies of administrative reform and expenditure reduction. A proper understanding of, and an effective struggle against, these policies is essential, not only from the Japanese point of view but also in the interests of the working classes throughout the world.[13]

Future Prospects

During the first half of the 1980s, despite the policies of economic austerity pursued by the government, Japan's growth rate not only maintained the levels of the "low-growth period" of the 1970s but actually recorded levels that were relatively high in comparison with those of other industrialized nations. An important element in Japanese growth during these years was the impact of Reaganomics, which maintained the value of the U.S. dollar at artificially high levels. The consequent undervaluation of the yen resulted in the rapid growth of Japanese exports to the United States, at the same time placing a brake on the expansion of imports.

From the beginning of 1985, however, the economic environment underwent a significant alteration. First, from the summer of 1985, as U.S. economic recovery peaked and Japan-U.S. trade friction intensified, technologically advanced industries were plunged into an ongoing state of recession. Second, as a consequence of agreements reached at the September 1985 Tokyo summit, the value of the yen was allowed to rise sharply against a wide range of other currencies. Within the single year to September 1986 its value had risen from 240 yen to the dollar to 155 yen to the dollar. Third, Japan came under increasingly powerful international pressure to restrain the level of its exports and increase its imports. As a result, the fall in oil prices that commenced at the end of 1985 and the concomitant decline in the cost of raw materials failed to provide the expected impetus for higher Japanese economic growth.

One may predict a continuation of the administrative reform policies that emerged as the basic strategy of big business and government during the 1980s. On the one hand, investment in labor- and energy-saving technologies will be expanded and "rationalization" pushed to its utmost limits. On the other, wage rises will be held at low levels and welfare provisions further reduced. Thus the competitive position of Japanese products, not only in terms of quality and technology but also in terms of labor costs, will be reinforced. Increasingly severe welfare cuts seem particularly likely, both because of the continuing crisis in government budget financing and because low growth, by restricting increases in tax revenues, will further aggravate that crisis.

It is also important to emphasize, however, that in these troubled economic circumstances Japanese monopoly capital still retains such overwhelming economic and competitive power that it can well afford to make compromises. It is therefore possible to conceive that the policies of administrative reform and expenditure reduction could be replaced by new strategies devised and supported by the working classes themselves. For these reasons it is more than ever urgent and essential that groups both within Japan and abroad should strive and campaign for the reversal of the current strategies of Japanese business and government.

Notes

1. The history of Japanese capitalism may be regarded as commencing with the Meiji Restoration of 1868. The Meiji Restoration was not so much a product of the internal development of the Japanese economy as the result of threats to Japan's independence from the pressure of the great powers of Europe and North America. It therefore possessed few characteristics of a bourgeois revolution. Consequently, the Meiji Restoration resulted in the emergence of the centralized, absolutist emperor system. The Restoration opened the way to the subsequent rapid development of capitalism in Japan, but the rights of Japanese citizens continued to be strongly restricted.

2. Japan's share in the total GNP of OECD member countries fell from 15.8 percent in 1978 to 11.8 percent in 1983. However, the figures for the early 1980s are unrealistically deflated by the artificially high levels of the dollar imposed by Reaganomics.

3. This point is made by the Soviet economist Kudrov in "Amerika gasshūkoku to Nihon: Teikokushugi kan kyōsō no senei-ka," *Sekai keizai to kokusai kankei* 70, p. 80, and is strongly supported by many contemporary economic analysts.

4. Initially, the intention had been for large amounts of Japanese heavy industrial equipment to be removed to China as war reparations. This plan was abandoned, however, and, with the changing direction of U.S. policy, Japan began to be turned into the arsenal and military base for U.S. Asian strategy.

5. The priority production system had already been used to increase capacity during the war. In the postwar period, however, when the technology, scale, and productivity of Japanese industries had fallen far behind those of other countries, this system began to be used, for the first time, specifically to protect and foster heavy industry and to raise its international competitiveness.

6. Muraoka Shunzō, "Sengo no taigai kankei no tenkai," in *Koza Nihon shihonshugi hattatsu shi*, pp. 205–206.

7. Between 1945 and 1949, U.S. aid to Japan reached the substantial level of $1.53 billion. (As will become clear from later comments, this aid was not an outright gift, but took the form of loans.) However, it is important to balance this aid against the so-called charges associated with the termination of hostilities. The flow of payments between the United States and Japan during the occupation period was by no means in one direction only.

8. Under the earlier system, price subsidies had been based upon the production costs of the least efficient enterprises (and were designed to ensure a target rate of profit). By contrast, the new subsidies were calculated on the basis of costs in "standard" enterprises with an average level of productivity. This policy thus aimed to concentrate production in larger enterprises: hence the name "concentrated production system."

9. The trade liberalization ratio is expressed in terms of the volume of imports of liberalized products, measured against the volume recorded in the base year of 1959.

10. This plan proposed a number of measures designed to alleviate overcrowding in Japan's Pacific Belt region, which was expected to occur as a result of an anticipated annual average GNP growth rate of 10 percent between 1970 and 1985. The major proposals included the transfer of basic heavy industries to outlying industrial zones and the construction of comprehensive nationwide transport and communication networks. To prevent urban overcrowding and rural depopulation, redevelopment plans for large cities were to be drawn up and the so-called industrialization of agricultural villages was to be promoted.

11. The reduction of the work force in large enterprises typically involves a number of successive stages. In the first stage, management responds to falling demand by reducing new recruitment to the company, cutting overtime, and shifting employees to other sections of the enterprise or to subsidiary companies. Next, temporary and part-time employees are dismissed, permanent employees are temporarily laid off or asked to take early retirement, and relations with subsidiary and

subcontracting enterprises are restructured. In the final stage, loss-making sections and inefficient factories are closed or converted into subsidiaries and permanent employees are offered "voluntary" redundancies (which are in practice very far from voluntary). These redundancies are directed particularly at workers with records of sickness or absenteeism, those with poor work records, married women, and older workers (whose wages are relatively high).

12. It had become accepted practice in large firms for workers recruited directly from high school or university to be guaranteed employment until the official retirement age of fifty-five or sixty.

13. This issue is more fully discussed in Seiyama Takurō, "Keizai kiki no shinko to keizai shakai seisaku no henyō: Senshin shihonshugi sho-koku ni okeru 80-nendai no atarashii dōkō to kanren shite," in *Shakai seisaku no kiki to kokumin seikatsu* (Tokyo: Keibunsha, 1986).

3

Land Reform and Postwar Japanese Capitalism

Teruoka Shuzō

Land reform in Japan was carried out from 1947 to 1950, under the terms of a law enacted in October 1946. The land reform policy was imposed by the Allied occupation forces after the defeat of Japan in the Second World War. It was planned under the direction of the U.S. Occupation Administration and was part of a series of reforms that included zaibatsu dissolution, antimonopoly policy, encouragement of the formation of trade unions, labor legislation, and so on. The purpose of these measures was the "demilitarization and democratization" of Japan.

Japanese Capitalism and Agriculture in the Prewar Period

Prewar Japanese colonialism had, on the one hand, a highly militaristic and imperialistic character: it had colonized Korea and part of China and had monopolized the commodity and capital markets of these countries. Yet, at the same time, it still contained many backward features. The textile industry was still predominant, and heavy industries were generally underdeveloped. By contrast, in the advanced capitalist countries of Europe and North America, heavy industries such as metal and machinery had already replaced textiles as the key industries after the First World War.

Table 3.1 shows that textiles, chiefly cotton and silk, occupied a central position in Japanese industrial production during the 1920s and 1930s. The share of textiles in industrial production reached a maximum of 46 percent in 1926. By comparison, the share of metals and machinery was a mere 15 percent. Even in 1934, when Japan had already experienced the world crisis of 1930 and the invasion of China had commenced, the textile industry still accounted for 35 percent of all industrial products, far higher than the 28 percent share held by metals and machinery. In terms of the composition of the work force, the textile industry also predominated. In 1926, 54 percent of industrial workers were employed in textiles, and even as late as 1934 the figure was 43 percent, easily surpassing the 29 percent employed in metals and machinery. While workers in the latter industry were almost all male, workers in the textile industry were usually women from rural areas.

The predominance of the textile industry and the inferior position of heavy industries were also reflected in the structure of foreign trade. In 1926–1929, 65 percent of all exports consisted of silk and cotton yarn and cloth, while exports of machinery accounted only for a little more than 1 percent, and even these were limited to the Chinese market. On the other hand, 6–8 percent of all imports consisted of machinery. At that time, the Japanese textile industry (to say nothing of heavy industries) still relied on imports of machinery from Europe and the United States.

As far as the export of textile goods is concerned, two interesting points need to be noted. First, cotton goods, chiefly cotton cloth, were exported mainly to Asian underdeveloped countries such as China and India, where the pound sterling was very influential. In other words, Japan, in relation to Asian underdeveloped countries, occupied the position of an advanced country with a developed cotton industry. The raw materials of the cotton industry were imported from dollar and pound sterling areas, such as the United States, India, China, and Egypt, and accounted for a considerable proportion (25–35 percent) of Japanese imports in value terms. The cotton textiles industry was, therefore, a typical "processing" industry. Second, silk products (chiefly raw silk) were the most significant export, comprising 43–44 percent of the total. These goods were directed almost wholly to the U.S. market. In contrast to cotton, the silk cocoons

Table 3.1

Distribution of Manufacturing Output and Work Force by Industry (factories with more than five workers)

Year	Total	Foodstuffs	Textiles	Chemicals	Metals	Machinery	Other
Output							
1926	100.0	17.3	45.5	12.0	7.8	7.4	9.9
1928	100.0	15.9	43.3	13.3	9.1	8.2	11.8
1930	100.0	16.1	38.0	15.3	9.6	10.6	10.4
1932	100.0	15.0	38.6	15.8	10.7	9.3	10.6
1934	100.0	11.2	35.2	15.8	16.9	11.5	9.4
1936	100.0	10.3	31.2	17.3	19.1	13.1	9.0
1938	100.0	9.1	21.7	17.5	25.2	18.2	8.3
1940	100.0	9.1	18.4	17.1	21.8	23.8	10.0
1942	100.0	7.7	12.6	15.4	22.7	32.2	9.4
Work force							
1926	100.0	9.2	53.9	6.0	5.8	12.9	12.3
1928	100.0	8.9	52.4	6.5	6.8	13.3	12.1
1930	100.0	8.1	50.9	7.1	6.4	13.2	14.3
1932	100.0	7.6	47.4	7.7	6.9	14.3	16.2
1934	100.0	6.7	42.8	8.9	8.4	16.2	14.6
1936	100.0	6.4	39.7	10.5	9.7	18.3	15.5
1938	100.0	5.9	31.0	10.0	12.0	24.4	13.9
1940	100.0	6.3	24.3	10.1	12.2	34.2	12.8
1942	100.0	5.0	18.0	9.5	11.9	43.6	12.0

Source: Keizai Kikaku Chō, *Nihon no keizai tōkei*, part 1, pp. 190–93.

that constituted the raw material of this industry were all produced and supplied by Japanese peasant farmers. Therefore, the silk industry played a very important part in securing foreign currency, especially dollars.

Foreign currency thus acquired by the Japanese textile industry was the resource that provided, on the one hand, the materials for the cotton and woolen industries and, on the other, machinery, iron, steel, and oil: goods whose production was either at an inferior stage or nonexistent in Japan. By using this resource, Japan intended to promote the development of heavy industries and to catch up with European countries and the United States. This process was further assisted by the strongly centralized state, which exercised considerable control over the national economy. As is shown in table 3.1, the share of the metal and machinery industries in total industrial production increased gradually, surpassing that of the textile industry after 1936.

Japanese textile exports expanded rapidly, pushing aside European (chiefly English) and American capitalists, as well as the "native capitalists" of Asian underdeveloped countries such as China and India. For example, the share of Japanese goods in the Chinese cotton goods market showed a rapid increase from 20 percent in 1913 to 60 percent in 1923–1927. The comparable figures for India were 1 percent and 11 percent; for the Dutch East Indies (Indonesia), 1 percent and 20 percent.

It was not the superiority of Japanese machinery or skill that accounted for Japan's competitive power in the international textile market. As already mentioned, Japan was at that time still importing machinery from Europe and the United States. Japanese competitive power depended mainly upon the existence of the many young female workers who poured into the textile factories from rural areas. Most of these workers came from poor tenant families and were employed under miserable conditions, with very low wage rates and long working hours.

Table 3.2 shows that the weekly wage rate of Japanese workers in the cotton industry in 1932 was much lower, not only than that of the United States but also than that of Western European countries. It was, in fact, on the level of Asian underdeveloped countries. On the other hand, Japanese productivity in terms of cotton yarn per worker was much higher than that of China and India, though a little lower than that of West European countries. This

Table 3.2

Wages, Productivity, and Wage Costs in the Spinning Industry

Country	Weekly wages (yen) (Dec. 1932)	Persons per 1,000 spindles	Productivity per person (bales)[a]	Wages per unit		Working hours in cotton industry (1935)	
				Yen per bale	Yen index (Japan = 100)	Daily	Weekly
China	3.7	8.9	0.31	11.8	89	10.30–12.00	—
Japan	5.8	6.1	0.44	13.2	100	8.78	—
India	9.7	15.0	0.16	56.7	424	—	60.0
United Kingdom	29.2	4.0	0.58	50.8	385	—	47.3
Italy	25.6	5.5	0.44	58.7	445	—	—
Germany	30.8	4.5	0.51	60.3	457	—	40.55–45.63
France	29.6	5.5	0.44	67.8	514	—	—
United States	84.0	3.4	0.71	119.0	902	—	35.5

Source: Takeshi Fujimoto, *Chingin to rōdō jikan* (Tokyo: Mineruba Shobō, 1959), pp. 14, 17; original source: ILO, *The World Textile Industry Economic and Social Problems* (1937), 1:208.

[a]1 bale = 400 pounds of yarn.

means that technically Japan was superior to Asian underdeveloped countries but inferior to European countries and the United States. The Japanese wage cost per unit of cotton yarn was only one-ninth of that of the United States, and one-fourth or one-fifth of that of Western European countries. The working day in the Japanese cotton industry (1935) was much longer than in the United States and Western Europe. In this respect also Japan was on the Asian level. Similar conditions existed in the silk industry.

The working conditions of Japanese industrial workers were not uniform but varied greatly from one industry to another during the 1920s and 1930s. As figure 3.1 illustrates, there was a great difference in wage rates between skilled workers in heavy industries (Group I) and unskilled workers in the textile industry (Group III). In regard to employment terms, too, the former had relatively greater stability than the latter. Textile workers experienced severe exploitation and were readily dismissed by employers. In the 1920s and 1930s, as already indicated, it was the unskilled and cheap workers of Group III who still constituted the largest and most representative section of the Japanese working class. Thus, Japan's superior competitive power in the international market for textiles and sundry goods at that time depended upon a combination of equipment technologically superior to that of Asian underdeveloped countries and unskilled labor whose wages were at an Asian level.

To comprehend the abundance of unskilled, low-wage workers (such as the young female textile workers), we need to examine the conditions of life in the rural areas of prewar Japan.

Table 3.3 shows that, according to the 1938 census, there were 5,441,000 farm households in Japan. Of these, only 30 percent were peasant proprietors who possessed their own farms, while 70 percent were tenant farm households who rented a greater or lesser proportion of their land. Of the latter, 26 percent were full tenants who owned no land at all, and 44 percent were part tenants who rented part of their holdings from landlords.

The First World War was a turning point for the Japanese landlord system, after which it entered a period of retrogression. Even in 1938, however, 47 percent of the total Japanese cultivated land area of 6,078,300 ha was leased to tenants.

The average landholding of Japanese farm households was only 1.1 ha, and that of full tenants was especially small. Fifty percent of

Figure 3.1. **Nominal Average Daily Wages by Industry.**

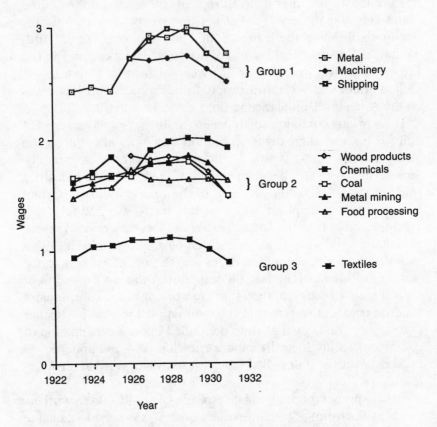

Source: Keizai Kikaku-chō, *Nihon keizai tōkei*, part 2, pp. 46–47.

them had holdings of under 0.5 ha; 78 percent, holdings of under 1 ha. Even in the case of part tenants, though the size of their cultivated land was a little larger than that of full tenants, the majority (54 percent) had less than 1 ha.

The chief products of prewar Japanese agriculture were rice and silk cocoons. Rice, as the staple food of the nation, was the most important product. It was cultivated mainly on paddy fields. In 1938, rice accounted for 56 percent of the total value of agricultural products and cocoons for 9 percent. Rent was generally paid not in money but in rice, the product of the paddy fields. Rent in the case of paddy fields had been tending to fall since 1916. But, even in 1933–35 and 1941–43, it still amounted to as much as half of the

Table 3.3

Number of Farm Households by Size and Ownership of Cultivated Land, 1938 (1,000 households, percent)

Ownership	Size of cultivated holding (hectares)						
	−0.5	0.5–1.0	1.0–2.0	2.0–3.0	3.0–5.0	5.0	Total
Total	1,859.3	1,614.5	1,466.2	308.9	117.3	74.8	5,441.0
	(34.2)	(29.7)	(26.9)	(5.7)	(2.1)	(1.4)	(100.0)
							(100.0)
Peasant proprietor	675.7	401.5	383.5	97.9	41.4	26.4	1,626.3
	(41.6)	(24.7)	(23.6)	(6.0)	(2.5)	(1.6)	(100.0)
							(29.9)
Full tenant	709.0	387.0	220.6	39.4	27.7	23.2	1,406.9
	(50.4)	(27.5)	(15.7)	(2.8)	(2.0)	(1.6)	(100.0)
							(25.9)
Part tenant	474.6	826.0	862.1	171.5	48.3	25.3	2,407.8
	(19.8)	(34.3)	(35.8)	(7.1)	(2.0)	(1.0)	(100.0)
							(44.2)

Source: Ministry of Agriculture and Forestry, *Wagakuni nōka no tōkeiteki bunseki* (September 1938).

total product. Thus tenants subsisted under the burden of an oppressive rent in kind. They were forced to bear this burden, clinging to their petty holdings, because of the existence of latent overpopulation in prewar Japanese rural areas. In these circumstances, if tenants delayed payment of their rent, or demanded rent reductions, landlords could readily take away their holdings and lease them to others. Tenants' rights to their holdings were precarious in the prewar period. The prewar Japanese state did not guarantee, either to workers or to farmers, the legal right to form combinations, to bargain collectively, or to strike, and the economic and social position of the tenant farmer was consequently weak. The status of the prewar landlord may be said to have been "premodern and semifeudal." He extracted a high rent from his tenant farmers for their small holdings and occupied an influential position in society, in political as well as economic terms.

The agricultural income of tenant farmers was especially low among small holders. This fact emerges strikingly when the agricultural income of tenants is calculated (subtracting the cost of materials and rent) and their per hour income is compared with the wage of agricultural day laborers (see fig. 3.2). Agricultural day laborers belonged to that group of unskilled workers earlier identified as the lowest-paid stratum of the Japanese working class (fig. 3.1). According to figure 3.2, however, the agricultural income per hour of full tenants who had no holdings of their own, was smaller than the wage of agricultural day workers from the late 1920s to 1930–34. This was, of course, a period of depression and crisis, but even after 1935 the earnings of tenant farmers rose only to a level comparable with those of farm laborers. The income of part tenants (II) who rented more than half of their holdings was almost the same as that of full tenants until 1932. Subsequently, it rose to a level of a little above the wage of the average agricultural day laborer. Peasant proprietors who owned their own land earned agricultural incomes that were much higher than the wages of agricultural day workers. Only in the years 1930–31, at the height of the economic crisis, was this situation briefly reversed. The smaller the tenant's holding and the heavier the burden of rent, the more the tenant's income fell behind that of independent peasant proprietors.

Under these conditions, tenants' agricultural incomes were not even enough to cover their very meager living expenses. Table 3.4 shows expenditure per household member for farm households from 1926 to 1940 (excepting the crisis years of 1930–31) and indicates the extent to which agricultural income was able to cover that expenditure.

Spending was closely related to landholding status, being highest for peasant proprietors and lowest for full tenants. Yet even the expenditure of peasant proprietors was much lower than that of urban workers, while that of full tenants was only about half the level of urban workers in 1926–1929 and 1937–1940, and less than 40 percent in 1932–1936. Their extremely low spending may be said to be a symptom of their poverty.

Furthermore, even this low expenditure could not be covered by agricultural income. It was possible for peasant proprietors and part tenants I to cover their expenditure, except in the crisis years, but impossible for part tenants II and full tenants to cover theirs even in comparatively normal years. Thus the latter were forced to borrow from landlords or merchants at a high rate of interest and

Figure 3.2. **Agricultural Incomes (hourly).**

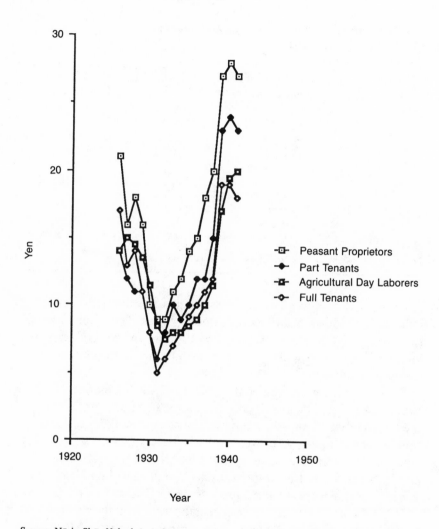

Source: Nōrin-Shō, *Nōka keizai chōsa.*

Note: For all but agricultural day laborers, the rate is calculated by dividing average agricultural income by number of working hours.

to complement their agricultural income with the wages of their daughters or younger sons who were sent out as cheap unskilled workers to be employed in the industry under miserable working conditions. Even tenant farmers themselves and their heirs were forced to earn supplementary income as day laborers. In some

Table 3.4

Trends in Farmers' Living Expenses and Incomes, 1926–1929 to 1937–1940

		1926–1929	1932–1936	1937–1940
Living expenses per household member (yen)	Peasant proprietor	173.1	113.9	171.4
	Part tenant I	157.7	103.0	159.9
	Part tenant II	119.5	98.4	158.6
	Full tenant	140.3	88.9	139.0
	Urban worker	292.1 (1926)	232.6	272.3
Living expenses as percent of agricultural income	Peasant proprietor	93.5	100.6	120.4
	Part tenant I	106.3	110.2	118.2
	Part tenant II	90.2	95.0	107.1
	Full tenant	85.6	78.1	94.9

Source: Nōrin-Shō, *Nōka keizai chōsa*, Naikaku Tōkei-Kyoku, *Kakei chōsa*.

cases they received several years' wages in advance. Thus the minuscule holdings of Japanese farmers (especially of full tenants), the exploitative landlord system, and the low and miserable working conditions of the Japanese working class were closely connected to each other.

It should also be noted that there was a close relationship between the militaristic and aggressive character of prewar Japan and the agrarian problem. According to the census of 1930, the largest share of the Japanese population (47 percent of those gainfully employed) was engaged in agriculture. Rural people, including landlords, provided an important source of "loyal and patriotic" soldiers and officers for the Japanese army. The crisis of 1930 and 1931 hit the agricultural sector especially hard, and the economy of all farmers, including peasant proprietors, collapsed. Moreover, the drastic fall of agricultural prices caused by this crisis dealt a serious blow to the economy of landlords who received their rent in kind. The Japanese landlord system was characterized by the existence of many small landowners. According to a 1920 inquiry by the Ministry of Agriculture and Forestry, there were 2,451 large landholding families who possessed more than 50 ha. The land they leased, however, represented only 14.5 percent of the total area of tenanted land in Japan. On the other hand, those small landlords who leased less than 3 ha were estimated to amount to as many as 1,665,000. It was these small landlords who typified the prewar Japanese landholding system. With incomes similar to those of the better paid group of industrial workers (see fig. 3.1), such landlords could not be described as affluent even in normal years. The depression had a severe impact on small landlords as well as larger landowners and made them eager to resume their leased land. As a result, these crisis years saw many serious tenancy disputes centering on the problem of land resumption. The social crisis occasioned by the bitter conflict between small landlords and poor tenant farmers was used by the Japanese governing class to promote military expansion abroad, as in the case of the "Manchurian Incident" of 1931. Not only landlords but also small tenants who had no land of their own came to see the vast *lebensraum* of the Asian continent as offering an escape from rural overcrowding and poverty in Japan, and they gave enthusiastic support to Japanese militarism.

Enforcement of Land Reform

In the early phases of the postwar occupation of Japan, the Allied forces of the international antifacism united front, and especially the United States, which had real control of the occupation, made the "demilitarization and democratization" of Japan the basic aim of their policy. Given the historical background, it was natural that they should have regarded the breaking up of the landlord system and the creation of a broad stratum of peasant proprietors as an essential element of this policy.

The substance of land reform as it was enforced in Japan was as follows. (1) The state compulsorily purchased all the land leased by absentee landlords, and that part of the land leased by resident landlords that exceeded a specified limit (4 ha in Hokkaido, 1 ha in other regions). This land was sold to tenant farmers. (2) As a general rule, the agricultural holdings of peasant proprietors were not to exceed a set limit (12 ha in Hokkaido, 3 ha in other regions). (3) Rent on the leased land that remained after the land reform was to be paid in money, and the level of rents was controlled. The maximum level was to be equivalent to 25 percent of the value of the produce of paddy fields, and 15 percent of the value of produce from other fields. (4) Tenants' contracts were to be in written form; the resumption of land by landlords was strictly regulated; and the transfer of tenancy was to be allowed only with the permission of the prefectural governor. (5) The purchase and sale of landlords' agricultural land was to be completed within two years. Agricultural land commissions were set up in cities, towns, and villages and were made responsible for planning the execution of the land reform in their areas. They were composed, in a manner that reflected the composition of rural society, of three landlords, two peasant proprietors, and five tenants. The opinions of tenants were therefore well represented on these commissions.

The land reform was planned and enforced "from above," under the direction of the United States, but making use of Japanese governing mechanisms that had survived virtually intact from the prewar period. It is particularly interesting to consider why such a sweeping and radical land reform, more thorough than any other conducted within the framework of the capitalist private property system, could be planned and enforced in postwar Japan. The following factors appear to have been particularly significant.

First, the United States, which was the main force behind the planning of the occupation policy, was the most developed capitalist country in the world. While its power rested on the international dominance of its monopoly capital, the ideology of "American Democracy" was still strongly influenced by the Jeffersonian concept of the independent farmer. These features of American capitalism helped to make it possible for the U.S.-controlled occupation administration to dissolve the Japanese landlord system.

Second, Japanese capitalism, as mentioned, had many backward aspects, including a despotic imperial regime, a powerful semi-feudal landlord system, a vast stratum of small and medium-sized enterprises, and an extremely oppressed and low-paid working class. On the other hand, however, unlike other Asian underdeveloped countries, Japan was by the late 1930s and early 1940s already making progress toward heavy industrialization. This progress had begun to erode the power of the landlord, and monopoly capital was gaining an increasingly dominant position in Japanese society. The dissolution of the landlord system, therefore, did not threaten the foundations of the power structure of capitalistic private property in Japan.

Third, the "demilitarization and democratization" policy of the occupation forces gave a considerable impetus not only to labor and citizens' movements but also to the farmers' movement. Struggles against land resumption by landlords, demands for land reform, and protests against the compulsory delivery of food at low prices and against heavy taxation all intensified. The capitalist system was menaced by the prospect of collaboration between workers and farmers adding momentum to the resurgent socialist and communist movements that emerged spontaneously after the defeat of Japan. Thus a land reform radical enough to defuse the demands of tenant farmers was necessary, not only to achieve the aims of "demilitarization and democratization" within the capitalist system, but also to preserve that system itself.

Fourth, the Soviet Union, as one of the Allied powers, had already made the first proposal for land reform. Their plan demanded the confiscation of all leased land from landlords and the confiscation without compensation of leased land in excess of 6 ha. It also called for the preferential distribution of the emancipated land to poor tenants. From the point of view of landlords this was a drastic proposal indeed. In opposing the Soviet plan, the United States had to put forward measures far-reaching enough to satisfy the tenant farmers' demands for land and to attract them to the "Free World." The United States reacted by pointing out that confiscation without compensation was incompatible with the principle of democracy. But, at the same time, it used the threat of the Soviet plan to make its own proposals acceptable to Japanese landlords, in effect implying that "our plan is at least a great improvement on the Soviet proposals."

Finally, in China, the civil war between the Nationalist government and the Chinese Communists had spread nationwide, and the area emancipated by the Communists was expanding rapidly. This was an unexpected situation for the United States. In the liberated areas land was confiscated from landlords and distributed preferentially to poor tenants. A socialist government was also established in North Korea, and a similar type of land reform involving the confiscation of land from landlords was enforced. In view of the rapid progress of communism in the immediate neighborhood of Japan, and of the thorough land reform that accompanied it, both the occupation forces and the Japanese ruling class recognized the urgent necessity of enacting a radical land reform "from above" to prevent the spread of communism and to maintain the capitalist private property system.

From 1947–48 onward, in the face of Communist advances in China and North Korea and the rise of radical movements in Japan itself, U.S. occupation policies underwent a transformation from the principle of "demilitarization and democratization" to that of "anticommunism and economic recovery." Land reform can be said to have been planned and enacted in the latter part of the "demilitarization and democratization" phase and enforced during the "anticommunism and economic recovery" phase.

With the transformation of occupation objectives, policies toward capital and labor also underwent major changes. The dilution of the initially stringent antizaibatsu and antimonopoly measures is discussed in detail in chapter 4. This, together with the great relaxation of reparations demands on Japan, made it possible for the Japanese economy, which had experienced almost total destruction in the closing phases of the war, to enter a new phase of rapid capital accumulation based on the provision of loan capital from large financial institutions to large industrial enterprises.

In the field of labor policy, too, there was a shift away from the democratic policies of the early period of occupation, such as encouragement for the formation of trade unions and official recognition of the right to strike, toward policies regulating the labor movement and restricting workers' rights. This trend became particularly evident after the decree of February 1, 1947, prohibiting a planned general strike. The policy of restricting workers' rights was directed especially at public servants, who were the bearers of official power. The new approach of the occupation administration was plainly revealed in July 1948, when government employees were deprived of the right to bargain collectively or strike, and the National Public Service Law was revised in accordance with this new approach in November of the same year.

Although important transformations took place during the later period of occupation in the policies toward capital and labor, there was no change in regard to the land reform, which formed the cornerstone of agricultural policy. Land reform "from above" not only was highly regarded as a step in the direction of the "demilitarization and democratization" of Japan but also effectively served the new objectives of "anticommunism and economic recovery."

In the words of Wolf I. Ladejinsky and Arthur F. Raper, who guided and advised the land reform as members of the occupation administration:

By strengthening the principle of private property where it was weakest, i.e., at the base of the social pyramid, the reform has created a huge class of staunch opponents of the communist ideology.[1]

Widespread land ownership makes the Japanese countryside almost impervious to communism. The concept of private property is strengthened enormously where it was weakest, at the huge base of the social pyramid. Communist promises of "land to the landless" do not entice farmers any longer. On the contrary, the new owners enlarged measurably the class of staunchest opponents of Communist economics and politics. It is fair to conclude that the agrarian reform has not only undermined that creed, but also strengthened the forces that make for a middle-of-the-road stable rural society, based on individual ownership of land.[2]

The Land Reform in Japan did not break up operating units, but rather more nearly conformed ownership units to traditional operatorship units. The Land Reform in Japan has provided a basis for increasing production, rather than reducing it; for the new owners there are taking more interest in the land they own than they did in the land they leased.[3]

Kenneth C. Royall, U.S. secretary of the army, gave a famous speech in January 1948 that is often seen as symbolizing the transformation of occupation policies toward Japan. In it, he made the following comment on the relationship between policies toward capital and industry and agricultural policy:

There has arisen an inevitable area of conflict between the original concept of broad demilitarization and the new purpose of building a self-supporting nation.

In the case of agriculture the two purposes do happen to run practically parallel. The breaking down of feudal holdings has ended a war-making influence. At the same time the wider division of lands tends to produce incentive on the part of the larger number of landowners and thereby to increase overall production.

But it is a different situation with manufacturing. The destruction of synthetic rubber or ship building or chemical or nonferrous metal plants will certainly destroy the war potential of Japan, but such destruction may also adversely affect the peace potential.[4]

As a result of the land reform, 80 percent (1,942,000 ha) of all leased land (which had amounted to 2,448,000 ha in 1945) was distributed to tenant farmers at low prices. Before the reform, in 1941, 53 percent of paddy fields, 38 percent of upland fields, and 46 percent of all cultivated fields were farmed by tenants, but after the reform, in 1949, rented land was reduced to 14 percent, 12 percent, and 13 percent respectively.

The land reform also created a broad stratum of peasant proprietors, in sharp contrast to the prereform landlord system. Peasant proprietors, who had constituted only 28 percent of all farm households in 1941, comprised the majority (55 percent) in 1949; while the percentage of full tenants declined dramatically to 8 percent, and the percentage of part-tenants also decreased from 41 percent to 35 percent.

Unlike the Soviet plan, the land reform as it was enacted offered compensation based on the private property system. However, as land prices were kept at an artificially low level, tenant farmers could obtain the means to become peasant proprietors relatively easily.

Under the land reform measures, the price of land was set at forty times the legal rental value in the case of paddy field, and at forty-eight times the rental value in the case of upland field. This produced an average price, per 10 ares of land, of about 760 yen and 450 yen respectively. In spite of the steep inflation of that period, land prices were held constant until the reform was completed. Thus the real value of land declined rapidly. As one observer noted, "the average official price of rice during the three years that covered the period of land reform (1947–49) was 3,232 yen per 150 kgm. Thus the price of 10 ares of paddy field equaled only about 34.5 kgm of rice. The cost of land was even lower when calculated in terms of black market prices, where 1.5 kgm of rice sold for over 100 yen. In this calculation the price of 10 ares of paddy field equaled only several kilos of rice at the most."[5]

Formally, the occupation administration emphasized its observance of the principle of private property, but in reality the reform was enforced on terms that amounted to virtual confiscation without compensation for the landlord and free distribution of land for the tenant.

While resident landlords were allowed to keep up to 1 ha of leased land, and some tenant farmers were not given the opportunity to become peasant proprietors, tenant rights on these remaining leased lands were greatly strengthened, and the level of money rents was kept at a low level. In 1948, for example, when the official price of rice was 3,600 yen per 150 kgm, the cost of rent on a field with average yield was equivalent to a mere 1 percent of the total product. Thus, even tenants who were unable to purchase their land could earn incomes little lower than those of owner-cultivators. On the other hand, it became impossible, even for those landlords who kept their 1 ha of leased land, to live off the rent received from tenants. The land reform therefore resulted in the irreversible dissolution of the Japanese landlord system.

Limitations and Consequences of Land Reform

In terms of its drastic impact on the landlord class and its effectiveness in creating a broad stratum of peasant proprietors, the Japanese land reform was without parallel among capitalist countries. Nevertheless, it had certain limitations.

First, as already mentioned, it differed from the Soviet plan in allowing resident landlords to keep 1 ha of leased land. It therefore made it impossible for some tenants to gain control of the land they cultivated.

Second, the reform was, in effect, limited to agricultural land and essentially involved the formal transfer of ownership of scattered small parcels of land from landlords to tenants. Thus the framework of small peasant farming with scattered holdings, characteristic of Japanese agriculture before the war, survived the reform, making it difficult to improve the level of agricultural development.

In Japan, with its restricted territory, forest occupies about 70 percent of the land area, five times as much as cultivated fields. It is important for the development of Japanese agriculture to make use of this vast forest area for cattle raising and dairy farming. But there were only exceptional cases in which forest was transferred to farmers and made use of to develop stockbreeding. Stockbreeding did develop considerably during the high economic growth period, but (except in Hokkaido) it has not been closely connected with land use and has depended chiefly on imported condensed feed. It was, as it were, a "processing industry."

The provisions of the land reform acts made it possible to create compact holdings and to rationalize farm management by the exchange and consolidation of land. But it was difficult to realize this objective (involving as it did a complex network of vested interests) within the two-year period specified for the land reform. The existence of remaining leased lands also made the attempt more difficult. Thus the scattered field system of the prereform period was preserved after the reform, although tenants had now become owners of land.

Third, and this is related to the second point, the small size of agricultural holdings characteristic of prereform Japanese agriculture was not remedied by the reform but was preserved. The land reform only transferred the ownership of land from landlord to tenant: it brought no change at all to the system of small peasant farming. On the contrary, the size of the peasant farms was generally somewhat smaller after the reform than it had been before the war. This tendency was the result of a combination of factors, including food shortages, the flow into rural areas of the unemployed, demobilized soldiers and civilians returning from abroad, and the resumption of land by landlords during the war and prior to the reform.

Despite these limitations, the land reform nevertheless played an important role for the development of postwar Japanese capitalism by bringing great changes to the structure of Japanese agriculture.

The peasant proprietor system created by the land reform proved an important precondition for an abrupt rise in the level of productivity of Japanese agriculture; the development of political support for the postwar conservative regime of the Liberal Democratic Party; and high economic growth (a high rate of capital accumulation) based on heavy industries, especially since 1960.

As far as the land reform's contribution to the remarkable rise of the level of postwar Japanese agricultural productivity is concerned, the following points should be mentioned. Land reform, though bringing no change to the small farm system inherited from the prewar period, dissolved the landlord system and transformed tenant farmers into peasant proprietors on very favorable terms. Farmers were therefore freed from the conditions of burdensome debts, exploitative rents, and weak tenants' rights under which they had labored before the war. They obtained full rights to cultivate their own farms, were better able to enjoy the "fruits of their labor," and had an incentive to improve the land and promote agricultural productivity.

Table 3.5

Increases in Agricultural Production, 1936–1938 to 1960–1962

| | Rice | | Mandarin oranges total production (tons) | Number of cattle (1,000 head) |
	Total production (1,000 tons)	Yield per 100 ares (kg)		
1936–1938	9,823 (100.0)	318 (100.0)	394,011 (100.0)	1,800 (100.0)
1946–1948	9,314 (94.8)	333 (104.7)	194,810 (49.4)	2,027 (112.6)
1955–1957	11,379 (115.8)	368 (115.7)	614,465 (156.0)	3,150 (175.0)
1960–1962	12,480 (127.0)	395 (124.2)	889,167 (225.7)	3,232 (179.6)

Source: Nōsei Chōsa Jinkai, Nihon nōgyō kiso tōkei (1977), pp. 194, 213, 258, 259.

The year 1955, when Japan had already completed the process of "postwar reconstruction" and laid the foundations of the "high growth" era, marked an epoch in the rise of Japan's agricultural productivity. Table 3.5 shows that in 1955 rice production, which comprised a substantial part of Japanese agriculture, realized the highest level ever, far surpassing the prewar peak. Thereafter this high level became the norm. After 1955, Japanese agriculture underwent multifaceted development, with high levels of productivity being attained in fruit and vegetable production, stock breeding, and so forth.

Agricultural policy during the occupation period was harsh on farmers: official prices for agricultural products were low and levels of taxation on farmers high. However, with the conclusion of the San Francisco Peace Treaty (1951) and reconstruction of Japanese capitalism (encouraged by enormous U.S. military demand during the Korean War) this policy was relaxed. The rise of agricultural productivity since 1955 was occasioned not only by this relaxation, but also by the land reform itself.

The land reform was planned and enforced "from above" under the direction of the U.S. occupation forces, who made use of the existing conservative governmental machinery to carry out the reform, and who intended their policy as a counterweight to the appeal of communism. It satisfied, for the time being, the strong demand for land from peasant farmers, transforming them into petty landowners, and, as Wolf Ladejinsky succinctly put it, "strengthening the principle of private property where it was weakest, i.e., at the base of social pyramid." As a result, it created among Japanese farmers a broad stratum of support for U.S. policies, for Japan's conservative (Liberal Democratic Party) rulers, and for the private property system as a whole.

Japan's small farmer class dissolved rapidly after 1955 when Japanese capitalism entered a phase of rapid capital accumulation based on heavy and chemical industries. Increased imports of agricultural products from the United States and other countries, together with severe competition at home, made it difficult for many small farmers to support themselves by agriculture alone and forced them to depend more and more on supplementary jobs, chiefly as wage laborers. The significance of landownership as the basis of farming and agricultural income clearly diminished.

Thus, under the Liberal Democratic government, farmers faced considerable economic difficulties. On the other hand, however, the price of their land rose swiftly under the circumstances of rapid capital accumulation, while job and employment opportunities for farm families expanded rapidly. These factors helped to maintain the support of most farmers for the Liberal Democratic Party government and for the capitalistic private property system.

The "high growth" phase of Japanese capitalism from the late 1950s to early 1970s was marked by expansion of the construction of factories, transportation networks, and dwellings, not only in urban and industrial areas but also in rural areas. As a result, the price of agricultural land soared after 1960. While the significance of agriculture for farmers diminished, land as property became much more important to them.

Furthermore, opportunities for nonagricultural employment expanded greatly during the high-growth period, and a large part of farm labor flowed out into manufacturing, construction, commerce, and services. Under these circumstances, in spite of the various difficulties facing Japanese agriculture, no serious social problems or peasant unrest occurred. The increase of nonagricultural wage labor expanded the income of farm households and raised their standard of living. The great difference in income and standards of living between urban workers and farmers, which had existed in the prewar period, disappeared after the war.

One part of the flow of farm labor away from agriculture took the form of rural people—mostly younger sons—migrating to cities, sometimes in distant parts of the country. But there were also many—chiefly householders and heirs—who commuted daily to work from their rural homes. During the 1970s, this latter group became considerably more significant than the former. These people are workers who own their own houses and land and continue to farm, on however small a scale; they therefore differ in their character from urban-type wage workers, and their existence has helped to "soften" the industrial confrontation between workers and bosses. Moreover, manufacturing and construction firms in rural areas are generally small or middle-sized enterprises, and their industrial relations are, on the whole, paternalistic. Besides, rural construction projects are chiefly financed by governmental public works budgets controlled by the Liberal Democratic Party. They are thus an important means of vote collecting in elections.

Nowadays, Japanese villages and farm households have been transformed into "mixed residential areas" of farmers and wage workers. In spite of the various agricultural problems that have emerged under the Liberal Democratic government, there exist miscellaneous mechanisms that help to maintain the support of rural inhabitants for that government. These include the fact that rural workers are also small-scale landowners, the paternalistic employer-employee relations that exist in country areas, the rising value of land, and the distribution of funds, in the form of subsidies and public works spending, to farmers and rural workers.

The consequences of all this become clearly apparent when one examines the contrast between urban and rural areas in terms of electoral support for each party in the general election for the Lower House of the Diet. In the 1980 election the Liberal Democratic Party held an overwhelming preponderance in every rural constituency (see fig. 3.3). In big cities, the Liberal Democratic Party obtained 23 percent of the vote, nearly equal to the 22.8 percent of the Socialist and Communist parties combined. On the other hand, in rural areas the Liberal Democratic Party's 49.7 percent was overwhelmingly greater than the Socialist and Communist parties' 20.3 percent.

It must also be observed that, in addition to the high electoral support for the Liberal Democratic Party in rural areas, the distribution of seats in both houses in Japan is very poorly related to population, giving too many seats to rural areas, and that this unequal representation is a further important factor supporting and maintaining the Liberal Democratic government.

Figure 3.3. **Electoral Support for Parties in 1980 Lower House Election.**

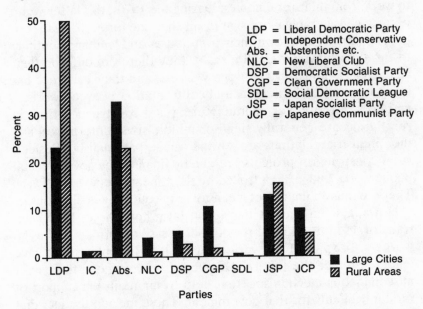

LDP = Liberal Democratic Party
IC = Independent Conservative
Abs. = Abstentions etc.
NLC = New Liberal Club
DSP = Democratic Socialist Party
CGP = Clean Government Party
SDL = Social Democratic League
JSP = Japan Socialist Party
JCP = Japanese Communist Party

■ Large Cities
▨ Rural Areas

Parties

Source: Hirose Michisada, *Hojokin to seikentō* (Toyko, 1981), p. 22.

In 1955, 44 percent of the population lived in rural areas. Farm households accounted for 41 percent of all households, and those engaged in agriculture were 34 percent of all working people. The rural element therefore constituted a large part of the total population. But after a quarter of a century, by 1980, the percentages had decreased to 24 percent, 18 percent, and 9 percent, respectively. Now rural people are numerically a minority, but, in terms of the "political population" they still hold a significant place.

The population of the four prefectures of the South Kantō district, including such big cities as Tokyo and Yokohama, was 28,690,000 in October 1980. This area elected 93 members to the Lower House and 20 members to the prefectural constituencies of the Upper House of the Diet, making a total of 113. On the other hand, the total population of the six prefectures of the Tōhoku district, the three prefectures of North Kantō, the four prefectures of Hokuriku, and the three prefectures of Tōzan (all rural areas) is 26,090,000. Yet these areas together elected 142 members to the Lower House and 44 members to the prefectural constituencies of the Upper House, making a total of 186, 1.65 times more than those of South Kantō.[6]

From the mid-1950s onward, Japanese heavy-industry-based capitalism rapidly transformed the farm population, using it as a source of the cheap and docile labor on which the "economic miracle" was based. During the period from 1951 to 1955, the Japanese economy, aided by the U.S. military demand accompanying the Korean War, completed the process of "postwar reconstruction." The social problem of relative overpopulation among small farmers remained, however, making it difficult to provide employment for the younger sons of farm households.

After 1955 the work force increased rapidly, while the proportion of employees in the work force expanded. The rate of increase was especially high in manufacturing and construction, followed by wholesale and retail trade, transportation and communication, public utilities, and services. By contrast, the number of people engaged in agriculture decreased rapidly from 14,890,000 (the largest percentage of the work force) in 1955 to 10,857,000 in 1965. By this year, the agricultural work force was already smaller than the manufacturing population of 11,507,000, and by 1970 it had decreased further to 9,274,000, smaller even than the number employed in wholesale and retail trade. Only a small share of this rapid growth of the nonagricultural (especially manufacturing) work force was accounted for by natural population increase. An important role was also played by the outflow of agricultural and farm household labor.

Table 3.6 shows the outflow of labor from farm households each year. According to this table, during the period 1960–1970, which was the peak of "high growth," as many as 750–850,000 members of farm households took up nonagricultural employment, but the number dropped to around 500,000 in the 1970s after the oil crisis and the beginning of the structural depression.

Before 1960, most of this outflow of farm labor had taken the form of people leaving home for urban areas. In the 1960s, however, this source of young workers began to dry up, and the absorption of labor by capital entered a new and more extensive phase. Transportation networks were improved, firms moved to rural areas, and the major outflow of labor from farm households took the form of people living at home and commuting to nonagricultural jobs.

This change was associated with other alterations in the flow of

Table 3.6

Outflow of Labor from Farm Households to Other Industries (percent)

		1958	1960	1965	1970	1975	1980
Total (thousands)		541.6	745.9	850.2	792.9	567.8	524.4
Type of outflow	Leaving farm	73.0	61.7	48.3	39.4	29.5	20.9
	Living on farm	27.0	38.3	51.7	60.6	70.5	79.1
Sex/age	Male	56.8	56.2	51.6	49.9	47.3	47.4
	(Under 20)	(69.6)	(61.4)	(66.6)	(60.7)	(52.0)	(47.2)
	(20–34)	(27.4)	(32.8)	(20.3)	(21.2)	(24.7)	(32.3)
	Female	43.2	43.8	48.4	50.1	52.7	52.6
	(Under 20)	(80.2)	(74.3)	(76.7)	(62.8)	(52.1)	(44.3)
Males' situation in household	Householder	—	10.5 (1961)	13.6	17.0	20.7	17.7
	Heir	—	29.0	35.9	40.1	43.5	46.3
	Other	—	60.5	50.5	42.9	35.8	36.0
New employment by industry	Construction	7.0	6.2	9.6	10.2	13.4	13.3
	Manufacturing	38.6	44.5	41.1	44.1	32.3	29.3
	Wholesale/retail	17.0	13.1	16.0	15.0	17.7	18.2
	Transport/ communication/ public utilties	5.6	5.7	6.7	5.6	4.8	5.2
	Services	19.8	15.7	16.4	15.2	18.9	22.6

Source: Nōrin-Suisan-Shō, Nōka shugyō dōkō chōsa hōkoku sho.

labor from agricultural to nonagricultural occupations. The proportion of male workers taking nonagricultural jobs decreased gradually and the proportion of female workers increased to become the majority. Young workers (under nineteen), though continuing to constitute the main stream of the outflow, gradually decreased in proportion to older workers. Concomitantly, the proportion of "household members other than householders and heirs," who had previously constituted the main flow of male labor from agriculture, gradually decreased, while that of "householders" and "heirs" increased and became the majority. In other words, the shift of the labor force away from agriculture was transformed from a process by which young people left their rural homes for the city to a process by which householders, heirs, and female household members went out to work while still living on the family farm. Thus, the labor force of the farm household became more and more deeply and comprehensively absorbed into the capitalist labor market in the process of rapid capital accumulation. As a consequence, full-time farm households became fewer and fewer, while part-time farm households, especially those whose members were engaged in wage labor, became increasingly numerous.

In which industries did these farm households' members find employment? During the high-growth period by far the largest share (41–45 percent) found jobs in manufacturing, though the construction sector also offered an increasing share of employment. Within the manufacturing sector, the metal and machine industries provided an increasingly large share of jobs for farm family workers. It is clear, then, that labor of farm household members was an important factor in the rapid, heavy-industry-based growth of Japanese capitalism.

From the point of view of capital, these peasant proprietors turned wage workers provided cheap and easily disciplined labor power. They thus came to constitute the base of the pyramidal wage and employment structure that is a marked characteristic of Japanese capitalism. This structure corresponds to the pyramidal organization of enterprises, with big firms at the top and a large number of subcontracting small or medium-sized firms at the base. Within the structure, the steady supply of rural-based workers served to push down the general level of wages and working conditions and to diminish the bargaining power of the Japanese working class as a whole.

It has already been shown that the typical Japanese workers of the prewar period were female textile workers who came from poor tenant-farmer households. Their educational level was low, and their wages were on a par with those of Asian countries and far below those of textile workers in European countries or the United States (see table 3.2). They worked extraordinarily long hours, usually more than ten per day.

After the war, workers in heavy and chemical industries came to occupy the central position in the Japanese industrial work force. The small peasant proprietors created by the land reform faced severe economic difficulties in an environment of fierce market competition. But, while prewar tenant farmers had been compelled by the burdens of poverty and heavy debt to generate wage labor with very low wage rates and miserable working conditions, postwar farmers could escape the debt trap and improve the educational and living standards of their families. Their wages rose relatively, to a level considerably higher than that of other Asian countries.

Compared with advanced European countries and the United States, however, the Japanese wage workers who were drawn from the mass of small peasant proprietors during the high-growth period from 1955 to 1970 were still "cheap labor." As is shown in table 3.7, the average wage in the Japanese manufacturing industry during the 1960s was from about one-sixth to one-fourth the U.S. level and one-third to one-half the British and West German level. There can be no doubt that peasant proprietor households as a source of supply of wage workers during this period were a significant factor in the low level of Japanese wages.

As noted, the outflow of farm household members gradually shifted its form from rural-urban migration to rural-based nonagricultural employment. Under the pyramidal structure of Japanese capitalism, most of the firms that were established in rural areas were small or medium-sized enterprises that operated as subcontractors to large manufacturing or construction firms. It was in such small subcontractors that most farm household members found employment.

As is evident from figure 3.4, there is a great difference in wage rates between big and small firms in the Japanese manufacturing industry. Even during the high-growth period of the 1960s, when

Table 3.7

Average Wage Rate per Working Hour, Manufacturing Industry (yen)

Year	Japan	United States	United Kingdom	West Germany	France	Italy
1950	—	— (1,092)	— (291)	— (225)	— (173)	— (170)
1959	81	799 (986)	312 (385)	209 (258)	144 (178)	126 (159)
1964	146	911 (624.0)	404 (274.7)	337 (230.8)	207 (141.8)	215 (147.3)
1965	163	940 (576.7)	441 (270.6)	371 (227.6)	219 (134.4)	224 (137.4)
1966	183	979 (535.0)	465 (254.1)	398 (217.5)	232 (126.8)	233 (127.3)
1967	205	1,019 (497.1)	687 (237.6)	414 (202.0)	246 (120.0)	248 (121.0)
1968	240	1,084 (451.7)	446 (185.8)	431 (179.6)	276 (115.0)	258 (107.5)
1969	287	1,148 (400.0)	483 (168.3)	519 (180.8)	273 (95.1)	284 (99.0)
1970	336	1,210 (360.1)	556 (165.5)	586 (174.4)	302 (89.9)	351 (104.5)
1971	388	1,096 (282.5)	578 (149.0)	637 (164.2)	312 (80.4)	373 (96.1)
1972	452	1,173 (259.5)	594 (131.4)	692 (153.1)	350 (77.4)	418 (92.5)
1973	563	1,140 (202.5)	583 (103.6)	832 (147.8)	419 (74.7)	444 (78.9)

Source: Tokita Yoshihisa, "Rōdōsha no rōdō to seikatsu," *Rōdōsha no kurashi to Shakai Hoshō*, Hōritsu-Bunka-Sha (1977), p. 53; original source, ILO statistics.

Note: ( ) = Index (Japan = 100).

Figure 3.4. **Wage Rates for Various Employment Categories (avg. wages in firms with 500 + workers = 100).**

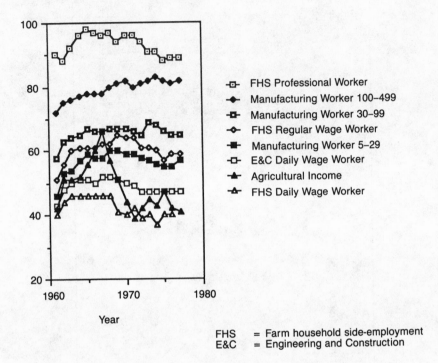

-□- FHS Professional Worker
-◆- Manufacturing Worker 100–499
-■- Manufacturing Worker 30–99
-◇- FHS Regular Wage Worker
-■- Manufacturing Worker 5–29
-□- E&C Daily Wage Worker
-▲- Agricultural Income
-△- FHS Daily Wage Worker

FHS   = Farm household side-employment
E&C   = Engineering and Construction

Source: Yoshiro Yoichi, *Sengo no nōminsō bunkai*, p. 261.

the difference is generally believed to have been at its smallest, the wage rate per hour was 55 to 65 in the case of firms with 30 to 99 employees, and 43 to 60 in the case of firms with 5 to 29 employees (on a scale in which wages in firms with over 500 employees equaled 100).

Workers from farm households are generally employed in these small firms on a temporary or seasonal basis. The rate of such workers' wages is restrained, even when they are constantly employed, between the level of manufacturing firms with 30 to 99 employees and those with 5 to 29 employees. Farm household members who are employed in constant work are in a relatively good position. Many, however, are employed as day laborers, in which case their wages are far below even the average for the smallest manufacturing firms (with 5 to 29 employees) and typically range between 36 percent to 45 percent of the average wages of firms with over 500 employees. Day workers' wage rates in construction (in which many farm household members are also employed) are on similarly low levels.

Low wage rates of farm household members at the base of the pyramidal Japanese wage structure are closely connected with the small agricultural income of peasant proprietors. Their agricultural income per hour is nearly the same as the wage level of day laborers from farm households or day laborers in the construction industry, who constitute the lowest paid category of Japanese workers.

The basic mechanism, in other words, is one in which the small agricultural income of peasant proprietors is too low to cover their costs. This forces them to sell their labor "piecemeal" (on a temporary basis) at very low wage rates. At the same time, the complementary income (however small) from their by-occupation makes it possible for the system of small peasant proprietors with low agricultural incomes to be reproduced. Japanese capitalism could thus achieve high growth and gain the strong competitive power in the international market by making use of cheap labor drawn from the vast number of small peasant proprietors.

Moreover, as workers in rural areas have their own land, houses, and farms, small though they are, capitalists can save on the outlay for workers' housing, social welfare, environmental provisions, and so forth. Because of the temporary nature of rural labor, it is also easy to adjust the amount of employment in accordance with trade cycles. Finally, rural workers have helped to make the base of Japanese capitalism apparently harmonious because they worked under paternalistic industrial relations and are not fundamentally antagonistic toward capital.

Thus, while the existence of a vast number of small peasant proprietors has prevented Japanese capitalism from reorganizing agriculture on a large scale with high productivity, it has on the other hand proved a factor of vital importance in the industrial expansion of Japanese capitalism in the postwar period.

Notes

1. Wolf I. Ladejinsky, "Land Reform in Japan: A Comment," in *Land Tenure*, ed. Kenneth H. Parsons et al. (Madison: University of Wisconsin Press, 1956), p. 228.

2. Wolf I. Ladejinsky, "Japan's Land Reform," *Foreign Agriculture* 15, 9 (September 1951): 189.

3. Arthur F. Raper, "Some Effects of Land Reform in Thirteen Japanese Villages," *Journal of Farm Economics* 33 (1951): 181.

4. Kenneth C. Royall's speech cited in *Shiryō sengo 20-senshi* (Documents, twenty years after the war) (Tokyo: Nihon Hyoronsha, 1966), 1:59.

5. Ōuchi Tsutomu, *Nihon shihonshugi no nogyo mondai* (Japanese capitalism and its agricultural problems) (Tokyo: Tokyo University Press, 1952), p. 268. Average rice yield per are of paddy field was 2.2 koku (326 kgm) in 1947–49.

6. Some redistribution of constituencies occurred in 1986, but the balance remains strongly weighted in favor of rural areas.

4

The Structure and Operation
of Monopoly Capital in Japan

SUMIYA TOSHIO

Big Business in Modern Japan

According to 1982 government statistics (compiled by the National
Tax Administration Agency) there are 1,542,299 corporate enterprises in Japan. Of these, "big businesses," capitalized at over one
billion yen, account for only 2,455, a mere 0.2 percent of the total.[1]
"Very big businesses" capitalized at over ten billion yen amount to
just 322 (see table 4.1).

This handful of giant enterprises includes manufacturing firms
(such as Toyota Motor Co., Hitachi, and Mitsubishi Heavy Industries), general trading companies (such as the Mitsubishi Corporation and Mitsui and Co.), big city banks (including Dai-Ichi
Kangyō and Fuji Banks), and many of the other leading names in
Japanese business. Each of these corporations individually can be
regarded as an example of monopoly capital: each exerts great
control over a sector of the economy—whether it be production,
marketing, or finance—and obtains large monopolistic profits
through its possession of technology, labor power, land, resources,
and so forth.

But the great individual power of these enterprises is augmented
by the fact that they are also members of enterprise groups. Two

Table 4.1

Number of Corporations (by size, 1982)

Value of paid-up capital (yen)	Number of firms	% of total number	Total capital (million yen)	% of total capital
Less than 5 million	986,078	64.0	1,703,705	5.5
5–10 million	267,174	17.3	1,589,579	5.2
10–100 million	270,316	17.5	5,766,162	18.7
100 million–1 billion	15,276	1.0	3,738,499	12.1
1–10 billion	2,133	0.1	5,970,623	19.4
More than 10 billion	322	0.02	12,051,233	39.1
Total	1,541,299	100.0	30,819,801	100.0

Source: National Tax Administration Agency, *The Substance of Corporations '82* (1984), p. 30.

main forms of enterprise groups can be distinguished. The first is a vertical grouping, within which each industrial, commercial, or banking firm has control over many subsidiaries (*ko-gaisha*, or "child companies") and affiliates.

But the largest of these monopoly enterprises also belong to a second type of group, the *kontserun* (from the German word *Konzern*) or horizontal interest group. The six big kontseruns at the center of Japanese finance capital are the Mitsubishi, Mitsui, Sumitomo, Fuji, Dai-ichi, and Sanwa groups.

The central management organ of each of these "big six" groups is the Shachō-kai or Presidents' Committee. As the name suggests, these meetings are attended by the presidents of the major enterprises in the group. (In all, 146 firms are represented in one or another of the Shachō-kai.) Each of the six Presidents' Committees has its own special nickname, often derived from the day of the week on which it meets (see table 4.2). Nevertheless, it is they who in fact define the common interests and coordinate the actions of each group.

In a narrow sense, then, one can say that the "big six" kontseruns consist of the large enterprises which are represented at their Presidents' Committee. But, since each of these enterprises in turn controls a whole hierarchy of subsidiaries and subcontractors, it can easily be imagined that the scope of the kontseruns is in reality far greater than it at first appears (see fig. 4.1).

Table 4.2

The Six Big Enterprise Groups and Their Shacho-kai (October 1, 1983)

Group name	Mitsubishi	Mitsui	Sumitomo	Fuji	Dai-Ichi	Sanwa
Shacho-kai name	Kinyō-kai	Nimoku-kai	Hakusui-kai	Fuyō-kai	Sankin-kai	Sansui-kai
Main manufacturing corporations	Mitsubishi Chemical Industries Ltd. Mitsubishi Rayon Co. Mitsubishi Steel Mfg. Co. Mitsubishi Heavy Industries Mitsubishi Motor Industry Mitsubishi Electric Corporation Mitsubishi Oil Co.	Mitsu Toatsu Chemicals Inc. Toray Industries Japan Steel Works Mitsui Engineering and Shipbuilding Co., Ltd. Toyota Motor Co. Toshiba Co.	Sumitomo Chemical Sumitomo Metal Industries Sumitomo Heavy Industries, Ltd. Nippon Electric Co.	Shōwa Denko K.K. Toyō Rayon Co., Ltd. Nippon Kōkan K.K. Kubota Ltd. Nippon Seiko K.K. Nissan Motor Oki Electric Industry Co. Ltd. Hitachi Tōa Nenryō Kōgyō K.K.	Denki Kagaku Kogyo K.K. Ashahi Chemical Industries Co. Kawasaki Steel Corporation Kawasaki Heavy Industries Ishikawajima-Harima Heavy Industries Isuzu Motors, Ltd. Fujitsu Hitachi Showa Oil Co.	Tokuyama Soga Co. Ltd. Unitika Teijin Kobe Steel Hitachi Shipbuilding and Engineering Co. Daihatsu Motor Co. Sharp Corporation Hitachi Maruzen Oil Co.
Others	Nippon Kōgaku K.K.			Cannon	Asahi Optical Company Nippon Columbia Co.	
General trading company	Mitsubishi Corporation	Mitsui and Co.	Sumitomo Shōji Kaisha	Marubeni Corporation	C. Itoh and Co.	Nisshō-Iwai Co.

Source: T. Sumiya, *Kokka to kigyō* (1984), pp. 82–83.

Figure 4.1. **Mergers in Postwar Japan (no. of cases).**

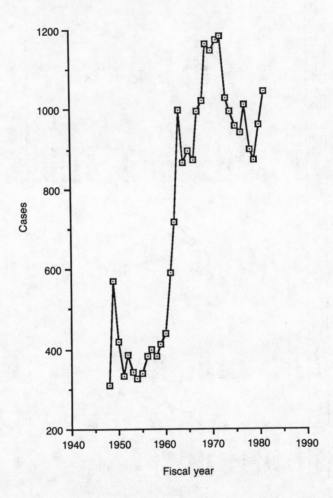

Cases

Fiscal year

Source: Fair Trade Commission, *Annual Reports* (various years).

A quick look at the statistics will help to illustrate the scale and cohesion of the "big six." In 1982, the 160 enterprises (excluding financial and insurance firms) represented in the six *Shachō-kai* accounted for 15.2 percent of the total assets of Japanese corporations; 14.4 percent of their total capital stock; 16.0 percent of sales; 13.9 percent of gross profits; and 16.6 percent of net profits. (The profit figures are based on data from 159 firms.)

The kontseruns are welded together, not only by the regular

Presidents' Committees, but also by cross-ownership of shares among member companies. On average, some 23.3 percent of the issued and outstanding shares of firms in the "big six" groups are held by other enterprises in the same group. In the modern large corporation, however, it is generally accepted that the main influence in shareholders' meetings is wielded by a relatively small group of significant shareholders. It is therefore of particular interest to examine the correlation between group-member shareholders and the largest twenty shareholders in the average kontserun-affiliated enterprise. On average, the top twenty shareholders hold 41.8 percent of the total shareholdings in firms belonging to the "big six" kontseruns. Of these, more than half (55.7 percent) are held by other enterprises within the same kontseruns. A similar picture emerges when one looks at bank loans.

Lastly, the cohesive force of each group is strengthened by the use of interlocking directorships. Directors and auditors are commonly posted from one group enterprise to another, and indeed at present some 45.6 percent of externally recruited directors and auditors in group-affiliated enterprises come from other firms in the same group.[2]

A general overview of the economic situation of the "big six" groups (as revealed by the investigations of the Fair Trade Commission) is given in table 4.3.

The Six Monopoly Enterprise Groups

Today, it is no exaggeration to say that these six monopoly enterprise groups exert enormous influence, not only on the economy, management, and industry, but also on government, society, and culture as a whole. As a modern form of finance capital they constitute the contemporary equivalent of the prewar zaibatsu, recreated after their dissolution by the Allied occupation authorities in the aftermath of Japan's defeat in World War II.

Among the "big six," the Mitsubishi, Mitsui, and Sumitomo groups can be identified as "descendants of the old zaibatsu." They represent the reconstructed, postwar form of zaibatsu that dominated the Japanese economy before the war. In these groups, economic coordination and cohesion are particularly strong. On the other hand, Fuji, Dai-ichi, and Sanwa are descendants of the so-called *shinkō-zaibatsu* (new zaibatsu) or *niryū-zaibatsu* (second-

Table 4.3

**Economic Position of the Six Big Enterprise Groups Including
Subsidiaries and Affiliated Companies (1981)**

Type of firm		Number of firms %	Total assets %	Capital %	Sales %
Shacho-kai members of "big six"		182 (0.011)	25.94	16.46	15.78
Subsidiary companies (more than 50%)		4,271 (0.249)	2.05	3.48	3.55
Affiliated companies	(25–50%)	4,251 (0.248)	2.65	5.75	4.01
	(10–25%)	3,278 (0.191)	3.36	6.95	4.29
Total		11,982 (0.699)	34.00	32.64	27.63

Source: Fair Trade Commission, *On the Substance of Enterprise Groups,* June 21, 1983.
Note: ( ) = % of all Japanese corporations.

rank zaibatsu), which began to appear in Japan in the 1930s. Compared with Mitsubishi, Mitsui, and Sumitomo, their coordination is relatively weak and diffuse.

Nevertheless, in examining their historical evolution and internal structure, one can identify many common features shared by the "big six" groups. These similarities are the product of a continuous process of competition and cooperation. On the one hand, they have developed against a background of intense intergroup rivalry over control of production and market shares. On the other hand, the challenges of democratic political movements at home and abroad and the structural crises of capitalism have compelled the groups to cooperate in developing business activities, formulating changed views on economic and industrial policy, exerting influence on foreign relations, and so forth.

In short, the "big six" groups constitute the modern form of Japanese finance capital. Without scientific analysis of their nature and operation, one cannot hope to elucidate the controlling structure and the development of contemporary Japanese capitalism.[3]

The Prewar Zaibatsu and Their
Postwar Reorganization

The Mitsubishi, Mitsui, and Sumitomo zaibatsu—ancestors of the contemporary enterprise groups—constituted the three major prewar zaibatsu. To their three names one might add a fourth, that of the Yasuda zaibatsu. In addition to this prewar "big four," however, there were also a number of lesser zaibatsu such as the Ayukawa, Asano, Furukawa, Ōkura, Nakajima, Nomura, and other combines. The prewar zaibatsu—particularly Mitsubishi, Mitsui, and Sumitomo—had differing origins and histories, and they also differed in the precise details of their internal constitution and structure. All, however, were closely linked to the government and military and contributed enthusiastically to the policy (first enunciated in the Meiji period) of creating a "rich country and a strong army." Within these groups, therefore, the outlines of a characteristic zaibatsu structure gradually emerged.

The prewar zaibatsu can be viewed as a more primitive precursor of the modern kontserun, in the sense that they were family owned and acted primarily as a vehicle for preserving and extending the wealth of the controlling family. They were financial forms of monopoly capital, whose purpose was to minimize the risks of investment by spreading their capital over a wide and diverse range of industrial sectors rather than concentrating it in a single area of production. At the same time, they can also be seen as successors to the *seishō* (political merchants). The continuing importance of commercial capital in the zaibatsu is apparent in the powerful role that zaibatsu-related general trading companies such as Mitsui Bussan (known in English as Mitsui Co.) and the Mitsubishi Shōji (Mitsubishi Corporation) came to play in Japanese commerce.

As will be apparent from these comments, the prewar zaibatsu had a number of distinctive characteristics that differentiate them from the forms of finance capital that emerged in other developed capitalist nations.

At the center of each of the prewar zaibatsu was the *zaibatsu honsha* or holding company. This controlled a large network of companies—some directly, others indirectly (as subsidiaries of directly controlled companies); others again were "associated companies" in which the zaibatsu holding company had a substantial, but not controlling, interest. In some cases, the stock of the holding company was wholly or almost wholly owned by a single family. This obviously endowed such families with very great power. Their enormous personal estates and incomes (some were billionaires) indicate the extreme concentration of wealth in prewar Japan. The zaibatsu-owning families included the imperial family, which occupied an exceptionally powerful position in the prewar Japanese economy, and whose economic position was further strengthened after the Second World War.

Some indication of the financial dominance of the zaibatsu families can be obtained from the available figures on the concentration ratio of the zaibatsu and their affiliated companies. For example, in 1945 the "big four" zaibatsu owned about one quarter (24.4 percent) of the total paid-up capital of all corporations in Japan. If the shareholdings of the other minor zaibatsu were added to this figure, the percentage would of course be much larger. It is particularly significant that this concentration ratio had risen rapidly during the war period. The "big four" zaibatsu more than quadrupled in size (a 430 percent increase) in the eight years between 1937 and 1945.[4]

During the Second World War, and the fifteen-year war in Asia that embraced it, Japan's ruling classes and militarists were responsible for the invasion of China and other Asian countries, on which they inflicted massive human and material damage. At the same time, the Japanese people themselves suffered greatly in terms of the destruction of life and freedom. This suffering culminated, in the final stages of the war, in the indiscriminate bombing by U.S. forces of cities and civilians, and in the destruction of Hiroshima and Nagasaki by atomic weapons.

On August 15, 1945, Japan surrendered and was placed under the direct occupation of the U.S. army as chief representative of the Allied powers. The Japanese economy, industry, and business lay in ruins as a result of wartime destruction and the continuous decline of production that accompanied it. Shortages of goods and severe inflation were also aggravated by the hoarding of goods by profiteers and sabotage of production by capitalists and enterprise managers. Ordinary people faced extreme hardship, and social unrest was rife. On the positive side, these conditions provided the basis for the creation of trade unions throughout the country, for the appearance and reconstruction of the Japanese Socialist Party and Communist Party, and for the rapid evolution of a variety of democratic-socialist movements. A new and turbulent age was beginning. The occupation policy of the General Headquarters of the Allied Powers (GHQ) was based on a series of measures of "democratization." These included the legalization of trade unions and the introduction of land reforms. The dissolution of the zaibatsu was an important part of this "democratization" process. Officially, the objective was to destroy the zaibatsu, which had been the driving force behind Japanese militarism. In fact, however, a fundamental objective was the weakening of the potential competitive power of Japanese monopoly capital vis-à-vis American monopoly capital.

The main elements of the zaibatsu dissolution program were as follows: First, the *zaibatsu honsha* and a number of other large holding companies were selected for dissolution. Their stocks were taken over by the occupation authorities (in return for certain compensation) and sold to the public. In all, eighty-three companies were dissolved in this way, including the holding companies of the Mitsui, Mitsubishi, Sumitomo, Yasuda, Fuji, Nissan, Asano, Shibusawa, Ōkura, and Nomura enterprises. By offering the stocks of these companies to the public, it was hoped to break up the zaibatsu into their component parts, which would then become independent, unrelated companies.

Second, members of the old zaibatsu families were barred from resuming positions as company officers in the ex-zaibatsu enterprises. This restriction applied to fifty-six individuals and aimed to break the human nexus of semifeudal control that had lain at the center of the zaibatsu structure.

Third, the use of the traditional zaibatsu trade names (Mitsui, Mitsubishi, etc.) and insignia was prohibited. Since names and trademarks had symbolized the cohesion of the prewar zaibatsu, this prohibition was clearly intended to discourage association between former zaibatsu-member firms.

Fourth, not only the Zaibatsu themselves but even some of their largest component enterprises were subject to dissolution. In particular, the giant zaibatsu-related trading companies, Mitsui Bussan and Mitsubishi Shōji, were divided into many small enterprises. In addition, the 1947 Law for the Elimination of Excessive Concentration of Economic Power opened the way for a sweeping plan to break up the Nippon Steel Corporation, Mitsubishi Heavy Industries, and some 323 other very large corporations.

Finally, the 1945 Law Concerning the Prohibition of Private Monopolies and Maintenance of Fair Trade Practices (usually referred to as the Antimonopoly Law) was enacted with the intention of preventing a future rebirth of the zaibatsu.

These zaibatsu dissolution measures achieved considerable

tangible results and dealt a severe blow to the system of Japanese finance capital. At this point, however, a dramatic change in world political conditions affected events in Japan. With the development of confrontation between the United States and the Soviet Union—centering on issues such as economic reconstruction in Western Europe and the rise of national liberation movements in China and elsewhere—the policies of American imperialism in Japan and the Far East began to take a new direction.

The old objective of keeping Japan's industrial and competitive power at a low level was replaced by a new desire to foster, in Japan, an Asian arsenal against "the menace of Communism." In these circumstances, antizaibatsu policies were gradually relaxed. One by one, companies that had been designated for subdivision were removed from the list; plans to break up the major banks and other financial concerns were dropped; and in the end, the powers of the 1947 Elimination of Excessive Concentration Law were applied only to eighteen large corporations. (This figure excludes the large electricity-generating companies, which were also dissolved under this law.) At the same time, purged members of the ex-zaibatsu families were gradually allowed to return to public life, and, in 1952, the prohibition on the use of zaibatsu names and trademarks was lifted.

The reversal of the earlier approach was also evident in the fate of the Antimonopoly Law. This was revised twice—once in 1949 and once, shortly after the end of the U.S. occupation, in 1953. The watering down of this law can be seen as part of a wider economic policy known in Japan as the "Dodge Line" (after U.S. banker and economic adviser Joseph Dodge). The main thrust of this policy was the promotion of heavy and chemical industries (dominated by large enterprises) at the expense of small and medium enterprises, farmers, fishermen, and workers. It therefore involved the creation of conditions in which industrial concentration could increase and monopoly capital be consolidated.

In June 1950, the Korean War broke out, and the U.S.-dominated United Nations forces in South Korea began a massive program of war-related procurements in Japan. These procurements proved a windfall for Japanese monopoly capital. Large firms pushed forward with new investment projects based both on internal accumulation of capital and on long-term loans from financial institutions. At the same time, the San Francisco Peace Treaty, by restoring Japan's political sovereignty, smoothed the way for the reconstruction of the old zaibatsu on new lines.

As has been seen, the dilution of the anticoncentration measures had left many large enterprises (particularly large financial enterprises) untouched. These firms soon emerged as the core of the new finance capital. Interlocking shareholding between the giant enterprises that had belonged to the zaibatsu increased, and the old zaibatsu-related city banks promoted the process of reconstruction by expanding their shareholdings in, and financing of, affiliated firms. From 1951 onward, the former zaibatsu trading companies, dissolved during the American occupation, began to reconstitute their dismembered parts. Mitsubishi Shōji was finally reunited in 1954, and Mitsui Bussan in 1959. Their reappearance was indeed symbolic of the revival of Japanese finance capital.

By about the mid-1950s, therefore, the major prewar zaibatsu had been remodeled into "modern" monopoly enterprise groups that corresponded to postwar economic and political conditions, and the first stage of their postwar development was complete.

It was around this time that the Mitsubishi, Mitsui, and Sumitomo groups (all descendants of the prewar zaibatsu) inaugurated their *shachō-kai* as a means of coordinating group policies.

Firms from prewar zaibatsu that had lacked an influential financial agency began to regroup around the other major city banks. Corporations that had been connected to the Asano, Nissan, Ōkura, Mori, and other interests developed links with the Fuji Bank. Similarly, Furukawa, Suzuki, and Fujiyama enterprises affiliated themselves with the Dai-Ichi Bank while several large firms from the Kansai (western Honshu) district formed financial connections with the Sanwa Bank. This process of consolidation went furthest in the Fuji Group. Nevertheless, none of these three bank-centered groups can be said to have become fully fledged kontseruns in this period. They remained at an intermediate stage of coordination that might be described as the "quasi-kontseruns" stage.

High Economic Growth and the Strengthening of the "Big Six"

The phase in the development of Japanese capitalism that is usually referred to as the "period of high economic growth" saw a rapid and profound transformation in the structure of the economy, industry, and enterprise. In the process, Japanese finance capital accumulated great economic power, perfected the construction of the modern kontseruns, and established firm control of the economic system. Simultaneously, however, the inherent contradictions of the system of state monopoly capitalism became increasingly visible and profound.

In the heavy and chemical industries—iron and steel, shipbuilding, electrical machinery, automobile manufacturing—oligopolistic enterprises grew ever more corpulent. Under the slogan of "industrial reorganization" or "strengthening international competitive power," large-scale amalgamation of enterprises took place (see fig. 4.2). This process enhanced the opportunities for major investments in new plant and equipment and made it possible to take advantage of economies of scale. Nor was it confined to the manufacturing sector: in transportation, commerce, and banking, major amalgamations also took place. Particularly striking examples of the advance of industrial concentration were the reunification of the subdivided Mitsubishi Heavy Industries Ltd. in 1964; the "reorganization" of the shipping industry in the same year reducing the number of major firms from twelve to six; and the merger of two firms in 1970 to form New Japan Steel, which at once became the world's largest steel corporation.

It is hardly surprising, in these circumstances, that the international ranking of major Japanese enterprises should have risen. According to the U.S. magazine *Fortune*, for example, in 1962 only eight of the two hundred largest foreign (i.e., non-U.S.) mining and manufacturing firms were Japanese. By 1966, the number had risen to thirty-eight; by 1970, it had reached fifty-one (table 4.4).

It was during this period that the kontseruns centered on the Fuji and Sanwa banks followed the lead of Mitsubishi and Mitsui and formed cohesive and self-supporting monopoly enterprise groups. In 1966, the Fuji Group established its own Presidents' Meeting—the "Fuyo-kai"—and the next year the Sanwa Group initiated its "Sankin-kai."

Under the conditions of high growth fostered by the Liberal Democratic government, intense competition between the big kontseruns took place. One after another, they advanced into new industrial fields: the petrochemicals industry; real estate and housing; the exploitation of marine resources, and so forth. In most

Figure 4.2. **Industrial Robot Production in Japan (1,000 units).**

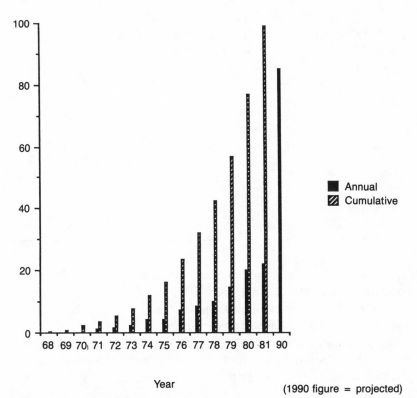

Year

(1990 figure = projected)

Source: Industrial Review of Japan 1984, p. 52.

cases, the constituent enterprises of the Presidents' Groups would jointly put up the money to finance these new ventures.

As their economic power strengthened in the 1960s, the representatives of these enterprise groups came to play a leading role in a variety of big business organizations such as Keidanren (the Federation of Economic Organizations), which help to weld together business and politics in Japan's capitalist system.

Because of Japan's extremely high dependence on imported raw materials, the 1973 oil crisis had a severe impact on the economy. In the wake of the oil crisis came the economic recession of 1974–1975. In terms of its depth and extent, this was the most serious crisis of overproduction in the postwar history of world capitalism. In Japan, gross national product registered negative growth in 1974 for the first time since the Second World War. Pro-

Table 4.4

The World's 200 Largest Industrial Corporations Outside the United States by Sales (distribution by country)

Country	1962	1970	1980	1982
Japan	8	51	39 (121)	46 (134)
Britain	19	46	36 (88)	36 (88)
Germany	19	26	31 (62)	27 (59)
France	10	21	22 (42)	20 (41)
Italy	5	7	6 (11)	7 (12)
Canada	—	11	11 (32)	13 (34)
Others	139	36	55 (144)	51 (132)

Source: *Fortune*, August 22, 1983, and others.

Note: ( ) = Share of 500 largest corporations.

duction and shipment of goods in many industrial sectors declined, while trade and overseas investment stagnated. The high economic growth that had been an almost continuous feature of the postwar Japanese economy had lost its momentum.

Japanese monopoly capital attempted to overcome this crisis by forcing through a program of "rationalization" (in Japan, usually referred to as *genryo keiei* or "slim-line management"). At the same time, the structure of the kontseruns was strengthened and consolidated. For example, the Dai-Ichi Kangyō Group (so called since the merger of the Dai-Ichi Bank and Nippon Kangyo Bank in 1970) reorganized and tightened its structure, and in 1977 a central Presidents' Committee (the Sansui-kai or Third Wednesday Club) was established. Simultaneously, the number of firms belonging to the Dai-Ichi Kanyō Group increased to forty-five. With the emergence of a unified Dai-Ichi group, it can be said that the evolution of Japanese monopoly capital is complete.

At the same time, the other kontseruns were expanding their networks of power. Firms that joined the Mitsui Group's Presidents' Committee in the 1970s include the Toshiba Electrical Company, the Mitsukoshi retail firm, and the Toyota Motor Company. Mitsubishi also added a new member firm to its Presidents' Committee in 1976 and, two years later, set up four ancillary Presidents' Meetings coordinating the activities of firms in specific industrial sectors. (The four groups are: the machine industry committee, the chemical industry committee, the service industry committee, and a fourth committee covering other miscellaneous industries.) Meanwhile, the Sumitomo Group and Sanwa Group increased the number of member firms represented in their committees by four and three respectively.

Like the 1960s, the 1970s and 1980s have seen the big monopoly enterprise groups move into new areas of economic activity: overseas resource exploitation, the information industry, and so on.

The Control System of the Big Six Groups

In the postwar period the development of new technologies and the economic recessions of 1956–1957 and 1974–1975 provided incentives for strengthening the internal cohesion of the "big six" groups. At the same time, they have also expanded externally, subordinating new enterprises to their control.

As has been seen, the major methods of internal integration have been the Presidents' Committees; interlocking shareholdings and financial transactions; the human networks formed by the movement of senior managers from one group firm to another; and the creation of joint group projects in new industrial sectors. This last method has become particularly significant in recent years, which have seen the appearance of group-centered joint ventures in areas such as overseas resource development and advanced technological research as well as in domestic industrial and infrastructure development (for example, the construction of the new Osaka airport).

External expansion has been achieved not only by the purchasing of shares and the provision of loans to companies (which then become drawn into group network), but also by other, less tangible methods. Major kontseruns may, for example, assist outside firms with marketing or with technological research and development. In this way, they expand the boundaries of their influence over the Japanese economy.

The Dominance of Monopoly Capital

Official figures reveal that "small and medium enterprises" account for an overwhelming 99.4 percent of all enterprises in Japan outside the agriculture, forestry and fishery sectors. Moreover,

63.9 percent of all corporations are capitalized at ¥ 5 million or less (about U.S. $38,000 at the 1988 exchange rate).[5]

From these figures it is obvious that a mass of small enterprises exist alongside the handful of giant firms that have been the main topic of discussion so far. A large number of people do indeed work in enterprises that are not corporations at all but are rather privately owned and operated. This vast substratum of small firms forms the foundation on which the power of the "big six" groups rests.

Small and medium enterprises are subordinated to giant corporations by subcontracting relationships (in the case of the manufacturing sector) or by affiliation (in the case of the commerce sector). According to the official figures, 84.2 percent of all large manufacturing enterprises subcontract part of their operations to outside enterprises, and 60.7 percent of small and medium-sized firms act as subcontractors to other companies. Of these, 81.3 percent depend on subcontracting relationships for more than 80 percent of their sales.[6]

To understand this relationship more clearly, one can look at the case of the motor vehicle industry. The production of a car or truck involves the assembly of an enormous number of parts (as many as twenty or thirty thousand in all). The Japanese automobile industry obtains most of these parts by placing orders with subcontractors. These subcontractors are organized into hierarchical levels: first-level subcontractors use the lower-level firms as a buffer against economic fluctuations, increasing orders from them in times of high demand and cutting them back in times of recession. Since wages and labor conditions in the lower-level subcontracting firms are poor, their existence also helps to reduce costs.

In the case of the Toyota Motor Company, for example, forty-seven thousand small firms are concentrated around, and dependent upon, its big modern factories. The use of subcontracting is a particularly marked feature of the Japanese style of management.

Japan's giant enterprises, however, do not only exert a dominant influence on small enterprises in industry, trade, and services. They also wield great control over agriculture. Although the majority of agricultural enterprises are operated on a family or small cooperative basis, they depend upon giant enterprises for inputs such as farm machinery, fertilizer, weed killers, and insecticides. Through its control of these products, monopoly capital is able to influence farm management policies. More recently, large firms have also increased their direct involvement in agriculture by setting up integrated poultry-farming, hog-raising, and other projects.

It is also fair to say that big business in Japan has considerable control over, and extracts substantial benefits from, the public enterprise sector. Although the number of state-owned enterprises in Japan is small by comparison with countries such as England, France, and Italy, public enterprises have until recently played an important part in certain areas of the economy such as the transport sector. In 1948 there were a total of ninety-nine state-owned, as well as some seven thousand local government-owned enterprises in Japan.[7] The means by which giant enterprises can utilize the public sector to their own advantage will become clear as the interaction between big business and politics in postwar Japan is considered.

"Japan, Incorporated": The Nexus of Business/Government/Bureaucracy

To safeguard their dominant position in the Japanese economy, the "big six" kontseruns have developed a complex and pervasive relationship with the political establishment. Close connections between business and government are not, of course, uniquely Japanese. They are a phenomenon common to all advanced capitalist countries in the period since the Second World War. The Japanese business-government nexus, however, has a number of distinctive features that are worth describing in some detail. Something of its character can be gleaned from the journalistic phrases that have been coined in recent years to describe it. It is frequently referred to as the *sei-kan-zai ittaikiko* (the amalgamation of politics, bureaucracy, and big business) or, more popularly, as *Nihon kabushiki kaisha* (Japan Incorporated).[8] Let us consider some of the mechanisms by which this amalgamation of political, bureaucratic, and big business interests is achieved.

First, there is the network of human relationships that links the management of large enterprises to the political and administrative leadership. This is partly based on family relationships (*kei-batsu*). For example, it is common for the daughter of a prominent politician to marry the son of a leading business figure, or vice versa. Even more important are the *gaku batsu* (academic cliques)—the "old school tie" connections that link fellow graduates of prestigious institutions such as Tokyo University.

These personal links are reinforced in a variety of ways. Senior management from the "big six" play a leading role in various lobby groups that represent the interests of monopoly capital in Japan, most notably the Federation of Economic Organizations (Keidanren), the Japan Committee for Economic Development (Keizai Dōyūkai), and the Japan Federation of Employers (Nikkeiren).[9] Prime ministers have made a practice of holding private meetings with representatives of these groups and with other prominent businessmen to discuss important political and economic matters.

Connections between bureaucracy and business are reinforced by the well-known system of *amakudari* (descent from heaven), whereby top-ranking government officials, on their resignation, are offered directorships or similar positions in large private firms.

Second, the intangible personal networks are backed up by a very tangible financial structure. Large enterprises are major contributors to the election funds of the ruling Liberal Democratic Party (LDP) and commonly put all their efforts into ensuring the election of LDP or Democratic Socialist Party candidates. (The Democratic Socialist Party is a small party whose political stance is close to that of the liberal wing of the LDP.) According to a report on political funding published in 1982, nearly 70 percent of the LDP's income is derived from big business sources. Large enterprises not only donate money to the central financial organs of the LDP but also provide funding for various individual factions within the party. It has been surmised that as much as 96 percent of donations to the major LDP factions come from corporate and industrial bodies.[10]

In return for their financial support, large enterprises have enjoyed the continued protection of Liberal Democratic governments since 1955. This has included subsidies, preferential finance and tax treatment, and government assistance for the development of technology through joint public and private research projects.

Monopoly Capital in Contemporary Japan: An Overview

Lenin, in *Imperialism: The Highest Stage of Capitalism*, defined "finance capital" as the fusion of monopolistic industrial capital with monopolistic banking capital. Does big business in Japan today constitute "finance capital" in this sense? I believe that, when one looks at the historical development and contemporary realities of monopoly capital in Japan, one finds that this traditional concept of "finance capital" is inadequate, and that a new definition is needed to encompass the functions of the giant Japanese kontseruns.

In essence they can be seen as representing the fusion of three types of monopoly capital: industrial, financial, and commercial. The role of commercial capital must be emphasized because of the importance of the big general trading companies (*sōgō shōsha*) in each group. These trading companies (Mitsubishi Shōji, Mitsui Bussan, Sumitomo Shōji, Marubeni, C. Itoh, and Nisshō-Iwai) not only perform normal sales functions but also purchase shares in and lend money to other enterprises, organize new investment projects, collect business information, and so forth. In this way they have come to be crucial to the coordination of each kontserun.

Since World War II a significant change has occurred in the nature of monopoly capital in Japan. Increasingly, the largest blocks of shares in major enterprises have come to be held not by individuals but by banks, life insurance companies, industrial corporations, and general trading companies. This was highlighted by a study conducted by the Fair Trade Commission in 1979 of one hundred major Japanese corporations. Of the top ten shareholders in these companies, 73.5 percent were financial institutions and 17.2 percent were other corporations.

In other words, the separation of ownership from control[11] has given rise to a new phenomenon, that of the "institutional investor." This phenomenon had induced some people to accept the mistaken view that contemporary Japanese society is noncapitalist, or is at least a form of "capitalism without capitalists."

But in reality, as has been seen, monopoly capital in the form of the "big six" enterprise groups exerts a dominant influence on Japanese society. The scale and economic power of these groups has increased rapidly, and the gap that once existed between Japanese big business and its U.S. and European counterparts has been narrowed. At the same time, the confrontation between monopoly capital, on the one hand, and working people—at home as well as in less developed nations and the socialist world—on the other grows steadily deeper, and with it the contradictions of capitalism are intensified.

The Crises of Modern Capitalism and New Tendencies in the Big Six Enterprise Groups

Since the mid-1970s, world capitalism has undergone a severe structural crisis. Inevitably, Japanese capitalism also has been caught up in this crisis.[12]

The ending of the period of high growth in the 1970s was accompanied by numerous symptoms of economic depression. Unemployment rose to the highest level since 1955: it became increasingly difficult for university graduates to find work; bankruptcies among small and medium enterprises reached a postwar high; local government finances were in chaos.

The roots of this crisis lie deep in the structure of the Japanese economy. The distorted nature of postwar economic growth has resulted in an ill-balanced industrial structure, energy crisis and agrarian crisis, excessive trade dependence on foreign countries, and the subordination of the Japanese economy to the U.S. imperialist order. During the period of high economic growth big business, supported by the Liberal Democratic Party, pursued a policy of extremely rapid accumulation of capital. To achieve this, they suppressed the wages and living conditions of working people. Consequently, while the GNP growth rate soared, standards of living lagged behind and environmental pollution worsened.

Since the 1974–1975 crisis, the six big enterprise groups have adopted a variety of measures in an attempt to overcome the severe problems they now face.

1. They have embarked on a massive program of promoting the development of science and technology. Research into advanced technologies such as electronics, optical fiber communications, industrial robots, biotechnology, and the development of new materials is progressing rapidly (on industrial robots, see fig. 4.2). The current "technological revolution" in some ways resembles that of the 1950s, which saw the emergence of transistor technology, jet transport, and computing. But the extent of the present technological advance is much wider, and its speed more rapid.

Intensified competition between giant enterprises and enterprise groups is leading to growing concentration and cartelization. On the one hand, large firms are entering into cooperative arrangements for the development of advanced technology. On the other, reorganization is occurring in the so-called structurally depressed industries, including parts of the vinyl chloride, aluminum, petrochemical, and paper and pulp industries. Here falling sales, excess capacity and bankruptcies have become common. For this reason, the LDP government has taken measures to encourage cooperation among enterprises in these industries, in the belief that increased concentration will promote restructuring and help to overcome the current crisis.

2. The big enterprise groups have set up a number of new, group-centered cooperative projects. It has already been seen that the formation of joint projects in new areas of industry was a feature of kontserun activity during the 1960s and early 1970s. The "big six" groups tend to pursue a policy of "one-set-ism"—that is, of attempting to ensure that they have some representation in every major industrial area. Thus, when one group establishes an enterprise in a promising new area of industry or services (such as microelectronics or the information industry), all the other groups are likely to follow suit. In recent years this tendency has been strengthened by the growth of international competition.

At present, the big enterprise groups are keeping a keen eye on the possibilities for "firm banking," "home banking," and so forth, which are being opened up by advances in a communications technology. The development of new credit and distribution systems, together with the liberalization of regulation of the financial sector, are promoting new links among the city banks, big securities companies, and other major enterprises.

In other respects, however, the principle of "one-set-ism" is being eroded. In many major industries (semiconductors, computers, automobiles, airplanes, atomic energy, weapons), the process of concentration has already reached the point where only two or three major enterprises remain. This obviously makes it impossible for every group to participate in such industries, and indeed this trend may ultimately force some restructuring of the kontseruns system itself.

3. Japanese corporations have sought to overcome the crisis by overseas expansion. Since World War II the fundamental pattern of activity has involved importing raw materials from overseas, processing them at home, and exporting the processed product.

Since the mid-1970s, this pattern has become increasingly marked. In many areas—for example, motor cars, semiconductors, and precision machinery—the technological level of Japanese enterprises has already overtaken that of their overseas competitors. In 1981, the share of Japanese semiconductors in the U.S. market was only 3 percent but in the case of 63-k RAM integrated circuits, Japanese firms had cornered 70 percent of the U.S. market.[13]

The international expansion of Japanese firms involves not only the export of goods but also, increasingly, the export of capital. By May 1980, 44.3 percent of all firms listed on the Tokyo Stock Exchange had direct overseas investments. Since the figure for 1972 was just 28.2 percent, it is clear that the multinational expansion of Japanese capital has been proceeding very rapidly in recent years.[14]

In an attempt to divert the frictions caused by the growth of their exports, many Japanese firms are setting up joint ventures with overseas firms. For example, General Motors and Toyota have set up a joint project for the production of small cars. Hitachi, Fujitsu, and other corporations are also developing joint projects with foreign firms in the fields of electronics and industrial robots.

None of this, however, has been sufficient to curb the rise of trade friction with the United States and the European Economic Community. Essentially, this friction can be seen as a manifestation of the laws of unequal development in the circumstances of contemporary monopoly capitalism. The United States and European countries, facing high levels of unemployment and profound structural problems, are putting increasing pressure on Japanese firms to restrain the level of their export increases.

The U.S. government and big business, in particular, have demanded not only that Japan impose "voluntary restraints" on its exports, but also that it open its domestic market to imports of U.S. beef, oranges, and other products. The liberalization of import restrictions on agricultural products, however, would result in a future fall in Japan's already low level of self-sufficiency in primary products. In 1982 Japan was already only 76 percent self-sufficient in marine products, and 32 percent self-sufficient in grains.

In addition, increased agricultural imports could cause disaster for Japan's small farmers, who still constitute some 10 percent of the work force (see chapter 3). Until now, the rural areas have constituted the cornerstone of the political strength of the ruling Liberal Democratic Party. The trade issue, however, places the interests of farmers in direct opposition to the interests of monopoly capital, and it could result in a drift in rural votes away from the big-business-oriented LDP.

4. Japan's giant enterprises (like big business elsewhere) are seeking to solve their problems by expanding their role as "merchants of death." The growth of armaments production by Japanese firms needs to be seen against the background of a world situation in which American imperialism is trying to strengthen its position, particularly vis-à-vis the Soviet Union, by expanding its nuclear arsenal. In this context, the American government has been pressuring Japan to increase its military spending, and the Japanese government, against the wishes of ordinary people, has acquiesced. In the nine years from 1973 to FY 1982, total defense-related expenditure increased 2.8-fold.

Fiscal 1982 saw severe cuts in the level of government spending. The official reason given for this was the need to reduce the budget deficit which had expanded under successive LDP administrations. As a result, social welfare and education spending was cut and the real level of taxes rose, placing heavy financial burden on working people. But in spite of all the talk of a "public spending crisis," military expenditure was increased by 7.8 percent over the previous financial year.

The growth of military expenditure is associated both with increasing U.S. armament production and exports and with growing domestic production of arms. A small number of big firms have a virtual monopoly of Japanese military production and of procurement orders from the Defense Agency. Not surprisingly, these firms have recently experienced rapidly rising profits. The value of Defense Agency contracts in 1982 was 42 percent higher than the previous year, and 3.7 times higher than in FY 1973. Over half of these contracts (in value terms) go to five firms: Mitsubishi Heavy Industries Ltd., Ishikawajima-Harima Heavy Industries Co. Ltd., Kawasaki Heavy Industries Ltd., Mitsubishi Electric Corporation, and Toshiba Co.

The position of Mitsubishi Heavy Industries is particularly dominant: it accounted for 16.9 percent of the total value of Defense Agency orders in 1982. The company is, of course, a member of the Mitsubishi group, which is the largest and strongest of the "big six" kontserns. The other enterprise groups also have their representatives in the armaments industry, although these are not quite on the scale of Mitsubishi Heavy Industries.

From the point of view of Japanese monopoly capital, armaments production, with its potential for large-scale orders and technological spin-off, is highly attractive. Increasingly, big business is pressuring government to increase armaments expenditure, relax the bar on armaments exports from Japan, and revise Article 9 of the constitution.

The development of microelectronic technology also has significant implications for the armaments industry. There is growing concern in Japan that high-level technological research might be diverted to military purposes. So far, however, the technological level of the Japanese industry is still far behind that of U.S. armaments makers, and Japanese weapons still contain much imported technology. The U.S.-Japan Security Treaty makes Japan militarily subordinate to the United States and inextricably involved in U.S. military strategies.

The growth of military spending and armaments production in Japan meets with widespread opposition from ordinary Japanese people. As the only country yet to experience the horrors of atomic bombing, Japan naturally has a strong tradition of opposition to nuclear arms, and the peace movement, supported by many diverse sections of the population, is growing nationally.

Rising Criticism of Monopoly Capital

Japan since World War II has experienced a level of economic growth unparalleled by other capitalist countries. This was achieved by the rapid development of heavy and chemical industries, a policy that involved the deepening of Japanese dependence upon imported raw materials.

At the same time, however, high growth aggravated the contradictions of monopoly capitalism. The destruction of the environment, proliferating pollution, the problems of rural depopulation and urban overpopulation, soaring land and housing prices, and so on all imposed heavy burdens on the Japanese people. The basic cause of this social crisis is the so-called amalgamation of politics, administration, and big business and the subordination of Japan to the military alliance with the United States. But the power of monopoly capital in Japan is also strengthened by the submissive attitude of many trade unions, particularly the company unions of large private enterprises. These unions pursue a policy of "labor-management cooperation," refrain from strike action, and evade the pressing problems of low wages, long working hours, and oppressive conditions.

Popular criticism of the government-business nexus is spreading, however. In recent years there has been a rising tide of protests at big business speculation, the political funding system, etc. These have become particularly marked in the aftermath of the Lockheed and Recruit case revelations. These cases, which exposed the depth of illicit financial links between politicians and big business, at home and abroad, have had widespread repercussions and caused considerable public questioning of the thirty-year dominance of the Liberal Democratic Party in Japanese politics. In these circumstances, there is a growing awareness of the fact that the problems of economic recession and political corruption can only be saved by a radical democratic change of the whole system of Japanese monopoly capitalism itself.

Notes

1. National Tax Administration Agency, *Hōjin kigyo no jittai '82* (The nature of corporations as revealed by tax statistics) (June 1984).

2. Tōyō Keiza Shinpōsha, *Kigyō keiretsu sōran '84* (Yearbook of enterprise groups) (1983).

3. T. Sumiya, *Nihon keizai to rokudai kigyō shūdan, gendai Nihon shihonshugi no shihai kōzō* (The Japanese economy and the six big enterprise groups, the controlling structure of modern Japanese capitalism) (Tokyo: Shinhyoron, 1982), chap. 4.

4. Holding Company Liquidation Commission, *Nihon zaibatsu to sono kaitai* (The Japanese zaibatsu and their dissolution, part 2) (Tokyo, 1950).

5. National Tax Administration Agency, *Hōjin kigyō no jittai '82*; Small and Medium Enterprises Agency, *Chūshō kigyū hakusho '82* (Annual report of small and medium-sized enterprises, 1982). The official definition of "small and medium enterprise"—*chūshō kigyō*—is firms that employ less than 300 workers, except in the case of the wholesale sector, where the cutoff point is 100 workers, and in the retail and service sectors, where it is 50 workers.

6. Small and Medium Enterprises Agency, *Chūshō kigyō hakusho '80*.

7. Administrative Management Agency, *Tokushū hōjin sōran '84* (Annual report of juridical persons having special status, 1984). The total for 1979 was 7,407.

8. U.S. Department of Commerce, *Japan, the Government-Business Relationship: a Guide for the American Businessman* (1972).

9. T. Sumiya, *Nihon keizai to rokudai kigyō shūdan*, chap. 5–6.

10. *Asahi shinbun* (Asahi news), August 31, 1983.

11. K. Marx, *Capital*, vol. 1 (1867), chap. 24; vol. 3 (1894), chaps. 23, 27; V. I. Lenin, *Imperialism: The Highest Stage of Capitalism* (1916), chap. 3.

12. See T. Sumiya, *Sengo Nihon no kigyo keiei, "Nihon-teki keiei" to sono tenki* (The management of enterprise in postwar Japan, "Japanese-style management" and its turning point) (Tokyo: Chuo Keizaisha, 1983), chap. 1.

13. *Shukan diayamondo* (Weekly diamond), May 1–8, 1982.

14. Tōyō Keizai Shinpōsha, *Nihon keizai to rokudai kigyō shudan*, chap. 7; *Sengo Nihon no kigyō keiei*, chap. 6; *Kokka to kigyō*, chap. 6.

5
Problems of the Japanese Working Class in Historical Perspective

KUROKAWA TOSHIO

Since the collapse of Japan's "economic miracle" workers have faced assaults on a number of fronts. These include wage restraint by monopoly capital, "rationalization" (or, as it is even more euphemistically called, "slim-line management"), and reductions in public spending (see chapter 6). In these circumstances, the labor movement has fallen into a state of stagnation, and since 1975 there has been a decline in the level of unionization. Not only is the work force being sacrificed by big business in its attempt to escape from the structural crisis of Japanese capitalism, it is also supporting levels of productivity that are so high as to cause international trade friction. Furthermore, Japanese workers now appear to be content to accept, almost without condition, the microelectronics revolution, whereby large enterprises are introducing industrial robots and other electronic equipment on an unprecedented scale. This acceptance is forthcoming despite the fact that the microelectronics revolution is having a serious effect on the problem of unemployment.

In light of these comments, how is one to understand the nature of Japanese workers? Often described as "workaholics who live in rabbit hutches," they are regarded with envy by the political and business leaders of the Western world, and with suspicion by Western workers and left-wing political parties. But, to both, they are objects of considerable bemusement and misunderstanding. To resolve such misunderstandings it is necessary to consider the cause of the present situation of the Japanese work force and the ways in which this situation may be transcended.

In the present analysis, it is of course important to examine the nature of the Japanese ruling class, which is responsible for the attacks on the working class mentioned in the first paragraph. The ruling class is supported by monopoly capital and the Japanese government, which together form the characteristically Japanese interlocking power structure of business, government, and bureaucracy, and acts to serve the needs of a state monopoly capital system subordinated to the interests of the United States. It is also important to analyze the role of the right-wing labor bosses who play an important part in some unions and mass-level organizations and who support the ruling class by pursuing a line, not simply of "cooperation between labor and management," but of the "unification of labor and management." The circumstances that have promoted the rise of these labor bosses are considered below.

If the Japanese working class is to resist the power of the ruling class and the labor bosses and is to avoid becoming a tool in their hands, it is essential also to analyze certain weak points inherent in the working class itself, and to suggest means by which these weak points can be overcome. For it is precisely at the time when the right-wing labor bosses are losing their mass support that shop-floor activists may seize the opportunity to play a leading role in labor organization, and to convert the present situation of stagnation into one of rapid progress. This will only be possible, however, if such activists appreciate the weak points in the present situation of the Japanese working class. It is therefore of particular importance that we should consider the nature and special characteristics of the Japanese work force. We must also define the weaknesses and potential strengths of the working class movement and explore possible alliances with other sections of society.

The Working Class in Postwar Japan

Changes in the Postwar Class Structure (I)

The primary characteristic of change in the Japanese class structure since the Pacific War has been the rapid decline in the number of self-employed farmers, fishers, and forestry workers, and the concomitant dramatic increase in the size of the working class. According to the late Ohashi Takanori, whose studies represent a major advance in our understanding of Japan's class composition, 16.189 million people (or 44 percent of the work force) were engaged in agriculture, fishing, and forestry in 1950, but by 1960 the figure had fallen to 13.486 million (30.6 percent) and thereafter it fell still more sharply, to 6.904 million (12.7 percent) in 1975, and to 5.592 million (9.8 percent) in 1980. Conversely, the size of the working class increased from 13.888 million (38.2 percent of the work force) in 1950 to 22.237 million (50.5 percent) in 1960, and to 38.008 million (66.6 percent) by 1980. In other words, within a mere thirty years, the size of the self-employed agricultural work force had decreased to a third of its initial level, while the size of the working class had almost trebled. No Western industrialized country has experienced such a dramatic transformation.

Sources of Weakness in the Contemporary Working Class

What consequences have arisen from these developments? The flexible labor market policy pursued by the the Japanese state, and the resultant shift of the work force from agriculture to manufacturing (particularly heavy manufacturing) has meant that an unusually large share of the industrial work force comes from a farming background. A somewhat similar situation existed before the war. Between 1888 and 1935, the size of the working class increased some sixtyfold, from 0.136 million to 8.001 million, while the number of peasant farm households, although increasing in absolute numbers, decreased as a percentage of the population.[1] The prewar situation, however, differed from postwar developments in that, since the war, both the number of farm households and the number of individuals employed in agriculture have shown an absolute decline. Before the war, many rural people (particularly women) who went to work in industry remained tied to the patriarchal family (*ie*) and returned to their villages as soon as their employment in industry was terminated. There was also, however, some increase in the number of male workers, particularly those employed in heavy industry, who established permanent residence in the cities.[2]

After 1945, the land reform resulted in the dissolution of the landlord system, and all farmers became self-employed. At the same time, the traditional patriarchal *ie* also disappeared. Consequently, with the exception of those who commute to outside work from their farms, workers who move out of the agricultural sector (be they blue-collar or white-collar) usually settle permanently in the cities. Nevertheless, they commonly continue to return to their "home village" for holidays and festivals, and thus their ties with agriculture have not been entirely severed. Unlike their counterparts in Western countries, there are many who have not yet put down roots in the urban community, and who are therefore slow to demand that local and central government meet their needs as urban residents by providing social security, public amenities, and services. They are also unfamiliar with a wage labor system, which involves the autonomous selling of one's own labor power. Many workers, therefore, fail to demand from their companies wages that reflect the value of their labor power, improvements in their hours and conditions of work, and so forth. They become, in other words, the type of "self-restrained" worker who, when confronted with problems, will merely murmur "oh well, we can't have everything our own way."

Even though the feudal elements of the prewar labor relations system have disappeared, it is still only *after* the signing of the employment contract that workers become aware of the precise form of work they are to perform, and only *after* they are employed that their precise occupation within the company is decided. They are also accustomed to a system whereby the company may shift them from one type of work to another. The power of capital over the workplace and the subordination of workers to company management is also strengthened by the fact that employees are forced to compete with one another for transfers and promotions. So, instead of pressing for their rights to higher pay, shorter hours, and better working conditions, there is a tendency for workers to make up for the inadequacies of their income by performing overtime, and even for many of them to forgo their annual leave entitlements. The situation is very different from that of workers in Western European countries, whose labor contracts spell out precisely the sorts of work in which they are to be engaged. Western workers also frequently undertake training on their own initiative before entering a company, and obtain employment that relates to their own, independently acquired, qualifications. This reduces the company's discretionary power over the placement of workers. It is particularly notable that, in the postwar period, Western unions have reduced the subordination of workers to the power of the company by securing arrangements whereby workers can take leave for educational and training purposes, and so raise the level of their qualifications.

As these comments indicate, the weaknesses in the contemporary position of the Japanese working class are, in no small measure, connected with the rapid decline in agricultural self-employment and sharp increase in industrial employment, which has been identified as the primary characteristic of social change in postwar Japan.

Links Between Workers and Farmers

As will by now be apparent, the situation of Japanese workers enables them to appreciate the interests of the farm population. This is true not only of the so-called landowning workers (farm owners in nonagricultural employment) and those who commute to work from farm households, but also of workers who live in the cities and return to their home villages for holidays and festivals. From the mid-1970s onward, however, there has been a growing tide of criticism directed against farmers and farm policy. These have suggested that the "high cost" of agricultural products and the "overproduction" of agriculture are responsible for trade friction, rising government expenditure, and the increasing cost of living. Such attacks have come primarily from the economic establishment (*zaikai*) and monopoly capital, but have also been supported by certain right-wing union bosses, whose policy of "cooperation between labor and management" is driving a wedge between the agricultural sector and the (mainly working-class) consumers.

The origins of current agricultural problems, however, lie precisely in the policies of high growth and heavy industrialization that were initiated by the *zaikai*, and which, as has already been seen, resulted in the rapid decline of the farm population. Since the beginning of the 1970s, although rapid growth has collapsed, there has been no fundamental change in the objectives of agricultural policy. Rather, these objectives have been further reinforced. Let us briefly examine these objectives and their impact on the relationship between farmers and the working class.

The policy of agricultural "modernization," introduced at the beginning of the 1960s, represented a major retreat from land reform's objectives of maintaining agricultural self-employment and expanding food production. The new policy, whose foundations were laid out in the Basic Agricultural Law (Nogyo Kihon Ho) imposed upon farmers a program of restructuring. This involved growing import dependence, which was specifically related to increased imports of surplus agricultural products from the United States. It also involved the introduction, under the auspices of monopoly capital, of large-scale agricultural machinery, fertilizers, agricultural chemicals, and feed developed in the United States, and the selective expansion of farm production. The consequence of these measures was an increase in managerial costs in the agricultural sector. Moreover, the evolving division and socialization of labor resulted in a change in the social expectations of farm families. Rural households began to demand living standards similar to those of urban households, and, since inflation was also running at a high rate, the consumption expenditure of farm families expanded. These trends led to an increase in the minimum viable size of farming operations. A handful of large-scale, full-time farmers succeeded in responding to this situation by expanding the size of their operations with the support of state assistance and financing. A far larger number of farmers, however, were obliged to respond by cutting back on the scale of their agricultural activities and placing an increasing number of family members in nonfarm employment. In other words, the drift toward part-time farming accelerated, with full-timers becoming part-timers, and those who were already part-timers devoting an increasing amount of time to nonagricultural work.

The effects of the policy of "structural reform" in agriculture were, clearly, to turn the villages into markets for sophisticated machinery and technology sold by monopoly enterprises at monopoly prices, and to provide a source of cheap labor for the process of heavy-industry-oriented high economic growth. The "reform" also lowered and destabilized the price of agricultural products other than rice and so encouraged farmers to overinvest in rice production. In response to this, the government, rather than altering its policy of expanding agricultural imports, introduced measures to restrict the area of rice paddy and to control rice prices. At the same time, the government-run rice distribution system was reorganized to allow increased independent distribution, and regional planning objectives were given precedence over the principles of the land reform, allowing the alienation of farm land for other uses. Thus, as it became increasingly difficult for farmers to earn a living in agriculture, so more and more rural people sought year-round jobs in industry, and a growing number of farmers were transformed into "landowning workers."

It is often suggested that, through growing participation in the nonagricultural work force, rural families have managed to raise their living standards to a level higher than that of urban workers. It is, indeed, true that since the early 1970s the average income of farm households has exceeded the average for wage-earning households as a whole. However, these statistics need to be seen in the context of the tendency, discussed above, toward the erosion of the independent economic basis of the farm family. Because of this tendency, the average number of income earners in the farm household is higher than that in the nonfarm household, and income per capita in farm households is still distinctly below average. Multiple employment means that the working conditions of farm family members are even worse than those of urban workers. Under the pressures of combining two or even three types of work, rural people increasingly find themselves subjected to the disintegration of family life.

Because of their participation in nonagricultural work, however, Japanese farmers are readily able to appreciate the interests of the industrial working class. They also possess a strong determination to rebuild and develop the basis of small-scale agriculture: a determination that has been revealed, for example, in recent protest actions in support of higher rice prices.

The various links discussed here mean that many members of the contemporary Japanese working class should be well able to identify with the problems of the rural sector. It is, in the first place, essential to realize that the aspects of the agricultural structure that are so stridently attacked by the *zaikai* and monopoly capital are precisely the consequence of policies pursued by the *zaikai*, large enterprises, and the Liberal Democratic administration themselves. The reconstruction and development of agriculture must be achieved, not by a liberalization of government controls, but by the extension of price support, not merely to rice but also to other farm products. To prevent such a policy from imposing excessive strains on the economy, however, it is necessary to reduce farm costs. This can be achieved by democratic regulations aimed at lowering the monopolistic prices currently charged for agricultural inputs such as machinery, fertilizers, chemicals, feed, and fuel. It is essential to reverse the trend toward increased dependence on imported farm products, and to increase self-sufficiency in food production. In this way the prosperity of all working people may be enhanced. Labor activists should endeavor to make these ideas understood, for they open up the possibility of joint political action by farmers and industrial workers.

Changes in the Postwar Class Structure (II)

A second significant aspect of social change in postwar Japan has been the growth, in both absolute and relative terms, of the stratum of "urban self-employed"—that is, of self-employed people outside the agricultural, forestry, and fishery sectors. The number of urban self-employed people in 1950 was 5.214 million, which was equivalent to some 14.3 percent of the work force. By 1960, however, the figure had risen to 6.614 (15.0 percent), and by 1980 to 9.984 (17.5 percent).

The increase in the size of the urban self-employed stratum has no parallel in the recent economic history of Western industrialized countries. As Ōhashi Takanori has observed, this upward trend takes place against a background of the continual establishment and collapse of small enterprises. Ōhashi's analysis also shows that the great majority of urban self-employed workers have previously been employees in other enterprises. The major share were formerly employed in small enterprises, but a quite substantial number are ex-employees of large firms. Of this latter group, many either have reached retirement age or, because of "rationalization," have been fired or accepted voluntary redundancy.[3] The lower levels of the urban self-employed stratum are, in other words, part of that surplus population constantly created and recreated by the process of capital accumulation. The growth of this stratum, therefore, must be seen as a consequence of the preculiarities of capital accumulation in Japan during the postwar high-growth era.

Characteristics of the Urban Self-Employed
Work Force

What, then, are the characteristics of this urban self-employed work force? There is a difference between prewar workers, who frequently maintained close links with their rural patriarchal *ie* and returned to the village when their urban employment was terminated, and postwar workers, who often settle in the city and return to their birthplace only for holidays and festivals. Among this postwar group there are a considerable number of workers who have found it impossible to obtain reemployment after retiring from, or being dismissed by, the companies in which they were employed. Such people have no alternative but to work on a self-employed basis. The substantial number of self-employed workers who have experienced employment in other enterprises are well placed to understand the interests and aspirations of the working class. On the other hand, the self-employed sector also includes those who have inherited family businesses established in the prewar period, and who have little or no experience of wage labor. Given the high risks and lack of security in self-employment, many of these people feel obliged to put in long and unregulated hours of work. Unlike wage workers, they have not yet reached the stage where they are willing to demand their rights to improvements in their present working conditions but rather tend to practice "self-restraint" in their approach to wages and conditions.[4]

In general, however, the private assets of the urban self-employed are more restricted than those of wage-workers, and their incomes are no greater. These considerations, as well as the fact that many have experienced wage-labor themselves, provide the basis for a certain degree of solidarity between the self-employed and other workers. Moreover, the self-employed have a positive role to play in the formation of urban communities and in the articulation of urban residents' demands for social security, public amenities, and services. Their importance here is reinforced by the fact that their workplaces and living quarters are normally integrated. In this sense, the self-employed differ from wage workers, whose places of work are usually far removed from their homes. With the increasing division and socialization of labor, the self-employed have also come to play a vital part in the production and distribution of consumer goods and services to wage-earning and other households within the local community. They thus have a variety of close links with the citizens of their local urban area. In this sense, their situation is far removed from that of the prewar urban self-employed sector. Before the war, the middle class of landowning farmers, fishers, artisans, doctors, priests and monks, professional people, middle-level bureaucrats, and so forth constituted around 40 percent of the work force. Apart from its very lowest segments, however, this prewar middle class tended to adopt a political position that supported the absolutist Emperor system.[5] The political role of the postwar urban self-employed sector is a very different one.

Links Between Workers and the Urban Self-Employed

The overwhelming majority of the expanding Japanese working class is made up of workers who have left the agricultural sector during the past thirty years. The fact that these workers have not entirely severed their links with their rural origins tends to weaken their position in class terms, but this weakness is not necessarily one that will determine the destiny of the Japanese working class. It is possible, indeed, that it will gradually disappear as succeeding generations of workers become further removed from their agrarian roots. Nevertheless, it is not enough simply to wait for the problem spontaneously to resolve itself. Nor is it helpful to try to overcome this weakness by repeatedly criticizing workers for their romantic attachments to their "home village."

Whatever the weaknesses of their positions, workers in contemporary Japan are, in an objective sense, sellers of labor power. The purchasers of labor power seek, by use of their own possession (capital), to pursue their own objective (profit). In this process, their aim is to exercise their rights as buyers of labor in such a way as to obtain the maximum amount of labor power at the minimum possible price. The workers, on the other hand, try to use their own possession (labor power) in pursuit of their own objective, which is the maintenance and re-creation of that labor power. They seek to exercise their rights as sellers of labor power to improve the price they receive for their labor and the circumstances (working hours and other conditions) under which that labor is consumed. There is, therefore, a confrontation between two contrasting systems of rights. In this situation, workers gradually become accustomed to the laws of the wage-labor market, within which they must autonomously sell their labor power. They learn to work with discretion, and to band together with other workers to protect their common rights. Thus there is increasing inter-worker solidarity aimed at limiting the mutual competition that could weaken their position as sellers of labor. By obtaining contracts that embody a legal recognition of the equal rights of the buyers and sellers of labor, workers may also strive for the recognition of a genuine equality between labor and management.

The existence of these conditions, however, does not mean that Japanese workers will, by themselves, be able to overcome the weaknesses of their position, pursue freedom and equality, and so realize their common interests. For this to happen it will be necessary for shop-floor activists to organize mass-level movements aimed at the achievement of specific rights and objectives. At the political level, it is also necessary to develop movements for the protection and strengthening of parliamentary democracy, and for the democratization of the economy. Such action should be based not on a wide and vaguely defined set of ideals, but rather on concrete demands which may provide footholds in surmounting the weaknesses inherent in the present situation of the working class. As I shall explain more fully below, in the present circumstances, when workers are being forced to accept longer working hours and a more intense pace of work, a specific demand for the shortening of working hours would offer such a foothold. It is necessary for Japanese workers to demand, on their own behalf, increases in the level of overtime payments, limits on the amount of overtime work, and the right to enjoy their full entitlement to annual leave. They must also demand that management maintain staffing levels adequate to support these objectives. By overcoming their traditional tendency to "self-restraint," workers will be able to develop joint struggles for shorter working hours and for better wages and economic conditions.

Furthermore, as discussed above, it is important for wage workers to contribute to the creation of urban communities, both in the areas where they work and in the areas where they live. These communities may include the urban self-employed, whose links with the working class have already been noted, and even the small-scale capitalists, who own financially insecure enterprises. Such citizens' movements could initiate joint actions, directed at local and national government, on behalf of their social rights. Pressing problems in this area include the inadequate social security system, which has been thrown into further crisis by recent expenditure cuts, the need for radical reform of the tax system, and the need for improved provision of public amenities and services. At the same time, it is also important for activists to work toward a change in the mental attitudes that promote "self-restraint" on the part of the work force.

On the political level, workers, the urban self-employed, and small business people may be united in movements on behalf of peace and democracy. Demands for peace and disarmament, aimed at the abolition of nuclear weapons, appeal to the desire of all these groups to protect their existence and livelihood. Such movements are given added significance by the fact that Japan is the only country to have formally renounced the use of military force.

Trade Unions and Changing Class Structure

How do the trade unions fit into these movements for economic and political change? In the prewar period, Japanese trade unions experienced severe repression at the hands of the emperor-centered absolutist system. They were thus unable to unite with revolutionary political parties into a joint antifascist front and were instead absorbed into a fascist-style labor organization—the "Industrial Patriotic Association" (Sangyō Hōkoku-kai)—which dealt the final death blow to the aspirations of organized labor.

In Western nations, working-class political action initially developed along different lines. There, the working class participated in the struggle to achieve a bourgeois democratic revolution. Although their efforts generally ended in oppression and failure, they learned from these failures valuable lessons: above all, lessons about the central importance of the strength of organization. In this respect, the Western experience differs from developments in Japan. There a universal suffrage movement emerged after the Russo-Japanese War (1904–1905), but the socialists were unable to participate effectively in this movement because of internal divisions between those who sought to work through the parliamentary system and those who favored direct, extraparliamentary action. Furthermore, the Japanese Communist Party, founded after the First World War, failed to fulfill the role of encouraging workers and farmers to participate in the universal suffrage movement and took no particular action to support the achievement of a bourgeois democratic revolution.[6]

In the wake of Japan's defeat in the Pacific War, under the auspices of the Allied occupation, the Japanese labor movement for the first time received legal recognition. Workers began to organize themselves, mainly on an enterprise basis, and the level of union membership rose to more than 50 percent of the industrial work force, a figure unprecedented in Japanese history. A joint struggle developed, led by the All-Japan Industrial Labor Union Congress (Sanbetsu Kaigi), but supported not only by the congress but also by other labor organizations such as the less radical General Federation of Labor (Sōdōmei). From the first, however, this struggle suffered both from the defects of the Sanbetsu Kaigi's leadership tactics and from weaknesses inherent in the postwar situation of the working class, who found themselves, after a long period of dormancy, suddenly facing the enormous challenges of the postwar "democratic revolution." These factors were exploited by the American occupation authorities, who launched a counterattack involving attempts to create a split within the workers' movement through support for an anti-Communist "Democratic Federation" (Minshū-ka Domei). The labor movement was unable to resist this attack, and the result was the formation of the Japan General Council of Labor Unions (Sōhyō), a new body jointly created by Sōdōmei and Minshū-ka Domei and designed to serve the objectives of the occupation authorities. Despite these changes, however, the attention of Japanese workers could not be diverted from certain fundamental issues, and once again, in opposition to the wishes of the occupation forces and of Japanese monopoly capital, they took up the struggle for better wages and an end to industrial "rationalization." They also based their movement upon objectives such as nuclear disarmament, peace, and democracy, and succeeded in developing joint actions with farmers and local citizens' groups. Nevertheless, the Japanese working class proved unable to transcend the weaknesses of its situation. One factor in this inability was Sōhyō's policy of focusing attention on the "spring offensive" (*shuntō*)—a single annual round of national wage bargaining which takes place in March–April. Another was the influx of peasant farmers into the industrial work force, which began to transform Japan's class structure as rapid economic growth took hold. Monopoly capital exploited these weaknesses to the limit in order to reassert their control over the work force. As a result, not only was enterprise opposition to rationalization undermined, but the wider movements for peace and democracy also experienced reverses. With the collapse of high economic growth in the 1970s, the labor movement was forced to retreat even on the wage front, and joint action with farmers and citizens groups diminished.

At present, therefore, it is essential to overcome the weaknesses mentioned by means of action based both in the workplace and in the local community. Within the workplace, such action must be founded upon opposition to the oppressive control of the enterprise and should involve practical demands for the shortening of working hours. More widely, it is important to develop and expand joint campaigns for peace and nuclear disarmament. In particular, it is vital that one confront the irresponsibility of the political, bureaucratic, and financial elite, who are preserving and maintaining the benefits received by monopoly capital from public contracts and government aid to industry, while at the same time carrying out spending cuts that undermine the basic human right to existence. Through opposition to this irresponsibility the consciousness of workers in relation to their own fundamental human right can be heightened.

The Position of Workers in Contemporary Japan

Changes in Wages and Working Conditions Since 1975

After the watershed of the 1973 oil crisis, high economic growth in Japan came to an abrupt end, and Japan, in common with Western industrialized countries, experienced the worst crisis of overproduction since the Second World War. As the government's 1984 White Paper on Labor points out, ever since 1975 (the year when the recession reached its height), the level of wage rises in Japan has been low. The paper also observes that, since 1975, there has been a tendency for the wage gaps between large and small firms, between male and female employees, and between older and younger workers to widen. Furthermore, differentials between large and small enterprises have widened not only in relation to wages, but also in relation to health and welfare benefits, severance payments, and so forth. According to the figures provided by the Labor Ministry's Monthly Survey of Employment Statistics, real wages increased at an annual rate of 1.3 percent between 1975 and 1980, and at a rate of 1.2 percent per annum between 1980 and 1983. This is far lower than the annual averages of 4.1 percent, achieved during the early part of the high growth era (1955–1965), and of 7.8 percent, attained in the latter phases of high economic growth (1965–1970). It is also well below the 6.4 percent per annum growth rate recorded in the years 1970–1975, which saw the collapse of the "economic miracle."

These figures reflect the success of the policy of "wage restraint" pursued by the Japan Employers' Association (Nikkeiren) from 1975 onward: success achieved through the support of right-wing union leaders, who advocated a path of "economic consolidation." The logic of the "economic consolidation" approach, which has received particularly effective support from the company unions of eight major enterprises (New Japan Steel, Japan Steel Tube, Hitachi, Toshiba, Toyota, Nissan, Mitsubishi Heavy Industries, and Ishikawajima Harima), is that low wage rises are necessitated by the low level of economic growth. According to the Finance Ministry's Statistics of Corporations, however, the total level of profits in all industries rose from 4,945.1 billion yen in 1975 to 17,895.8 billion in 1981 and 17,727.5 in 1983. This is much higher than the total of 10,997.7 billion attained at the peak of high economic growth in 1973. Besides, a major share of these profits accrues to a few very large firms. Within these firms, increases in the level of internal reserves have been several times as high as the levels of reported profits. These facts make it clear that monopoly capital has taken advantage of low growth and structural crisis to limit wages and cut back the size of their labor force (the so-called slim-line management policy) and has thus reorganized enterprises in such a way as to ensure high profits in a period of low growth.

Not only have the pay claims put forward during recent "spring offensives" been severely restricted, but the "slim-line management" policy has also implied a trend for firms to reduce the size of their permanent work forces and increase the number of "marginal workers"—temporary workers, day laborers, part-timers, and contract workers—all of whom work under insecure employment conditions. Moreover, working hours have been lengthened, and employees have been forced to accept increases in the speed and intensity of labor. According to the Monthly Survey of Employment Statistics, the index of manufacturing workers in regular employment fell from 105.9 in 1973 to 97.0 in 1983 (1975 = 100). The Labor Survey compiled by the Prime Minister's Office also reveals that, between 1975 and 1983, while the number of regular nonagricultural employees (including sectors other than manufacturing) increased by just 12.7 percent, the number of "temporary workers and day laborers" increased by 46.9 percent. At the same time, the total length of real working hours in manufacturing increased by 6 percent and the index of productivity of manufacturing labor increased by 63.3 percent. (These last two statistics are derived respectively from the Monthly Survey of Employment Statistics and from the Japan Productivity Center.)

Inevitably, as the hours and pace of labor have been increased, the size of the work force pared to the bone, and the uniquely Japanese employment system intensified, unreported industrial health problems, accidents, occupational diseases, and suicides have also increased. In particular, the 1980s have seen a rapid expansion in the use of robots and other microelectronically controlled equipment, and this has been accompanied by further extensions in working hours in the form of overtime, shift work, and night work. Workers are often forced to work for unnecessarily long continuous periods of time, and these trends have given rise to new forms of industrial accidents and health hazards.[7]

Worsening Unemployment and the Changing Structure of the Low-Wage Sector

Since 1975, employment problems have been aggravated not only by the dismissal of workers from large firms—the so-called slimline management policy discussed in the previous section—but also by the frequent failure of small and medium enterprises. According to the Tokyo Commerce and Industry Research Group, the number of bankruptcies rose from 8,202 in 1973 to 12,606 in 1975, and to a record high of 19,155 in 1983. The great majority of these bankruptcies were accounted for by small or medium-sized firms.

As a result of these developments, there has been a steady worsening in the employment situation. The Work Force Survey published by the Japanese Prime Minister's Office excludes from its category of "unemployed" a number of groups who would be treated as unemployed in U.S. or European statistics. Nevertheless, this survey shows that the number of "wholly unemployed" people rose from 680,000 in 1973 to 1,000,000 in 1975, and to 1,560,000 in 1983. It is this rise in unemployment that is responsible for the trend, discussed in the previous section, for wage gaps to widen, and in particular for the gap between large and small firms to increase. This reverses the tendency, apparent in the 1960s and early 1970s, for scale-related wage gaps to narrow. According to the Monthly Survey of Employment Statistics, the index of average wages in firms with 30–99 employees fell from 89.7 in 1975 to 84.2 in 1984. (Average wages in firms with 500 or more employees = 100.) This means that the gap between large and small firms had, by 1984, returned to the level at which it stood in 1973. Moreover, although male workers were in general being forced to work harder and for longer hours, their real wage levels were stagnating. It therefore became increasingly necessary for married women to seek paid employment. Many, however, were unable to find regular employment and joined the ranks of the "wholly unemployed." Those who did find work were often obliged to accept low-paid part-time employment. The consequence has been an increase in the gap between male and female wages since 1975.

It is also important to observe that these increases in wage gaps have altered the structure of the wage-earning sector. The Labor Ministry's Basic Statistical Survey of the Wage Structure shows that the lowest-paid manufacturing workers are predominantly employed in the following industries: garments and other textile products, electrical machinery and appliances, textile products, and food processing. Of these, the largest number are women workers. But whereas in the past most were girls who had recently graduated from middle school, this group is now declining, and older women workers (age forty or above) are coming to constitute an increasingly important share of the lowest-paid stratum. In a time of low growth and structural crisis, however, the unit prices received by subcontractors declines, and for this reason, many small enterprises have found that even the employment of very low-waged labor cannot save them from financial difficulties. The growth of the low-wage stratum is also associated with the increasing importance of the so-called tertiary sector in the industrial and employment structure. A particularly striking case is that of the office service industry, which performs such functions as the maintenance of office buildings. In this industry there has been both a decrease in demand from the public sector and a decline in the prices paid by large private firms to their subcontractors. These trends have resulted in the increased employment, through agency contracts, of very low-paid workers. At the same time there has been a phenomenal growth in the employment of low-paid women part-time workers in the manufacturing, wholesale, retail, and service sectors, while the number of outworkers employed on a piecework basis has shown little decline. This latter group, which receives even lower wages than part-time workers, constitutes the very poorest-paid sphere of employment. Recently, the micro-electronics revolution has resulted in the appearance of a new low-wage group whose working conditions represent a cross between part-time employment and outwork. In addition to these groups, one should not overlook the existence of a substantial number of students who perform side-jobs outside the sphere of the formal labor market.

Some Problems for Consideration

These special characteristics of the situation of the working class since 1975 raise a number of problems the labor movement must tackle at a mass level. The principal issues are: (1) the decline in the power of organized labor to campaign for higher wages; (2) the further decline in the already inadequate power of organized labor to campaign for shorter working hours; (3) the weakening and dissolution of resistance to monopoly capital; (4) the inability and failure of organized labor to take up the case of the unemployed and irregularly employed low-wage workers; and (5) the lack of concern displayed by organized labor toward the problems of the self-employed, and still more toward the financial and other difficulties of the owners of small firms. In the following section I shall consider the causes underlying these issues.

The Contemporary Situation of the Working Class

Wage Campaigns

First, let me consider the reasons for the declining power of organized labor to campaign for high wages.

As has already been seen, substantial rises in real wages accompanied the period of high economic growth. It can be argued that this rapid improvement in wage levels weakened the desire of workers to press for further rises. The impression of substantial improvements in income levels is reinforced if one takes a longer perspective. On an index where the prewar (1934–1936) level of wages equals 100, average wages in the immediate postwar period (December 1945) equaled a mere 13.1, and for some months after that they fluctuated between 20.0 and 30.0. Wages, in other words, were literally at starvation level. Thereafter, according to studies by the Labor Ministry, real wages rose to 66.3 in 1949, to 85.4 in 1950, and to 92.1 in 1951, before finally exceeding the prewar level in 1952. The start of high economic growth in 1955 took place at a time when real wages were only 14.5 percent higher than they had been before the war. During the short space of twenty years, however, rapid economic growth brought with it substantial rises in real earnings. Older workers, therefore, are in a position to draw a very favorable comparison between the present situation and the days when wages were lower than they had been in the 1930s. The consequence is a tendency for such workers to feel that they have received as much as they are entitled to hope for. The desire to press for higher wages is eroded.

There is, however, nothing inevitable about this weakening of the pressure for wage rises. For one thing, the government statistics only refer to increases in the average level of wages. Because high economic growth was accompanied by rapid heavy industrialization, and therefore by a radical alteration in the composition of the work force, these statistics distort the real picture. A more detailed analysis of the way in which the real earnings of each individual worker have risen may help to overcome any reluctance to press for higher wages.

It must, in the first place, be explained that the rise in disposable income (minus tax, social security payments, etc.) was lower than the rise in real wages. From 1965 to 1970, while real wages rose by 7.8 percent per annum, real disposable income rose by 5.2 percent per annum. The comparable figures for the period 1970 to 1975 were 6.4 percent and 4.4 percent respectively. Moreover, after 1975, when real wage increase were running a low level of 1.2 percent or 1.3 percent, real disposable income in several years actually recorded negative growth: –0.9 percent in 1976, –1.4 percent in

1980, and –1.0 percent in 1981.[8]

Looking at the other element in the equation, between 1973 and 1983, while the consumption expenditure of employee households increased 2.9-fold, their nonconsumption expenditure increased 3.2-fold. Thus the ratio of nonconsumption expenditure to total household spending rose from 9.3 percent to 11.3 percent. This trend was reinforced after the collapse of high economic growth in 1975, and by 1979 the ratio of nonconsumption to total expenditure had soared to 15.5 percent.[9]

Thus, working-class families have had to bear the growing burden of nonconsumption expenditures such as taxes and social security payments. In Japan, income tax is largely deducted on a pay-as-you-earn basis. It is therefore important for workers to develop an awareness of the tax problem, and, along with farmers as well as small business people, to demand a system in which their living expenses can be treated as deductible "necessary expenditure." It should also be possible to organize a joint movement of workers, farmers, the urban self-employed, and the owners of small firms, to halt and reverse the great increases in the burden of social security contributions. Such a movement, however, should not regard decreases in nonconsumption expenditure as a substitute for wage rises. On the contrary, it should aim to direct attention to the structure of the household budget, and so reinforce demands for higher wages. In this way, we can create the conditions for the development of a unified approach in which workers strive not only for their own personal interests, but for the common interests they share with farmers, fishers, and the nonagricultural self-employed. This need for a common approach applies also to the second problem relating to wage rises, which will be discussed in the following paragraphs.

The second issue to be considered is this. The substantial rise in real wages that occurred during the high growth period was accompanied by a change in consumption patterns. By means of the "demonstration effect" and of advertising, large enterprises succeeded in making consumers increasingly dependent upon products such as household electrical appliances and automobiles. To "keep up with the Joneses," households and individuals were obliged to indulge in "social-pressure spending" on items such as hairdressing, cosmetics, entertainment, appliance repairs, and leisure activities. The levels of fixed social expenditure (which includes charges for public services such as transport, communications, heating, water, rents, insurance, medical care, and education) were also rising. All of these elements came to occupy an increasing share of household expenditure. Between 1960 and 1973 the share of social-pressure spending of the type described above in household expenditure rose from 26.0 percent to 36.2 percent, while the share of fixed social expenditure rose from 15.3 percent to 16.0 percent. After the collapse of high growth, these expenditures continued to rise rapidly, reaching 39.3 percent and 18.0 percent respectively by 1980. Meanwhile, the share of expenditure directed to the purchase of food, clothing, and so forth was decreasing, particularly among lower-income earners.[10]

In light of these circumstances, it is important for workers to initiate campaigns, like those that have taken place in some Western countries, for reductions in the cost of public services, and for these services to be more fully supported by state or local spending. At the same time, they should also press for democratic controls to reduce the monopolistic prices charged by large enterprises for their products.

The third point to be made about wage rises during the high-growth era is that they were associated with the increasing use of income for purposes not classified as "expenditure" but rather as "increases in assets." These include savings, the repayment of loans, and the payment of insurance premiums, credit installments, and so on. Between 1963 and 1979 the level of such "increases in assets" rose 10.3-fold, while the level of loan repayments alone rose 12.6-fold. In 1963, "increases in assets" had accounted for 20.7 percent of household spending, but by 1979 their share had risen to 32.5 percent. In other words, the growth of consumer credit systems designed to promote mass consumption, and the Japanese government's policy of encouraging home ownership, were forcing workers to sustain the burden of increasing housing loan repayments and rising levels of savings. The underdevelopment of the social security system also meant that workers were obliged to increase their savings and life insurance payments to prepare for eventualities such as ill health and old age. According to the Bank of Japan's *Statistics of the Japanese Economy in an International Context*, Japanese households save approximately 20 percent of their disposable income, a far higher figure than the average level of savings by Western European households, which stands at around 10 percent. The reason for this difference lies in the policies of the Japanese government. Unlike the governments of Western European nations, the Japanese government has sought to promote private home ownership rather than to provide public housing for low income earners. Its social security policies have also been quite unlike those of many European countries, where the burden of insurance payments is borne by public finances or by corporations, and where a uniform national minimum level has been maintained. In Japan, on the contrary, the principle of "beneficiary pays" has meant that the workers bear the increasing burden of insurance premiums, while the level of benefits falls. As workers develop a greater awareness of these facts, they will come to demand changes in government housing and social security policies, in order to protect their own fundamental rights to existence. They may also begin to press for wage rises and even for the establishment of a national minimum wage system embracing all branches of industry.

When one looks in detail at the real nature of the rapid wage rises that occurred in the high-growth era, therefore, a new picture emerges. As wages rose, the products of large enterprises entered increasingly into the consumption patterns of workers. The processes of daily life, which enabled workers to maintain and reproduce their labor power, broadened in scope, and the methods by which workers financed these processes also altered. Instead of using wages to pay directly for their requirements, workers increasingly had to resort to credit and savings.

The substantial rises in real wages that took place during the high-growth period were not a straightforward reflection of increases in labor productivity. Indeed, while the real wage index (1955 = 100) rose to 300.0 by 1973, the index of labor productivity in manufacturing for the same period rose to 572.7. It cannot be denied that the "spring offensives" which began in 1955 had a significant effect on the level of earnings during the "economic miracle." However, these "offensives" restricted their attention to direct wage rises. Consequently, not only did wage rises fail to keep up with increases in productivity, but also problems associated with nonconsumption expenditure, conspicuous spending, public service charges, savings, and loans multiplied. Since the end of high economic growth, while the level of real wages has stagnated, these problems have continued to increase. Exposure of this fact can help to inspire demands by workers for wages that reflect the real value of their labor and enable them to support consumption patterns commensurate with their levels of skill. In addition, it is important to impose limits on the levels of expenditure that are necessary for workers to reproduce their labor power. Rather, there should be increased demands for a right to maintain expenditure levels appropriate to real needs. For these purposes, joint campaigns for improvements in social security, housing, and other public services and amenities must be developed by workers and citizens.

The Campaign for Shorter Working Hours

Next, it is necessary to consider why Japanese workers have been less effective than Western workers in pressing for shorter working hours.

First, as already observed, many Japanese workers are not yet accustomed to the laws of a wage system under which they must autonomously sell their own labor power. They have therefore not yet reached a stage at which they feel about to demand increased leisure time from the purchasers of that labor.

Second, Japanese workers are unlike their Western counterparts in that they are not normally hired by the company to fill a specific position. Instead, the company is able to decide where they will work and what tasks they will perform, and it is free to alter their position at any time. This strengthens the control of the enterprise over the employee.

Third, Japanese workers have had to face the problem of rapidly rising expenditure on housing loans, and on credit repayments for household electrical appliances and cars. To sustain their household incomes, they have therefore been forced to take on more overtime and to work during holiday periods. Paradoxically, however, ownership of electrical goods, cars, and other consumer products has increased the demand for leisure time in which to use these products.

It is therefore important for those active in the labor movement to concern themselves with demands for increased leisure, the full utilization of annual leave, increased overtime payments, and restriction of overtime hours. In pursuing these objectives, it is possible for workers to identify their own interests with a wider

common interest. Such a campaign for shorter working hours
could also, as suggested, provide a focus for the creation of local
community actions in which workers cooperate with residents of
the areas in which they live or work.

Resistance to Rationalization

After the demise of high economic growth in 1975, monopoly capital pursued a policy of rationalization or "slim-line management,"
which involved drastic reductions in the size of the work force.
Such reductions were made possible by the absence of resistance
from those "pillars of Japanese-style management," the enterprise-
based unions. At the same time Japanese corporations were themselves weakening the other major pillars, the age-related wage
system (whereby wage rises and promotions occur automatically
with length of service to the company) and the lifetime employment system (whereby the company accepts a commitment to re-
tain the employee until retirement age). These latter peculiarities
of the Japanese management system were features that, if used effectively as bargaining tools by organized labor, might have operated in the interests of the workers.

The rationalization policy was also pursued by means of the
"self-management" or "small group" system, under which groups
of perhaps seven or eight employees would become responsible for
monitoring aspects of their own work, while competing with one
another to increase productivity. (Quality control circles constitute
the best-known example of this system.) These innovations
resulted in longer working hours and greater intensity of labor, and
also strengthened the authoritarian control of management over
the workplace. In the following section the workings of such
groups will be examined in more detail. But first, to appreciate the
reasons why the labor movement offered relatively little resistance
to these changes, something must be said about the history of
union attitudes to rationalization.

The so-called peculiarities of Japanese management were not in
fact widespread before the high-growth era, and it can be argued
that it was rapid economic growth itself that provided the material
and economic foundations for age-related promotions and lifetime
employment in large enterprises. It is also true, however, that prior
to the high-growth period and even after rapid growth had begun,

the Japanese union movement had possessed an organizational structure that enabled it to offer effective resistance to rationalization.

The "spring offensive" system of annual wage bargaining commenced at the beginning of the period of rapid economic growth. Prior to that, Japanese unions did not conduct their wage bargaining at one particular time of the year. Moreover, they already had considerable experience of conducting campaigns against rationalization and layoffs, and they continued to conduct such campaigns for some time after the start of high growth.

In the immediate postwar period, when the left-wing Sanbetsu Kaigi was in control of the Japanese union movement, resistance to rationalization was of course effectively organized. The power of Sanbetsu Kaigi was undermined, however, and leadership of the trade union movement was taken over the the less radical Sōhyō, which was expected to support the policies favored by the U.S. occupation authorities. The outbreak of the Korean War in 1950 brought with it the initiation of special war procurements in Japan and enabled Japanese monopoly enterprises to embark on a period of rapid capital accumulation, while at the same time subordinating the Japanese economy more firmly then ever to U.S. economic dominance. At the same time a rationalization movement was launched against the work force. Under the leadership of Secretary General Takano Minoru, however, Sōhyō put up a broad-based resistance to this attack. Typical examples of this resistance, in which many workers participated, include the campaign against firings in the Nissan Motor Company (May–September 1953), and the "113 day" campaign by the Mitsui Mine Workers' Union (August–November 1953). In the post–Korean War period war procurements ceased, and large enterprises anticipated that the new security treaty with the United States would provide an opportunity to convert to armaments production. Further rationalization occurred and was resolutely resisted by organized labor. In 1954, for example, workers campaigned against the closure of the Amagasaki Steel Works, and in December of the same year a major movement to oppose firings was initiated at the Muroran Works of Japan Steel Tube.

These campaigns scored some successes. The Mitsui Mine Workers' Union, for example, forced the company to withdraw 1,815 dismissals. In other cases, although the union movement was unable to prevent firings, it did succeed in limiting the ability of management to exert arbitrary control over the workplace.

Thereafter, however, a change in leadership resulted in alterations in Sōhyō policy. Ōta Kaoru became Sōhyō president and Iwai Akira replaced Takano Minoru as secretary general. The new leaders had been critical of Takano's antirationalization stance and favored a policy that concentrated on organizing integrated campaigns throughout all industries for increases in wage levels. The outcome was the initiation, in 1955, of the "spring offensives." These offensives were successful in the sense that they compensated for the organizational weakness inherent in the Japanese enterprise-union system and enabled labor to confront the structures of monopoly capital in an effective manner. However, while they operated along regional lines, with various local factories working together in support of higher wages, the offensives were still unable to overcome the contradictions of the enterprise-union system. They therefore failed to develop into an adequate form of resistance to Japanese monopoly capital. The restriction of union activity to wage demands resulted in a weakening of the organizational basis for antirationalization campaigns, a fact that indeed attracted criticism from within Sōhyō itself. Even after the initiation of the "spring offensive" system, however, a number of unions organized fairly powerful antirationalization campaigns, the most notable case being the Mitsui Miike strike of 1960, which sought to oppose major closures in the coal industry. As a result of such actions, monopoly capital came to fear the power of workplace unionism and found itself unable to withdraw the rights it had already granted to its employees.

In particular, from the second half of the 1960s, monopoly capital began to develop new methods to undermine the rights of the work force. These involved the education and training of the procompany unionists who favored "cooperation between management and workers" and who were placed in leading positions in the unions. During the late 1960s and early 1970s large numbers of young workers were recruited into corporations. Some of these workers were given extensive training both within and outside the enterprise, encouraged to participate in various informal company activities, and selected as leaders of small work teams. They then provided a corps of right-wing leaders who took a nonconfrontational view of trade unionism. These policies made it possible for management to strengthen its control over the workplace, eliminate opposition to rationalization, and erode the rights that workers had earlier won for themselves. These developments help us to understand the weak or nonexistent opposition of workers to the present wave of rationalization.

The Contemporary Rationalization Movement

This weakness, however, should not be regarded as irremediable. In Western Europe, where monopoly capital has been attempting to "humanize" labor relations by means of QC circles, and so forth, workers have responded by developing "solidarity through autonomy." To achieve this objective they have sought shorter working hours, training opportunities, and employment security. This style of union action is criticized by the Japanese Employers' Federation (*Nikkeiren*) as placing excessive emphasis on individual rights. In Japan, monopoly capital has rather been attempting to strengthen what they call "meritocratic management" (*noryoku-shugi kanri*)—a system whereby workers are made to compete with one another and so hindered from achieving workplace solidarity. At the same time there has been a move toward increasing use of the self-management or small-group system in factories. These trends have made it possible for management to increase its control over employees, to extend hours and intensify the pace of work, and to reduce to a minimum the size of the work force.

To illustrate the nature of meritocratic management let us consider the case of the Mitsubishi Electrical Company. There a so-called New Qualification System has been established. Rather than receiving automatic promotion by seniority, workers are urged to compete with one another in a promotion race based on tough examinations, assessments by superiors, personal interviews, and written reports in which they are expected to assess their own achievements. The result is that employees become individualistic and self-centered, and it is increasingly difficult to develop a sense of workplace solidarity.

The workings of the "self-management" or "small-group" system can be illustrated by the case of the Nippon Electrical Company (NEC), which initiated this approach in 1965 with its so-called ZD (zero defect) movement and has been active in promoting the small-group system ever since. The NEC ZD movement is described by the Japan Productivity Center's publication *The ZD Plan: An Outline of Its Introduction and Development* as "offering returns that range from 47 times to 170 times the amount invested in its implementation." The zero defect movement was introduced at a time when the NEC union was becoming increasingly subservient to the enterprise. The movement, while giving workers an illusion of participating in management, in fact subordinated them more firmly than ever to the objectives of the corporation. Employees were expected to devise and attain their own production targets, and in one instance the pressures of responsibility were so great as to drive a sixteen-year-old female worker insane.[11] The small work-teams, which were established to eliminate defects, were not only involved in the setting of production targets but also became responsible for achieving the company's slogan of "autonomy through consensus." To fulfill this responsibility, the small work-teams were expected to keep a check upon the behavior of workers both on the shop floor and in their family lives. The smallest-scale groups, known as "units," were treated as individual entities, and the profitability of each unit was calculated separately. Great emphasis was placed on the "autonomy" of the work teams, each of which had its own special functions.

This ZD movement, however, conferred no real autonomy on the workers. Instead, feelings of dissatisfaction among the work force were suppressed by sending selected workers on extramural training courses where they were groomed for leadership, or by creating informal "self-improvement" groups in which the small-group leaders were exposed to right-wing ideas designed to bring out their capacity to exert authority over others. Basic objectives were drawn up by meetings of a managerial group consisting of the leaders, unit chiefs, supervisors, and section chiefs, while the small groups became responsible only for the practical details involved in attaining these objectives.

What would happen if the workers were to use the small-group system to make autonomous proposals for improvements in working conditions? If the company felt that these threatened its profitability, it would farm out that particular process to subcontractors, reduce the work force through severances or transfers, and increase profits by lengthening working hours and intensifying the pace of work. In effect, the workers would be cutting their own throats.

Nevertheless, the small-group system does create certain possibilities for action. In the first place, it offers the illusion of "autonomy." It is possible that, as workers find it harder and harder to tolerate the increasing hours and intensity of work, they may come to experience growing dissatisfaction at the gap between illusion and reality. This would create contradictions for the group leaders, who would be obliged to make concessions aimed at meeting such dissatisfaction.

Second, since the self-management or small-group systems give workers certain decision-making functions, they do allow employees to accumulate increasing knowledge of the labor process. Workers acquire a growing multiplicity of skills through their participation in discussion circles that bring together different work groups, and so come to have a wider appreciation of a variety of work processes and their interaction with one another. In this sense, the small-group system may create possibilities for Japanese workers, who face lengthening working hours and limited opportunities for leisure or education, to campaign for the rights that are currently sought by various Western European unions. These include a reduction in the length of the working week from forty to thirty-five hours; an increase in annual leave from four to five weeks; the right to take leave for training and educational purposes; and the establishment of effective skill development systems. Such reforms would help the worker, as Marx termed it, to "strip off the fetters of his individuality and develop the capabilities of his species."[12]

It is only through the organizational role of workplace activists, however, that the potentialities of the self-management or small-group system can be converted into reality. In the development of such an organizational role, it is important to take into consideration a number of contradictions of the small-group system. The first contradiction is the fact that, in the process of rationalization, many active unionists have been removed from the shop floor; but the removal of such workers in some sense prevents the small-group system from achieving its avowed objectives. The second point to be appreciated is that the system obliges managerial and supervisory employees to become more closely involved in production-line work and so increases their understanding of and sympathy with shop-floor workers. Third, the cooperation between union and management in the rationalization movement has undermined worker confidence in the procompany union leaders. It was these leaders who were responsible for transmitting the grievances of workers to management. The current situation therefore means that, as they press forward toward higher levels of rationalization, managers are increasingly unaware of the dissatisfaction that exists on the production line. The consequence is a sense of instability and crisis at the shop-floor level.

In these circumstances, labor activists should not deliberately seek to antagonize management. Instead, they should attempt to gain their support in listening to the grievances and demands of the workers. Rather than impatiently forcing their own views on other workers or criticizing those workers' opinions, they should try to open up dialogue that will enable workers to transform their demands into effective rights. In this way the company slogan of "autonomy through consensus" may in fact provide the basis for "solidarity through autonomy."

Moreover, the lengthening of hours and intensification of work that have accompanied the current wave of rationalization have resulted in increases in industrial accidents, occupational diseases, and suicides, to an extent that is not adequately reflected in the official statistics. This trend has been intensified by the introduction of microelectronic equipment and the associated expansion of overtime, shift work, and night work. As a result of these developments, shop-floor workers who previously tended to attribute industrial accidents and ill health to individual carelessness are now more ready to criticize the company and to recognize the inescapable responsibility of the company to protect industrial health. By raising the issue of industrial health problems, unionists can help to overcome the spirit of intense individualistic competition between workers induced by the policy of meritocratic management. Employees can be encouraged to develop a greater sense of responsibility for their fellow workers. The analysis of rationalization presented in this section, therefore, provides some indication of ways in which the weakness of workers' resistance to the rationalization process may be overcome.

Organizing the Marginal Work Force

Further issues to be considered are the problems of the marginal work force and the unemployed, problems that organized labor has

so far failed to confront. In Japan, so-called marginal workers—temporary and seasonal workers, day-laborers, part-timers,
subcontracting employees—constitute a substantial share of the
work force, and this share has been increasing with the introduction of rationalization policies since 1975. In particular, the
"microelectronics revolution" has resulted in an expansion of the
marginal work force (including workers employed through agency
contracts) and a decline in the proportion of full-time permanent
employees. In Japan, this technological revolution has also been
associated with an increasing standardization and uniformity of
labor processes and therefore with a growth in the number of
semiskilled workers. Most Western industrialized countries have
technical training institutions that are integrated with the school
system and skill-based minimum wage scales for each industry.
Japan, however, lacks such institutions, and, as a result, the definition of semiskilled labor is unclear. Consequently, with the erosion
of the seniority-based lifetime employment system, not only have
unskilled workers been forced out into marginal employment, but
even the semiskilled, who would previously have formed part of
the permanent work force, are increasingly forced to work on a
temporary or subcontracting basis. Thus workers who lose their
jobs as a result of reductions in the permanent work force can only
hope to be reemployed as temporary workers, even though the
content of the work they perform may be virtually unchanged.

In the present conditions, where divisions and discrimination between full-time employees and others are increasing, unionized
workers, the vast majority of whom are in regular employment,
tend to regard themselves as a "labor aristocracy" in relation to the
marginal work force and the unemployed. Unionized workers have
failed to take up the problems of these latter groups. The lack of
interest displayed by organized labor toward the marginal work
force and the unemployed is reinforced by a variety of other factors. For one thing, the changing structure of the workplace has
tended to increase discrimination and exploitation of nonperma-
nent workers. The restructuring of the system of promotion qualifications also creates an illusory hierarchy within the work force.
At the same time, the fostering of a corps of procompany union officials, drawn from managerial and technical employees, has created a right-wing trend within the union leadership.

Most temporary and contract workers, however, form part of

the growing structure of semiskilled workers to which many full-time regular employees also belong. Moreover, with the increasing pace and scope of factory work, part-time and contract workers are expected to develop a variety of skills that enable them to be used as reinforcements in various parts of the highly pressured production process. They are therefore in a position to provide important support for resistance by full-time employees to the rationalization process examined above. Such semiskilled temporary workers are also particularly well able to understand the discrimination and economic insecurity faced by the unskilled sections of the marginal work force.

By joining with semiskilled temporary workers in the struggle against rationalization, full-time regular employees can begin to overcome their sense of belonging to a "labor aristocracy." Thus they may open the way for the creation of a movement that would articulate the demands of unskilled temporary workers and the unemployed. The most important demands of such a movement would be radical overhauling of the present minimum wage legislation to create a unified national system for all industries, fundamental improvements in the unemployement insurance system, and revised employment policies. If such a movement were organized on a regional basis, it would also provide scope for cooperation between workers and their local society and could thus emphasize the need to maintain the social rights necessary for the development of the human personality.

Semiskilled temporary and contract workers are difficult to organize because they are isolated and often subject to the control of employment agencies. Despite such difficulties, however, it is necessary for union activitists to direct their energies to the task of overcoming these problems.

Cooperation with Other Social Classes

Finally, it is necessary to examine the relationship between the working class and other social classes in contemporary Japan. Organized labor at present pays little attention to the problems of farmers and the urban self-employed, despite the fact that they face similar problems in seeking to maintain their livelihood. The labor movement, moreover, has been even more reluctant to consider the needs of the owners of small enterprises. If organized

labor, however, begins to create regional movements, encompass-
ing temporary workers and the unemployed and directed toward
the establishment of a minimum wage system and of effective employment policies, they will inevitably find themselves confronting
the problems of farmers, the urban self-employed, and the small
business sector.

At present, large manufacturing enterprises in particular are
pursuing the so-called slim-line management approach, while the
zaikai and the Liberal Democratic Party have developed a strategy
for the 1980s that involves cuts in public spending and the "upgrading of the industrial structure." The result of these measures is
a rapid increase in the size of the tertiary sector, which acts as a
"sponge" to absorb excess labor squeezed out of manufacturing.
The number of self-employed, small business people, and marginal
workers engaged in commerce, finance, construction, transport,
communications, and services is expanding. Simultaneously, the
economic crisis faced by such workers is deepening. For these reasons, it becomes ever more impossible for organized labor to dis-
tance itself from the problems of the self-employed and the owners
of small enterprises.

As the "tertiarization" of the economy progresses, rationalization occurs not only in manufacturing itself but also in industries
such as wholesale trade, finance, transport, and communications,
whose demand structures are strongly influenced by trends within
the large-scale manufacturing sector. Worsening problems face the
growing number of small enterprises and marginal workers in areas
such as the information industry (computer services, advertising,
etc.) and office services (office maintenance, security, etc.), and
also in catering, insurance, health care, transport, communications,
entertainment, education, and other personal services, which rely
heavily on spending by members of the employed work force.

In these circumstances, workers must organize to realize the objectives, not only of minimum wage and employment policies but
also, as discussed earlier, of a revised agricultural policy.
Temporary and contract employment must be more tightly controlled, and the power of monopoly capital must be regulated in such a
way as to protect the livelihood of the worker. This can be
achieved by basing such organization upon the sense of shared interests that already exists among workers, farmers, and the urban
self-employed. By linking together places of employment and

places of residence, positive steps can be taken toward the development of local communities, and so toward the development of concerted action by all these groups.

Conclusions

By way of conclusion it is, I believe, important to make one point. In this essay I have frequently used expressions such as: "It is important for activists to do such-and-such." In using this phrase, I am not only referring to those who are currently involved in the left wing of the union movement, but also to activists who exist within labor organizations in the small-business sector and within the large enterprise unions whose leadership is at present in the hands of right-wingers. It is such people who must extend their horizons beyond the limits of their company or organizations to the regional and national level, and who must develop connections with their counterparts in consumers' groups, cultural organizations, women's groups, youth groups, farmers' organizations, and small-business associations. If campaigns are developed within each of these loci and based upon the actual experiences of each specific group, the necessary conditions will be created for practical strategies leading to the development and strengthening of local communities.

Notes

1. *Nihon shigaku ronsō*, vol. 9 of *Kōza Nihon-shi* (Tokyo: Tokyo Daigaku Shuppan, 1971).

2. Kurokawa Toshio, *Nihon no teichingin kōzō* (Tokyo: Ōtsuki Shoten, 1974).

3. Ōhashi Takanori, *Nihon no kaikyū kōsei* (Tokyo: Iwanami Shinsho, 1971).

4. Watanabe Mutsu, "Shōkō jieigyo fujin no shūrō to seikatsu no jittai," *Meiji daigaku shakaigaku kenkyū-sho kiyo* 19.

5. Kurokawa Toshio, ed., *Gendai Nihon no keizai kōzō* (Tokyo: Hōritsu Bunka Sha, 1982), p. 33.

6. Ichikawa Seiichi, *Nihon kyōsanto tōsō shoshi* (Tokyo, 1945).

7. Kurokawa Toshio, "Gendai no ME kakumei to Marukusu no rōdō katei ron," *Mita gakkai zasshi* 77, 2 (1984).

8. *Rōdō hakusho* (1984).

9. Eguchi Eiichi et al., "Konnichi no dokusen shihon to kakei," in *Kōzō konnichi no Nihon shihonshugi* (Tokyo: Ōtsuki Shoten, 1982), pp. 150–54.

10. Eguchi Eiichi et al., "Shōhi seikatsu no tenkai to sono genchi ten," in ibid., pp. 108–45.

11. Tomioka Takashi, "Musume-san o hakkyō sareto ZD undō," *Keizai* (February 1966).

12. K. Marx, *Capital* (London: Pelican Marx Library, 1976) 1:447.

6

Foreign Trade, Investment, and Industrial Imperialism in Postwar Japan

FUJIWARA SADAO

Japan's international economic activities have been divided into three stages. The first stage is the period 1955–1971, the era of the old IMF-GATT system, when "export for export's sake" and heavy and chemical industrialization dominated every aspect of economic activity. The second is the period 1971–1980, which includes the collapse of the old IMF system, the two oil crises, and the world depression. In this period almost all Japanese firms tried to undertake severe rationalization measures, while the government made desperate efforts to adjust its economic policies to the new international circumstances. The third stage runs from the beginning of the 1980s to the present. During these years, while Japan has been successful in gaining greater economic power, economic confrontations involving Japan have been considerably intensified.

"Export for Export's Sake" and Heavy Industrialization, 1955–1971

At the end of the decade of economic reconstruction that followed Japan's defeat in World War II, the government's *Economic White Paper* (*Keizai hakusho*) of 1956 declared: "The postwar period is over. . . . Growth through reconstruction has ended. From now on, growth should be supported by modernization."[1] From 1955 to 1971, Japanese economic growth proceeded at a very fast rate, the so-called economic miracle. As a result of this high-speed growth, by 1970 Japan ranked second in the world to the United States in terms of size of GNP. In essence, the "economic miracle" meant the expansion of the industrial sector and a shift in its structure toward heavy and chemical industries. This process was made possible by a very high level of capital accumulation. Moreover, if we examine the matter a little further, it becomes obvious that Japan's overseas trade provided crucial support for rapid growth by offering extensive foreign markets for Japanese industrial products and by supplying the large quantity of natural resources essential for heavy industrialization.

In postwar world trade, the share of heavy industrial goods in world exports increased steadily, from 28 percent in 1953 to 38 percent in 1960, and to 46 percent in 1970. This worldwide trend indicates that, without heavy and chemical industrialization, Japan would almost certainly have been unable to expand its exports. In effect, then, heavy industrialization was synonymous with the export expansion that constituted Japanese capitalism's basic strategy for economic reconstruction.

Professor Sinha defines the causes of Japan's high economic growth in the period after World War II as "efforts by the Japanese elite," "the Japanese preference for thriftiness and frugality," "the special relationship between government and business," and "the international situation."[2] Given the intimate connection between industrial growth and trade expansion, these four elements can also be seen as being causes of Japan's success in foreign trade. In light of these comments, therefore, some of the factors that enabled Japanese trade to grow so quickly during the period of the "economic miracle" will be examined below.

Factors in the Rapid Growth of Japanese Foreign Trade

Japan's business leaders realized that the lack of natural resources was an Achilles' heel that always threatened to jeopardize the success of Japanese heavy industrialization, and that, from the point of view of capital accumulation, the supply of investment funds was not as serious a bottleneck as the supply of raw materials. Private plant and equipment investment increased from a mere $3.5 billion in 1955 to \$15.7 in 1965, and to \$42.9 billion in 1970 (1970 constant prices). Japanese companies could not finance this massive growth in investment entirely from intracompany resources and therefore had to seek outside funds. The biggest capital suppliers were private financial organizations, particularly the city banks, which provided about 70 percent of external capital in this period. As is well known, the "Japanese preference for thriftiness and frugality" created a massive source of capital that was channeled into private industry through city banks (with the backing of the Bank of Japan).

Japan, however, had virtually no domestic sources of fuel or raw materials and had to import these if the rapid growth of industry was to be maintained. This is reflected in the fact that Japan imported only 5.5 million metric tons of iron ore in 1955, but 115 million in 1971. Likewise, in the same period, imports of coal increased from 2.9 to 47 million metric tons, crude oil from 8.5 to 197 million kiloliters, and copper from 44 to 1,926 thousand metric tons.[3] A substantial share of the deposits of these natural resources was located in less developed countries, which, with the rise of political and economic nationalism, had strengthened restrictions on the foreign exploitation of their raw materials. Furthermore, many large multinational mining and oil companies already had concessions for the extraction and sale of these resources. For Japanese capitalism, therefore, the securing of foreign supplies of raw materials constituted a major problem.

During the 1950s, the Japanese government began to rebuild diplomatic relations with the Southeast Asian countries that had been the victims of Japanese wartime imperialism. Japan succeeded in concluding a series of reparations and economic cooperation agreements with Burma (1955), the Philippines (1956), Indonesia (1958), and Vietnam (1960). Economic cooperation agreements (without reparations provisions) were also signed with Laos and Kampuchea (1959) and the Republic of Korea (1965). By improving political relations with these countries, Japan obtained access to their natural resources; cooperation with national development policies opened up Southeast Asian markets to Japanese products.

Despite considerable efforts by the Japanese government and by private companies to obtain a stake in foreign resources, however, such resource investments proved unable to satisfy the increasing demand of Japanese heavy industry. In the case of a number of natural resources, the relative importance of imports from overseas mines in which Japan had a financial stake reached a peak around 1960. Imports of iron from such overseas mining ventures, for example, constituted about 24 percent of all iron ore imports in 1959. The comparable figures for copper (1958) and bauxite (1961) were 66 percent and 22 percent respectively.[4] But in the 1960s, while total imports of these materials increased rapidly, the share supplied by Japanese investment projects declined. Japan now began to pay less attention to possibilities for direct investment in raw materials, and more to securing other stable sources of supply. The fruits of this effort proved an important factor in the rapid growth of Japanese foreign trade. During the 1960s the prices of raw materials, including agricultural products, showed remarkable stability, and there was little concern over the possibility of resource shortages. The policy also involved certain costs, however. The obvious need for foreign earnings to pay for raw material imports induced the government to implement a variety of measures to support and expand exports, many of which had a negative effect from the point of view of workers, farmers, and small enterprises. At the same time, through its search for security rather than ownership in resource-based projects, Japan chose to become dependent on the U.S. oil majors for most of its oil imports, thus ultimately increasing its vulnerability in this area.

A further factor in the expansion of Japanese trade in this period was the competitive situation within the Japanese economy, which created considerable pressures for export expansion. The most conspicuous feature of the home market in the fifties was that the reconstruction of oligopoly and the development of intensive competition were proceeding simultaneously. A handful of companies had market control over most industries, and the competition between the leading companies in each industry was so intense that it may be termed (in the words of Professor Miyazaki) "overcompetition."[5] As the government gradually altered its trade and exchange policies in the early 1960s and its policies on capital transactions in the late 1960s, the oligopolistic situation intensified, with big companies enlarging their capacity and sometimes merging with others in order to resist international competition. Since competitive advantage in the leading industries of the 1960s—iron and steel, shipbuilding, electric machinery, petrochemicals, synthetic fiber—depended on economies of scale, companies in these industries made desperate efforts to enlarge their share in both domestic and foreign markets. On the one hand, this resulted in an improvement in the international competitiveness of these industries; on the other, it produced those sudden influxes of Japanese goods that often provoked criticism in the importing countries.

Foreign Trade: Export Promotion and Trade Liberalization

A third factor in the rapid growth of trade was the decisive role of the Japanese government. In the 1960s, as the Japanese economy expanded and international censure of Japan's trade restrictions developed, these trade policies, which included import restrictions and export promotion measures, were gradually liberalized.

Japan's complex export promotion system is well described by the statement that "the Japanese government tends to provide specific policies to cover specific needs, thereby making the scale of each measure small."[6] The Export Council was established in 1954 for the purpose of planning and managing exports, and it can be said to have "played a central role in the expansion of Japanese exports."[7] This council was established in conjunction with a Supreme Export Council, a secretarial board, and individual export councils for each industry. The chair of the Supreme Export Council was the prime minister, and the vice-chair was the minister of international trade and industry. Other members of the Supreme Council included the presidents of the Bank of Japan and Export-Import Bank of Japan and the minister of finance. The council decided policies and set export targets on a half-yearly basis, while the secretarial board, consisting of the vice-ministers (administrative heads) of the relevant ministries, was responsible for coordinating the interests of various departments of government. The export councils of twelve major industries operated under the supervision of the Ministry of International Trade and Industry (MITI). In 1970, the Export Council changed its name to the Foreign Trade Council, dealing with both imports and exports.

Two financing systems were used to promote exports. The first provided short-term finance, such as export advance bills and foreign exchange funds loans, while the second provided medium-

and long-term finance from the Export-Import Bank of Japan. Since the terms of these financing systems were more favorable than those available for domestic activities, they provided Japanese firms with a strong incentive to export. In the fifties, short-term finance was of greater importance to Japanese firms, but in the sixties, as the export of plant and equipment expanded, medium- and long-term loans became increasingly significant. During this period, exports were also encouraged by a variety of tax measures, including the Export Income Deduction System (in operation from 1953 to 1963), the Export Loss Reserve Fund System (from 1953 to 1959), and an accelerated depreciation system for the overseas branches of trading companies (from 1953 to 1959). Among other efforts to promote exports one might also mention the establishment of the Japanese External Trade Organization (JETRO), a government-funded body with offices around the world providing information on Japanese products, enterprises, and so forth.

It should be noted that under the provisions of the Export and Import Trading Law of 1958, MITI suspended the application of the 1947 Anti-Monopoly Law to any agreements, associations, or cartels established for orderly export purposes. MITI thus had an extremely important role in the expansion of exports and in reducing conflicts, both among Japanese firms themselves and between Japan and its foreign trading partners. Since intense competitive pressures in the home market tended to spill over into export competition, the ministry did not always succeed in its objective of maintaining "orderly exports." Its common solution to the problem, however, was to use its administrative guidance to induce companies to pursue a course of "voluntary restraint."

Japan became a signatory to the International Monetary Fund (IMF) treaty in 1952, and to the General Agreement on Tariffs and Trade (GATT) in 1955, but during the 1950s the realities of Japan's trade policies were still far removed from the ideals of these organizations. As shown in table 6.1, Japan's trade balance was in deficit for most of this decade, and gold and foreign exchange reserves stood at only about one billion dollars. The Foreign Exchange and Foreign Trade Control Law of 1949 (referred to below as the Control Law) provided the basic framework for most of Japan's international activities, and, together with many other ordinances, endowed the government (particularly MITI) with great power to influence foreign trade. In principle, the Control Law permitted free trade, but at the same time it prohibited private foreign exchange transactions. All foreign exchange was deposited in the government's Foreign Exchange Funds Special Account, from where it was allotted to traders and overseas investors in accordance with current government policy. During the 1950s the government's allocation of foreign currency to specific industries was determined in the light of half-yearly trade targets and of the need of industries for imports of raw materials and machinery. This mechanism allowed imports and foreign investment to be more severely restricted in times when foreign currency reserves were low.

The year 1959 marked a turning point for Japanese foreign trade policy. At an August meeting with Trade and Industry Minister Ikeda, U.S. Ambassador MacArthur pressed strong demands for the liberalization of trade and foreign exchange, and in November Japan's trade restrictions again came under heavy fire at a GATT general meeting in Tokyo. As pressure against Japanese trade restrictions increased, the August general meeting of Japan's major business organization Keidanren (the Federation of Economic Organizations) decided to support an approach reducing regulation and building Japan's economic strength to a point where it would be able to survive international competition. In the same month, eight prominent business leaders and economists issued a joint statement emphasizing that trade liberalization was in Japan's long-term interests.[8] Most of the businessmen who favored liberalization were managers of relatively large companies or of firms with strong comparative advantage, and it was they who succeeded in taking the initiative in pressing for the liberalization of Japanese trade and foreign exchange.

In April 1970, Japan's import liberalization ratio was just 41 percent. Soon after, the government announced general principles for increasing the ratio to 80 percent by mid-1963. This was not sufficient, however, to satisfy the IMF Council for Japan, which persuaded the government to accelerate the speed of liberalization to reach a level of 90 percent by October 1962. In 1963 Japan became an Article 11 member of GATT, which meant that it was necessary to abolish general quantity limitations on the balance-of-payments deficit. Then, the following year, Japan became both an Article 8 member of the IMF and a member of the Organization for Economic Cooperation and Development (OECD). It could therefore

Table 6.1

Balance of International Payments, 1951–1970

Annual average	1951–1955	1956–1960	1961–1965	1966–1970
Current balance	104.8	5.0	−271.6	1,240.2
Trade balance	−396.6	93.0	391.0	2,725.2
Exports	1,503.6	3,119.6	5,887.4	13,454.2
Imports	1,900.2	3,026.6	5,496.4	10,729.0
Long-term capital balance	−10.8	−22.2	63.0	−721.0
Overall balance	92.8	27.8	−120.0	905.0
Gold and foreign exchange reserves	769.0	1,090.4	1,862.6	2,973.0

Source: To 1961: I. Yamamoto, *Chōki-keizai-tōkei 14: Boeki to kokusaishushi* (Foreign trade and balance of payments, estimates of long-term economic statistics of Japan since 1868), vol. 14 (Tokyo: Tōyō Keizai Shimposha, 1979). From 1962: Bank of Japan, *Balance of Payments Monthly*.

no longer deal with balance-of-payments problems by limiting capital movements and payments on current transactions. Despite these changes, however, Japan did not lift restrictions on some 170 import items (even though 123 of these restrictions were in violation of GATT rules) and, even by the mid-1960s, had still failed to fulfill some of its obligations to liberalize capital movement.

Japan's policy of heavy and chemical industrialization did not proceed entirely smoothly. By 1965 output was exceeding demand, and a major crisis threatened. Attempts to solve these problems made Japanese business more dependent both on deficit financing by the government and on foreign trade. Consequently, the government was obliged to take a more positive approach to the liberalization of trade and investment. In response to censure at the 1968 general meeting of GATT, the Japanese government promised to remove as many of the remaining restrictions as possible within the next few years. Indeed, by October 1971, the number of restricted import items was reduced to 40 (from 120 in April 1969) as compared with 5 in the case of the United States, 25 for Britain, 39 for Germany, and 74 for France.

As far as foreign investment was concerned, all overseas investors had to receive permission from the Foreign Investment Council in the years from 1949 to mid-1967. In 1967, however, the first round of investment liberalization removed the need for investment licenses in fifty specified industries, on condition that the project concerned was a new venture in which the foreign partner held no more than 50 percent of the equity. The second round, in 1969, added a further 204 industries to the list, and the third, in 1971, an additional 675. Foreign holdings in existing Japanese firms, however, were restricted to 25 percent. Overseas investment activities by Japanese enterprises were also liberalized. With the rapid improvement in the balance-of-payments situation in the late 1960s, approval for purchases of overseas securities and bonds under a specified value became automatic, and limitations were abolished altogether in July 1971. By October 1972 overseas portfolio investment had been almost entirely liberalized.

The government, however, made sure that Japanese industry was well prepared for liberalization. In 1961, the government made the first overall revision of the tariff system since the end of the occupation.[9] The purpose of the revision was to cope with liberalization and to protect domestic industry. Protective tariff rates, emergency tariffs, tariff quotas, and provisional tariffs were all strengthened by this revision. In place of the earlier, blatant export promotion policies, new and more subtle policies such as extra depreciation for exports (1964–1969) and overseas market development reserves (1964–1969) were introduced. The government was particularly concerned at the possible negative effects of liberalization on small firms, which were mostly engaged in labor-intensive light industry, and which often supported larger firms through the subcontracting system. A Small Enterprises Modernization Promotion Act was therefore introduced in 1963 to help finance the modernization of viable small and medium-sized firms.

Meanwhile, Japanese overseas aid was helping to expand the market for Japan's exports in Southeast Asia. About three-quarters of the $2,432 million official development assistance provided by the Japanese government between 1966 and 1971 went to that area, while Japan also played a central role, in cooperation with the United States and other Asian countries, in the 1967 establishment of the Asian Development Bank, in which Japan became the largest investor.

The International Economy in the "Golden Sixties"

It should be emphasized that the rapid growth of Japan's foreign trade was partly a consequence of a favorable international environment. In the first place, the IMF and GATT systems were at their zenith during the 1960s. The Kennedy Round of 1964–1967 cut tariffs on the 30,000 tax items of the forty-six GATT signatories by some 45 percent, thus contributing to the expansion of world trade. Indeed, throughout the 1960s, the average growth of trade in the developed world was more rapid than the growth of mining and manufacturing. Trade thus acted as an engine of economic growth, particularly as far as Japan was concerned.

Second, the Japanese economy was helped by the close political ties that existed between Japan and the United States. The United States needed Japan as a stable capitalist country that would provide a bulwark against communism in Asia. It therefore supported Japanese membership of the IMF and GATT in 1955 and assisted Japan in improving relations with other Asian countries in the late 1950s and early 1960s, while at the same time keeping its own market open to Japanese goods and making technology and capital available to Japanese enterprises. Japanese capitalism could thus pursue its own interests on the international stage under the umbrella of U.S. world strategy.

Third, Japan also benefited from the improvement of economic relations with European countries during the first half of the 1960s. Although Japan had become a signatory of GATT in 1955, certain nations, including Britain, France, and Australia, had made use of Article 35 of the treaty in their economic relations with Japan during the latter part of the 1950s. The article allowed these nations, which placed little faith in Japan's trade dealings, to maintain differential high tariffs on Japanese goods (a situation that was regarded as damaging to Japan's political prestige). With the conclusion of the Japan-United Kingdom Commerce and Navigation Treaty in 1963 and the Japan-France Commerce Agreement in 1964, bilateral negotiating organs were set up to deal with these issues, and the Article 35 problems were largely resolved.[10]

In this favorable environment, Japan rapidly grew to be one of the world's largest producers of heavy industrial goods. By 1971 Japan's GNP had reached a level of $259 billion—larger than that of West Germany, and approximately one-quarter of the size of the U.S. GNP. Japan was second only to the United States in terms of the production of crude steel, electrical power, and passenger cars. This situation, however, contained the seeds of future international economic conflict.

The Structure of Imports and Exports

Between 1955 and 1971 Japan's exports increased from $2 billion to $24 billion (f.o.b. at current prices). At the same time, as shown in table 6.2, the composition of exports underwent dramatic changes. Fibers, the traditional mainstay of Japan's export trade, accounted for 37 percent in 1955 but had declined to a mere 11.5 percent in 1971. The decline was particularly sharp in the case of cotton textiles, which had comprised 31 percent of all textile exports in 1955 but were down to 7.6 percent in 1971. By contrast, synthetic fibers, an archetypal oligopolistic industry of the high growth era, expanded to occupy 47.5 percent of textile exports by 1971. It is also interesting to note that exports of light industrial products (toys, footwear, plywood, apparel, etc.), which were mostly produced by small firms employing low-paid labor under poor working conditions, occupied the same 16 percent of exports in 1955 and 1965, though their importance subsequently declined.

Not surprisingly, heavy industrial exports showed the greatest expansion. They accounted for just 38.0 percent of all exports in 1955, but by 1971 their share had risen to 74.6 percent, a percentage similar to that of other advanced industrialized countries. The composition of heavy industrial exports changed continuously: changes in the nature of machinery exports, in particular, provide a clear indication of the achievements of industrialization. Whereas in the mid-1950s these consisted mainly of relatively simple products such as sewing machines, binoculars, and cameras, by the mid-1960s ball bearings, TV sets, machine tools, and cars had been added to the list of major exports, and by 1971 items such as telecommunications equipment had become important.

Japan's main export markets had traditionally been the United States and Southeast Asia. These two areas together took about half of all Japanese exports throughout the period under consideration. Apart from some increase in the role of Western Europe as a market, there were few sharp changes in the geographical structure of Japan's exports in these years.

One interesting characteristic of Japanese export trade during the 1950s and 1960s, however, was the relatively great dependence on less developed nations as markets. This was in part a reflection of the fact that many of Japan's heavy industrial products were not yet competitive enough to obtain a strong foothold in developed

Table 6.2

Exports: Commodity and Destination, 1955–1970
(U.S.$ millions, percent)

	1955	1960	1965	1970
Total exports	2,001	4,055	8,452	19,318
Foodstuffs	6.6	6.6	4.1	3.4
Raw materials & fuels	1.9	1.6	1.5	1.0
Heavy & chemical industrial products	38.0	43.4	62.5	72.4
Machinery & equipment	13.9	25.4	35.1	46.3
Metallic goods	12.9	13.4	20.3	19.7
Chemical goods	4.7	4.2	6.5	6.4
Light industrial products	53.5	48.4	31.9	22.4
Textile goods	37.2	30.2	18.7	12.5
Developed areas	39.6	47.3	50.8	54.0
United States	22.7	27.2	29.3	30.7
EEC	4.1	4.3	5.7	6.7
EFTA	4.5	5.6	5.4	5.5
Developing areas	58.5	50.9	43.5	40.5
Southeast Asia	26.6	37.0	21.9	23.8
Middle & Near East Asia	4.3	3.5	3.4	3.3
Africa	8.8	7.3	8.0	5.2
Latin America	9.2	7.5	5.8	6.1
Communist bloc	1.9	1.8	5.7	5.5

Source: MITI, *White Paper on International Trade, Japan.*

markets. In the early 1960s this problem was an issue of considerable concern to MITI. In 1965, for example, while the proportion of heavy industrial goods in exports to less industrialized countries was 64.8 percent, their share in exports to industrialized countries was only 56.7 percent. With the expansion of investment in plant and equipment during the second half of the 1960s, however, this gap was overcome, and by the 1970s the share of heavy industrial goods in exports to developed and less developed countries was, respectively, 75.6 percent and 72.9 percent.

Imports, too, were rising rapidly, from $2.5 billion (c.i.f. at current prices) in 1955 to $19.7 billion in 1971. Changes in the composition of this trade are shown in table 6.3. Imports of foodstuffs followed a U-curve determined by developments both in domestic agriculture and in Japanese eating habits. Increases in agricultural productivity (particularly the productivity of rice farming) within Japan resulted in falling food imports at the beginning of the 1960s, while the subsequent rise reflects both a slowing of agricultural development and an increasing demand for imported, nontraditional foodstuffs including meat.

Industrial raw materials accounted for about half of all imports in 1955, but their share decreased gradually to 32.5 percent in 1971. As might be expected, the declining international competitiveness of the textile industry resulted in a decline in importance of raw cotton as an import item. Among metallic raw materials, the share of iron ore and scrap also fell from 78 percent in 1955 to around 50 percent by 1971. In 1960 Japanese industry switched from coal to petroleum as its major energy source; however, because of the low level of petroleum prices during the 1960s, the share of crude oil in imports remained constant at around 10 percent, despite rapid increases in the quantity of oil imported.

Manufactured goods, although increasing in importance, still occupied just under a third of the import total in 1971. Of these imports, more than 80 percent consisted of heavy industrial products. Imports of machinery and equipment were particularly essential for Japan's own industrial expansion, and technologically sophisticated, large-scale equipment such as aircraft engines, electronic computers, and electricity-generating equipment became a major component of Japan's manufactured imports.

As in the case of exports, so in the case of imports Japan's main trading partners were the United States and Southeast Asia. The United States accounted for 34.6 percent of imports at its peak in 1960, but this proportion fell to 25 percent by 1971. The United States was the biggest supplier of foodstuffs, manufactured goods (especially machinery and equipment), and some other raw materials. Southeast Asia was primarily a supplier of raw materials and mineral fuels but was of less importance to Japan as a source of imports than as an export market. As a whole, throughout the period, Japan depended on less developed countries for 40 percent of its imports, with the Middle and Near East being the biggest suppliers of petroleum.[11]

Immature Direct Foreign Investment

Japan's postwar direct foreign investment commenced in 1951, and by the end of 1960 the cumulative value of overseas direct invest-

Table 6.3

Imports: Commodity and Source, 1955–1970
(U.S.$ millions, percent)

	1955	1960	1965	1970
Total imports	2,471	4,491	8,169	18,881
Foodstuffs	24.8	12.2	18.0	13.6
Materials	51.1	49.1	39.4	35.4
Fiber materials	23.7	17.0	10.4	5.1
Metallic materials	7.5	15.0	12.5	14.3
Mineral fuels	11.7	16.5	19.9	20.7
Coal	2.3	3.1	2.6	5.3
Crude oil	6.0	10.4	11.4	11.8
Manufactured products	12.4	22.2	22.7	30.3
Developed areas	51.5	58.2	51.7	55.2
United States	31.3	34.6	29.0	29.4
Western Europe	6.8	8.8	8.9	10.4
Oceania	8.2	9.0	8.0	8.8
Developing areas	44.9	39.0	41.8	40.1
Southeast Asia	21.1	16.5	14.5	13.6
Middle and Near East Asia	6.4	9.4	13.1	12.4
Africa	2.5	3.7	4.3	3.7
Latin America	9.8	6.9	8.7	7.3
Communist bloc	3.6	2.8	6.5	4.7

Source: See table 6.2.

ments was only $283 million. (Note: the figures given in this section are based on Ministry of Finance approvals, and years referred to are financial years.) This total gradually increased to $4.4 billion by the end of 1971, but even at this time Japan's stock of overseas investment was considerably lower than that of the other main members of the OECD's Development Assistance Committee (DAC). (The figures for West Germany, Britain, and the United States, for example, were $7.4 billion, $21.8 billion, and $86.0 billion respectively.) It is appropriate, therefore, to focus here upon the reasons for the comparative immaturity of Japan's foreign investment.

First, capital accumulation within Japan was still at such a low level that the government sought to restrain overseas investment except in cases where it could contribute directly to the expansion of foreign markets or the acquisition of natural resources. The restriction of capital outflow was essential to maintain a balance-of-payments equilibrium. Second, Japanese enterprises lacked the managerial resources necessary to establish manufacturing projects overseas, particularly in advanced industrialized countries. Third, economic growth within Japan was proceeding so rapidly that companies were able to find abundant investment opportunities within the domestic economy. In other words, foreign direct investment had little appeal to Japanese firms themselves. Fourth, the "export for export's sake" policies pursued by the Japanese government during the 1950s and 1960s encouraged firms to concentrate on expanding exports rather than on seeking to produce overseas. Fifth, the strong export competitiveness of the "elite" large enterprises was based upon economic conditions peculiar to Japan. These firms had the benefits of "Japanese-style" management practices, the low wage costs associated with the subcontracting system, and the advantages (by the late 1960s) of an undervalued yen, but they could enjoy these benefits only if they located their productive facilities within Japan itself. Finally, the international environment for Japanese foreign direct investment was not inviting, since the Southeast Asian countries that constituted Japan's nearest and largest regional trading partners were in a state of economic and political instability. It was only in the late 1960s, when these countries adopted a policy of utilizing direct foreign investment to support their export-oriented industrialization, that Japan began to invest in them on a large scale.

The Collapse of the Bretton Woods System and Japanese External Expansion, 1971–1980

During the 1970s a host of worldwide economic and political phenomena attested to the fact that the era of comparative stability in the world capitalist economic system—the so-called golden decade of the international economy—was over, and that a new period of international instability had arrived.

The fixed exchange rate that had been the basis of the IMF system had virtually collapsed by the second part of 1971, and by the end of spring 1973 all major currencies had adopted a floating exchange system. The fact that fluctuations in value under this system were greater than had been anticipated only served to aggravate instabilities both in international transactions and in the domestic economic policies of the major trading nations. Stagflation proliferated, and the advanced industrial economies experienced a decline in their real growth rates, rising prices, and massive increases in unemployment. If one compares the annual average growth rates of GNP in the decade 1961–1970 and 1971–1980, for example, one finds that the figure fell from 4.0 percent to 3.1 percent in the case of the United States, from 2.9 percent to 1.9 percent in Britain, from 4.9 percent to 2.9 percent in West Germany, and from 5.8 percent to 3.7 percent in France. Meanwhile, by 1980, the consumer price index (1970 = 100) had risen to 212 in the United States, 361 in Britain, 164 in West Germany and 251 in France.[12] In both advanced and less developed countries, the drastic oil price rises of 1974–1973 and 1979–1980 proved a powerful trigger to worsening stagflation.

Another factor that shook the international economy was the changing nature of the North-South problem. Less developed countries were demanding a new world economic order,[13] and the industrialized nations were forced to make certain concessions to these demands. Some countries of the South—the so-called newly industrializing countries (NICs)—experienced remarkable capitalist development, thus at once becoming competitors of the older industrialized countries in many areas, and offering these countries new markets for trade and investment. At the same time, however, this capitalist development brought about many severe contradictions within the economies of the NICs—contradictions exemplified by rising international debts, deepening rural poverty, and urban hyperexpansion.

Inevitably, the collapse of the old order and the emergence of new economic crises resulted both in international confrontation and in new forms of cooperation. Rather than large groups representing diverse interests, such as the IMF, GATT, and the United Nations, bilateral negotiations or smaller-scale group cooperation emerged as the new axes of international politics. The summit conferences held between the major advanced capitalist nations every year from 1975 to harmonize economic policies repeatedly addressed the problems of trade friction, exchange rates, unemployment, and aid to less developed countries.

Japanese capitalism was obliged to adapt itself to this new situation. The yen was revalued by a margin of 16.8 percent in 1971, and the shift to floating exchange rate in March 1973 had a substantial influence on the Japanese economy. Initially, the government tried to pursue expansionary policies to counter the recession induced by the yen's rising value, but, as a result of rampant speculation by Japanese enterprises and the first oil crisis of 1973, these policies ended in failure. Thereafter the government introduced deflationary policies and measures to promote industrial restructuring. Japanese companies, too, began to pursue drastic rationalization measures, their justification being that such steps were necessary to enable them to export with the yen at its new higher value. The success of these efforts is clearly illustrated by the fact that the index of labor productivity showed a higher rise in Japan than in any other major industrialized nation during the 1970s. In 1980 the figure for Japan (1970 = 100) was 183, while the figures for the United States, Britain, and West Germany were 133, 124, and 146 respectively.[14] At summit conferences in the 1970s the leaders of other industrialized countries repeatedly urged Japan to introduce expansionary policies to reduce exports and increase imports. The Japanese government, however, did not comply, mainly because of its apprehensions that expansionary measures would fuel inflation, and so lower the international competitiveness of Japanese goods. Consequently, although Japan's annual average growth rate in the 1970s was a mere 4.9 percent (less than half the level achieved in the 1960s), this figure was the highest rate for any major industrialized country during that decade, and Japan's growth during the 1970s was in large measure dependent upon success on the world export market.

By the beginning of the 1970s, both government and enterprises in Japan recognized the necessity of converting the industrial structure from one based on heavy industry to one based on knowledge-intensive and technology-intensive industries. Overemphasis on heavy industrialization had already made Japan dangerously dependent upon overseas supplies of raw materials. In 1969, for example, 41.6 percent of all coking coal imports by OECD countries went to Japan, while the comparable figures for iron ore, copper, and crude oil were 39.3 percent, 19.1 percent, and 15.6 percent respectively.[15] These figures suggested that Japanese capitalism was extremely vulnerable to world shortages or sudden price rises of raw materials. Furthermore, increasing wages associated with high economic growth had weakened the comparative advantage of Japan's traditional labor-intensive industries, particularly vis-à-vis the NICs. At the same time, concern within Japan over worsening pollution problems made it increasingly difficult for enterprises to find domestic sites for heavy industrial expansion. The oil crisis, and the worldwide stagflation that followed it, affected heavy industry particularly severely and therefore focused increased attention on the need for radical industrial restructuring.

The figures for the decade 1970–1980 indicate some success in the implementation of this restructuring policy. In that period, manufacturing output as a whole increased 1.5-fold, but, while production of electrical machinery increased 2.8-fold and that of transport equipment 1.8-fold, output increased only 1.3-fold in the iron and steel and petroleum products industries, and the textile and pulp industries showed no growth at all. In other words, labor-intensive industries and those that were heavy consumers of raw materials were decreasing in importance, while more technologically sophisticated assembly industries were expanding. Many Japanese enterprises also increased their international competitiveness by managerial rationalization and the development of new products and energy-saving production technologies and techniques.

One ominous feature of this decade from the point of view of Japanese management, however, was the growth of protectionist sentiments in the United States. During 1969 and 1970 alone, it was reported that as many as 590 bills for the restraint of imports were introduced in Congress.[16] The Trade Act of 1974 and the Trade Agreement Act of 1979 were clearly aimed at making it easier for the government to execute measures restricting imports. Japan responded with efforts aimed at averting the U.S. tendency to protectionism and maintaining the free trade system. These included the further liberalization of Japanese trade and investment. The number of items affected by residual import restrictions was reduced from eighty in January 1971 to twenty-seven in December 1980, and tariffs were also cut, with the result that the tariff burden ratio fell from 6.6 percent in 1970 to 2.5 percent in 1980. The last figure was considerably lower than the United States's 3.1 percent, and indeed lower than the figures for most industrialized countries.[17] It should be noted, though, that the Japanese figure tends to appear smaller because a large share of imports is made up of raw materials, which carry low tariffs or none at all. On imports of foreign manufactured goods, however, Japanese tariffs were not always particularly low.

In 1972 the government abolished a number of nontariff measures (NTMs), including extra depreciation for exports, the export preference bill, and the practice of limiting government procurements to Japanese goods. But, although direct and explicit NTMs were removed, a number of indirect measures remained in force. These included the strict application of quality checks under the Plant Epidemic Prevention Act, the Food Hygiene Act, and so forth, which could be used as a means to restrict access to imported goods. It was not until the beginning of the 1980s that serious efforts were made to dismantle these invisible trade barriers. In December 1980 the final overall revision of the Control Law resulted in the liberalization, in principle, of all international transactions. In practice, the implications of this measure were slight, since liberalization had been proceeding in a piecemeal fashion over the past two decades. But it is worth noting that the freeing of controls on international transactions had taken thirty years to complete. Japan's growing fears of international protectionism were indicated by the relatively active role played by the government in the GATT Tokyo Round of multilateral trade negotiations from 1973 to 1979.[18] In 1978, for example, Japan proposed that member nations should cut their weighted average of tariffs by 40 percent, and Japan took the initiative in cutting tariffs on 125 items itself.

A further problem confronting Japanese capitalism related to Japan's increasing economic influence in less developed countries, particularly those of the Asian region. In September 1971 the government resolved to raise Japan's official development assistance (ODA)/GNP ratio to a level comparable with that of other DAC countries. It also aimed to improve the conditions of Japanese government loans, reduce the level of tied aid, and improve the efficiency of aid programs. Japan's ODA increased more than sevenfold in the 1970s, and, as a consequence, Japan's share in the total sum of aid provided by DAC nations rose from 6.7 percent in 1970 to 12.3 percent in 1980.

Throughout, Japan's aid was heavily concentrated on Asia. In 1980, 70.5 percent went to Asia, 18.9 percent to Africa, and 6.0 percent to Latin America. Moreover, four Asian countries alone—Indonesia, the Republic of Korea, the Philippines, and

Thailand—received approximately half of Japan's total aid in 1980. Despite the 1971 measures, Japan's reputation as an aid donor remained a poor one. Major complaints included the relatively unfavorable interest rates and conditions associated with direct government loans (which constituted the largest share of Japanese aid); the continuing use of tied loans, which forced recipients to purchase expensive Japanese products; and the rumors of corruption that surrounded many aid programs. The Japanese government was generally more willing to extend aid to Asian countries than to open up Japanese markets to imports of Asian goods, since it feared that these might have an adverse effect on Japanese agriculture and light industry. ODA can also be seen as having played an important role in creating the infrastructure necessary for the expansion of Japanese overseas investment, and in providing a market for Japan's exports of industrial plant and equipment.

The Changing Structure of Foreign Trade

Japan's export trade experienced rapid expansion during the 1970s, with the annual average growth rate of exports running at 21.6 percent, the highest level among major industrialized countries. At the end of the 1960s, Japan's exports had accounted for 6.5 percent of the total value of exports from nonsocialist countries, but by the end of the 1970s this proportion had risen to 7.3 percent.

Table 6.4 illustrates the marked changes that were occurring in the composition of this trade. Exports, not only of textiles but also of iron and steel, experienced a relative decline, while machinery and equipment exports rose sharply. This, of course, parallels the shift in Japan's industrial structure away from basic heavy-industrial goods and toward more technology-intensive products.

Japan's major export markets were still the United States and Southeast Asia, although the importance of the former declined somewhat during the 1970s. In the case of Southeast Asia, rapid industrialization was making the region a particularly important market for Japan's exports of plant and equipment. The most significant change in Japan's overseas markets in this period, however, was the increasing importance of the oil-exporting nations of West Asia, which took 10.3 percent of Japan's exports in 1980, as compared with 2.8 percent in 1970.

mmodity and Destination, 1971–1984
ions, percent)

	1971	1975	1980	1984
Total exports	24,019	55,753	129,807	170,114
Foodstuffs	2.8	1.4	1.2	0.8
Textile goods	11.5	6.7	4.8	4.0
Chemical goods	6.2	7.0	5.2	4.5
Nonmetallic mineral products	1.6	1.3	1.4	1.3
Metal goods	19.0	22.5	16.4	11.3
Machinery & equipment	49.4	53.8	62.8	70.4
Miscellaneous	9.5	7.4	8.1	7.7
Asia	29.0	36.7	38.0	33.5
Southeast Asia	24.0	22.5	23.8	21.6
Europe	16.4	18.6	19.4	16.0
EC	6.8	10.2	12.8	11.4
North America	38.1	26.4	29.3	41.3
United States	31.2	20.0	24.1	35.2
South America	3.4	4.2	3.7	1.5
Africa	8.6	10.0	6.2	3.7
Oceania	4.0	4.1	3.4	4.1

Source: JTA, Summary Report of Japanese Trade.

A crucial feature of the expansion of Japanese exports in this period was Japan's success in capturing an increasing share of the world automobile market. Japan's exports of motor vehicles topped the million mark for the first time in 1970 but by 1980 had risen to over 6 million. In value terms, motor vehicles accounted for 6.9 percent of exports in 1970 and 17.9 percent in 1980, by which time Japan had emerged as the largest car producer in the world. The United States constituted Japan's major motor vehicle market, and by the start of the 1980s Japan was producing over 21.1 percent of all passenger cars sold in the United States, and 61.3 percent of all U.S. motor vehicle imports.[19] The principal reason for the expansion of Japanese car exports was the rising price of petroleum. This encouraged customers in the United States and elsewhere to purchase small cars, in whose production Japanese firms had an edge in terms of experience, price, and quality. A further important factor, however, was the drastic rationalization that had occurred within the Japanese car industry, with the introduction of large-scale robotization, the exploitation of the subcontracting system, and the development of close cooperation between management and labor unions. Similar factors were also at work in the electrical goods industry, which likewise experienced rapid export expansion in the 1970s.

But if Japan's exports rose sharply, so did imports. Indeed, here again Japan's growth rate was the highest among major industrialized nations (24.1 percent per annum). The rise in oil prices had a dramatic effect on the composition of Japan's import trade (see table 6.5). Crude oil accounted only for 11.8 percent of imports in 1970, but 33.9 percent in 1975 and 37.5 percent in 1980. By this time, payments for imported crude oil (at $52.8 billion) were far exceeding Japan's export earnings from motor vehicles and electrical appliances ($46.0 billion). In the latter part of the 1970s, mineral fuels, industrial raw materials, and foodstuffs together consistently accounted for around three-quarters of all imports, while manufactured goods constituted the remaining quarter. Not surprisingly, the oil crises also affected the geographical structure of Japan's import trade: West Asia's share jumped from 2.8 percent in 1970 to 31.3 percent in 1980, while all other areas except Southeast Asia declined in relative importance.

Two further aspects of Japan's trade at this time deserve consideration. The first is the degree of export and import specialization for various industries.[20] The levels of export specialization were as high as 3.88 in shipbuilding, 2.41 in steel production, 2.09 in electrical equipment manufacturing, and 1.87 in vehicle manufacturing. Conversely, rates of import specialization in manufacturing were as low as 0.55 in shipbuilding, 0.20 in steel production, 0.35 in electrical equipment manufacturing, and 0.008 in vehicle manufacture. But the rates for raw materials, fuel, and foodstuffs were 2.29, 1.94, and 1.19 respectively. These figures highlight the fact that Japan has an extraordinarily high degree of vertical division of labor with its trading partners, a fact that is liable to provoke trade conflicts.

A second factor to be considered is the fluctuation in Japan's balance of trade during the 1970s. For the decade as a whole the export surplus reached $113 million, but for five out of the ten years Japan's trade was in deficit. It is clear that, while export expansion was mainly caused by quantitative increases, import expan-

Table 6.5

Imports: Commodity and Source, 1971–1984
(U.S.$ millions, percent)

	1971	1975	1980	1984
Total imports	19,712	57,863	140,528	136,503
Foodstuffs	14.8	15.2	10.4	11.7
Fiber materials	4.9	2.6	1.7	1.8
Metallic materials	12.8	7.6	6.0	4.8
Other raw material goods	14.8	9.9	9.2	7.7
Mineral fuels	24.1	44.3	49.8	44.2
Chemical goods	5.1	3.6	4.4	6.1
Machinery & equipment	12.2	7.4	7.0	8.8
Miscellaneous	11.3	9.3	11.4	14.8
Asia	34.0	49.0	57.1	51.9
Southeast Asia	17.3	18.3	22.6	23.4
Europe	13.4	10.0	8.9	10.9
EC	5.8	5.8	5.6	6.8
North America	32.6	25.8	21.8	25.5
United States	25.3	20.1	17.4	19.5
South America	4.5	2.9	3.0	3.1
Africa	5.0	4.0	3.2	2.3
Oceania	10.4	8.3	6.0	6.3

Source: See table 6.7.

sion was mainly caused by price rises. The terms of trade of most industrialized countries declined continuously during the seventies, and Japan was particularly severely affected. The index of Japan's terms of trade (1970 = 100) fell to 75.2 in 1974 and to 54.5 in 1980.

Japan's Emergence as a Major Overseas Investor

Fiscal year 1972, in which overseas direct investment suddenly increased 2.7-fold over the previous year's figure, can be seen as marking the emergence of Japan as a major foreign investor. Thereafter, foreign investment ran at an annual rate of around $3 billion until 1977, and rose to an average of $4.8 billion in fiscal years 1978–1980. By the end of 1980 Japan's total stock of accumulated overseas direct investments amounted to $36.5 billion, and 87.9 percent of this sum had been invested since 1972.

Changes in both external and internal economic environments contributed to this expansion of investment. First, the revaluation of the yen both reduced the cost of overseas projects and made it more difficult to export goods produced in Japan. This was an important factor particularly in the expansion of manufacturing investment projects in Southeast Asia, which were geared to taking advantage of low labor costs. In the period 1971–1975 nominal and real wages in Japan increased, respectively, 2-fold and 1.6-fold, and the wage gap between Japan and many other Asian countries became an increasingly significant consideration for overseas investing firms. In the Republic of Korea, for example, where a large share of Japanese manufacturing investment was concentrated, the monthly nominal wage of laborers in the period 1972–1974 was only one-seventh of the Japanese level,[21] and the gap between Japan and many other Southeast Asian countries was even greater.

At the same time, less developed Southeast Asian countries were operating a number of policies designed to attract overseas investors. In 1970, South Korea opened a free trade zone and prohibited industrial action in affiliates of foreign firms, while Malaysia and the Philippines also established free trade zones in 1971 and 1972. Incentives to foreign investors were not always consistent, and, particularly in the second half of the decade, a number of measures restricting some areas of activity by foreign investors were introduced. In general, however, it is clear that the environment for Japanese investors was more favorable than it had been in the 1960s.

Third, direct foreign investment was also stimulated by growing trade conflicts with developed nations. Increasing restrictions on imports of Japanese products induced Japanese firms to establish ventures in these countries even in situations where there was no clear gain to be made in terms of costs of production. Color televisions in the late 1970s and automobiles in the early 1980s were typical examples of industries where this type of investment strategy became important. Between July 1977 and June 1980, exports of Japanese TV sets to the United States were restricted to an annual level of 1,750,000 sets. In response, the major producers (Hitachi, Sharp, Toshiba, Mitsubishi, and Sanyo) one after the other established television manufacturing subsidiaries in the United States. Likewise, between 1978 and 1980 the major Japanese integrated circuit makers—NEC, Toshiba, Hitachi, and Fujitsu—established IC manufacturing facilities in the United States to avoid trade friction. With rising unemployment, developed nations, like less developed countries, were increasingly offering investment incentives to multinational enterprises, and Japanese companies took advantage of these schemes in the industrialized world as well as in Southeast Asia.

A fourth factor in the growth of overseas investment was the changing world environment for natural resource extraction. On the one hand, less developed countries were seeking to expand control over their own natural resources, while, on the other hand, world resource prices were rising. Despite slower growth, industrial restructuring, and energy-saving measures, the Japanese economy remained highly dependent upon foreign sources of raw materials, and Japanese enterprises during the 1970s became involved in a number of giant resource extraction projects, most operated jointly with overseas governments or private interests.

Lastly, overseas investment was made possible by rapid capital accumulation within Japan. Japan's foreign currency reserves during the 1970s were greater than those of any other industrialized country except West Germany. Large Japanese companies were also building up their levels of internal financing. Between the first half of 1971 and the second half of 1980 the ratio of internal to external funding in the 420-odd largest manufacturing companies increased from 110.6 to 152.4.[22] Capital for overseas investment was thus becoming increasingly available, and from July 1972 the government took measures to promote foreign investment by Japanese firms. The narrowing of the technology gap between Japan and other industrialized nations was also a factor in decisions to invest, particularly in developed nations. R & D expenditure was expanding rapidly: from $3.9 billion in 1971 to $20.7 billion in 1980, by which time Japan's research spending was second only to that of the United States. Many Japanese producers now felt that their overseas projects in industries such as electrical goods and electronics could compete successfully with local U.S. or European producers,[23] particularly if they took advantage of the Japanese management techniques and high levels of robotization that they used to such effect at home.

This account of the causes of rapid increases in Japanese overseas investment during the 1970s also helps to explain the patterns and peculiarities of Japanese multinational activities (see table

6.6). First, whereas a large share of U.S. and European overseas investment went to other advanced regions, a substantial proportion of Japanese foreign investment was located in less developed countries, particularly those of Asia, which accounted for 26.9 percent of the total by 1980. Manufacturing investment was particularly heavily concentrated in Asia: 36.4 percent of all manufacturing investment to 1980, and as much as 56.2 percent of textile investment, was located in the Asian region. The United States accounted for about a quarter of Japanese overseas investment, but it was of particular importance where investments in commerce were concerned. Commerce investment, which was carried out by general trading companies (*sogo shosha*), manufacturers, and other commercial interests, was generally aimed at expanding the market for Japanese exports and ensuring reliable supplies of imported foodstuffs and raw materials, and some 60 percent of these projects (in value terms) were located in the United States. Commerce-related projects could also be of importance in collecting information about new technological and market trends, and in establishing bridgeheads for local production.

As far as manufacturing was concerned, the United States accounted for less than 20 percent of investment to 1980, but in qualitative terms these projects were important to Japan. Successful production in the U.S. market required high levels of competitiveness in both production and distribution, and the fortunes of these U.S.-based projects were therefore a sensitive indicator of the potential for investment in other advanced nations.

A relatively large share of Japanese overseas investment was resource related. Although mining only accounted for 19.4 percent of the total, investments in the chemicals, iron, and nonferrous metals industries were commonly related to the development of overseas resource inputs for Japanese manufacturing (such as petrochemicals and aluminum refining). A large share of investment in both mining and resource processing was located in Asia.

The size of Japanese foreign investment projects was typically rather small. The average value of each project increased from less than $1 million in 1971 to $1.9 million in 1980, but if inflation is taken into account it is clear that the increase in real size was not as significant as these figures would suggest. Investment projects in Asia were particularly small, being on average half the value of those in the United States. It was also characteristic of Japanese,

Table 6.6

Japan's Foreign Direct Investment: Industry and Region (U.S.$ millions, percent)

	North America	Central- South America	Middle & Near East	Asia	Europe	Africa	Oceania	Total
Manufacturing	2,428	2,781	4,571	1,064	844	96	789	12,573
Textiles	181	351	920	4	138	38	5	1,637
Chemical	243	501	721	944	105	14	99	2,626
Iron & nonferrous metals	371	735	1,032	52	156	20	254	2,619
Electrical	662	212	544	10	127	4	21	1,579
Miscellaneous	119	79	524	39	97	6	30	894
Mining	578	1,185	3,022	39	859	471	915	7,171
Commerce	3,493	439	401	10	817	3	248	5,409
Finance insurance	951	296	266	25	822	2	62	2,426
Other service	1,402	1,084	1,085	77	988	793	378	5,808
Total	9,789	6,168	9,830	2,359	4,471	1,445	2,525	36,497

Source: Ministry of Finance.
Note: Cumulative value on basis of notification and sanction of MOF at end of FY 1980.

as opposed to U.S. or European, overseas investment projects that they were often established jointly with one or more local partners. Where the commerce sector and manufacturing investment in developed countries were concerned, wholly owned subsidiaries were common, but in developing countries minority-owned subsidiaries were the rule. To 1980, 50.2 percent of manufacturing projects and 53.5 percent of mining projects in less developed countries took the form of subsidiaries in which the Japanese side held a minority of the stock.[24]

Growing International Conflict and Japanese Industrial Imperialism Since 1981

The Japanese economy did not suffer as severe a blow from the second oil crisis as did other economies. Deflationary policies and industrial rationalization within Japan minimized the effects of rising oil costs on domestic prices. Other industrialized countries, by contrast, were more reluctant to take such measures because of their fears of rising unemployment. As a result, the competitiveness of Japanese goods relative to those of most major developed nations increased, Japanese exports expanded (see table 6.7), and, during the first half of the 1980s, Japan came to play an increasingly central role in the world economy.

Rapid Expansion of Exports and Foreign Investment

Japan accounted for 9.1 percent of the total exports of the capitalist world in 1983, and for 14.0 percent of the exports of advanced industrial nations in 1984. The growth of exports represented a real increase in the quantity of goods traded, rather than a mere increase in export prices. Indeed, the price index of Japanese exports (yen basis, 1975 = 100) fell slightly, from 117.8 in 1981 to 115.2 in 1984.

During this period there was a marked change in the composition of Japanese exports. Passenger cars still constituted the major export item, although it was noteworthy that the export of car components, needed to supply the foreign affiliates established by Japanese makers during the late 1970s and early 1980s, increased rapidly. Among the new leading exports were video cassette recorders (VCRs), thermionic tubes, semiconductors, and automatic data-processing equipment. These products shared the characteristics of being technologically sophisticated, produced by oligopolistic and intensely competitive enterprises, and (particularly in the case of semiconductors and data-processing equipment) very important in industrial automation. In recent years, Japanese companies have effectively monopolized the production of VCRs and have provided about 30 percent of world exports of semiconductors and around 40 percent of world exports of business machines (including automatic data processors). These figures demonstrate that, at least in some respects, the industrial restructuring and development of high-tech industries that had been pursued during the seventies had proved successful.

At the same time, Japan's role as an overseas investor was also expanding. Foreign direct investment in the period 1981–1984 totaled $34.9 billion, and by the end of FY 1984 the cumulative total had reached $71.4 billion. It was in the late 1970s that many Japanese companies could be said to have adopted a multinational

Table 6.7

**Japan's External Performance, 1981–1984
(U.S.$ millions)**

	1981	1982	1983	1984
Balance of payments (IMF basis)	19,967	18,079	31,454	44,257
Trade balance				
Exports	149,522	137,663	145,768	168,290
Imports	129,555	119,584	114,014	124,033
Long-term capital balance	−9,672	−14,969	−17,700	−49,651
Direct investment (net)	−4,795	−4,101	−3,196	−49,651
Securities investment (net)	−4,443	2,117	1,816	−23,601
Investment income balance	−763	1,718	3,082	4,231
Direct investment income (net)	816	992	1,354	1,428
Overall balance of payments	−2,144	−4,971	5,177	−15,200
External assets and liabilities				
Direct investment (assets)	24,506	28,969	32,178	37,921
Securities investment (assets)	31,538	40,070	56,115	87,578
Net assets in private sector	−18,537	2,046	11,928	47,069
Total net assets	10,918	24,682	37,259	74,346

Source: Bank of Japan, *Balance of Payments Monthly*, no. 232 (November 1985); Ministry of Finance, *Financial Statistics Monthly*, no. 398 (June 1985).

strategy, integrating domestic and overseas production. This strategy, however, is still being developed, and, as multinationals, Japanese companies remain fragile in terms of their accumulation of experience, organization, and personnel. The top twenty companies engaged in overseas manufacturing projects in 1983 produced about $10 billion worth of goods overseas, but this was only equivalent to 6.8 percent of Japanese exports.

During the first half of the 1980s, a particularly large share (just over half) of Japanese manufacturing investment went to the United States and Europe. Numerous electrical machinery and motor vehicle producers, concerned at the dangers of rising protectionism, moved to set up local production facilities in their major developed markets. Conversely, although manufacturing investment in less developed countries continued to expand, its growth rate was comparatively low. This slowdown was caused by increased economic and political risks in some host countries (especially in Latin America) and by the narrowing of the wage gap between Japan and certain of the Asian less developed countries. The increasing regulation of foreign subsidiaries in some of the latter group of countries also proved a disincentive to investment by Japanese companies. At the same time, the introduction of labor-saving equipment into factories within Japan reduced the pressure for formerly labor-intensive activities to be relocated overseas.

Outflows of resource-related investment declined somewhat during this period, mainly because of reduced resource demands resulting from the world recession, the restructuring of Japanese industry, and the introduction of new energy saving technologies. However, rising domestic production costs (particularly electricity costs) and measures by producer nations to strengthen local processing induced Japanese processors of petrochemicals, nonferrous metals, and aluminum to locate facilities overseas.

Overseas financial operations also showed great expansion in this period. Here, major factors were the liberalization of the financial sector in Japan and the high interest rates prevalent in the United States. Some of the major banks, such as the Mitsui and Fuji banks, expanded their worldwide networks by purchasing smaller U.S. banks, while medium-sized banks and security companies, as well as their larger counterparts, set up subsidiaries in the cities of Europe and the United States.

A particularly striking feature of the early 1980s was the massive growth of Japanese overseas portfolio investment. Net foreign indirect investment (total acquisitions minus disposals of foreign securities) touched the $10 billion mark for the first time in 1981, and reached $35 billion in 1984. A large share of this outflow of capital went into U.S. securities, particularly U.S. Treasury bonds. The major reason was the substantial difference in interest rates between Japan and the United States (estimated in 1984 at 4 percent net on long-term investments). As a result of the rapid growth of foreign securities investment, the net external assets of the Japanese private sector became positive in 1982 and amounted to $47.1 billion in December 1984.[25]

The government's 1984 White Paper on International Trade stated that Japan should "fulfill its duty" as an international supplier of capital.[26] This amounted to recognition by the government that Japan's current account surplus—totaling $67.4 billion in the period 1981–1984—had made it possible for Japan to export a growing amount of capital in the forms of both direct and indirect overseas investment, and that such activity was desirable to avert the conflicts provoked by growing Japanese trade surpluses.

Trade Conflict with the West and Growing Influence in Asia

The development of Japan's external activities caused severe trade friction with industrialized countries and criticisms of Japan's excessive influence within Asia. From the late seventies onward, trade disputes with the United States became increasingly serious, mainly because of the massive expansion of the U.S. deficit in its trade with Japan. This amounted to an average $2.3 billion per annum from 1971 to 1975, $9.6 billion per annum from 1976 to 1980, and $22.6 billion per annum from 1981 to 1984. During the 1980s, a number of Japanese exports became the subject of lawsuits or of protective legislation within the United States, while the U.S. government placed increasing pressure on Japan to open its domestic market to imported goods. At the same time, it has become more and more apparent that Japan-U.S. trade friction involves fundamental structural problems that cannot readily be resolved by government negotiations.

The report of an official U.S. investigation of trade friction with Japan published in the late 1970s (the first Jones report) discussed Japanese market restrictions and industrial policies and demanded market liberalization, the revision of industrial policies, and greater Japanese investment in the United States.[27] Other reports, on the contrary, while noting the existence of Japanese trade barriers, placed greater emphasis on the declining competitiveness of U.S. industry as a cause of the trade imbalance. Such reports pointed to the fact that Japan accounted only for 30 percent of the U.S. trade deficit in 1984, and that deficits with other trading partners were also increasing. A document published by the General Accounting Office in 1979, for example, suggested the following reasons for America's declining competitiveness.[28] While the Japanese government had carried out long-term industrial and foreign trade strategies that provided a framework for the development of technologically sophisticated manufacturing activities by private enterprise, the United States had no tradition of coherent industrial policy making, and U.S. enterprises had tended to concentrate upon overseas investment rather than developing domestically based export industries. The "second Jones report" of 1980 recognized that even if Japan met U.S. demands for a removal of trade barriers, this would provide only a partial alleviation of trade problems.[29] These reports argued that Japan's economic structure, which excluded many U.S. and other manufactured imports, was detrimental to the liberalization of world trade. But at the same time they emphasized the U.S. government's responsibility for pursuing policies that would restore the nation's industrial strength.

The reports had some influence on the policies of the Reagan administration, but, while that administration claimed to be committed to "reindustrialization" and to recreating a "strong America," the short-term effects of its policies may be said to have damaged U.S. competitiveness. Enormous budget deficits, resulting mainly from high military expenditures, raised interest rates and so maintained the dollar at a high value on international money markets until the end of 1985. Some prominent government officials admitted, indeed, that the high exchange rate of the dollar was responsible for around half of the U.S. trade deficit.[30]

But although the U.S. trade deficit must in part be attributed to American government policies, it is also clear that the highly vertical nature of Japan's trade structure is a major source of friction. This trade structure has emerged for a number of reasons. In the first place, the combination of a large population with an almost total lack of domestic sources of raw materials induced Japanese capitalism to export in order to earn the foreign exchange needed for resource imports. The existence in Japan of competing oligopolist enterprises was also a factor in the tendency for sudden "floods" of new Japanese exports to hit a single market simultaneously. As far as Japan is concerned, it is unlikely that trade problems could be resolved without some rather fundamental structural changes. For example, as long as prices of foreign raw materials remain high, Japan will need to maintain large export surpluses with non-resource-exporting countries if it is to avoid a perpetual overall balance-of-trade deficit. The division of labor between Japan and other Asian countries is also unlikely to change until these countries arrive at a higher level of industrialization.

Because of its fears that rising protectionism in the United States and Europe would obstruct exports, the Japanese government has gone some way toward complying with the demands of its trading partners. Japanese companies have, in certain instances, voluntarily restricted their exports and have set up local production facilities in their industrialized markets. Furthermore, in response to the threat of trade conflict, the Japanese government in 1985 reached agreement with the British and French governments on proposals to promote the transfer of technology and to participate in cooperative technological development projects. Joint committees have been set up by the U.S. and Japanese governments to handle trade complaints and to deal with problems of nontariff barriers. Perhaps a more significant step in preventing trade friction from escalating into political conflict, however, has been the expansion of Japanese military expenditure. This, of course, is aimed at defusing U.S. criticisms of Japan's reluctance to "share the burden of defending the West." In essence, however, trade friction between Japan and other advanced nations is a reflection of the unbalanced development of contemporary world capitalism, and as such is not susceptible to simple solutions.

Meanwhile, Japan is also exerting an ever-greater influence over the economies of its Asian neighbors, and this influence, too, may well be a source of increasing future conflict. Japan is not only the largest trade partner and direct foreign investor, but also the largest supplier of overseas government assistance to Southeast Asia (see table 6.8). Economic relations between Japan and that region are, naturally, more vertical than Japan's relations with advanced industrialized nations. Southeast Asia is primarily an importer of capital and intermediate goods and consumer durables from Japan, and an exporter to Japan and the United States of foodstuffs, natural resources, and labor-intensive manufactured goods. A triangular trade relationship exists among Japan, Southeast Asia, and the United States: Southeast Asian countries (except Indonesia) have a trade deficit with Japan, while their trade balance with the United States is, in general, favorable. In other words, surpluses with the United States are balanced against deficits with Japan and are important in providing the foreign currency needed for the import of Japanese industrial equipment and other items. This situation, needless to say, is a source of trade friction between the United States and Southeast Asia.

The Asian NICs have now reached a fairly high level of industrialization, but, for further industrial growth, they require higher levels of technology and wider markets for their products. As is well known, the industrialization strategies of the Asian NICs

Table 6.8

Japan's Share in Southeast Asian Economies (U.S.$ millions, percent)

	Exports to Japan			Imports from Japan			Japan's foreign direct investment	Japan's official funds cooperation
	Value	Japan's share of total	Ranking	Value	Japan's share of total	Ranking		
Republic of Korea	41.2	15.7	2	69.4	24.7	1	15.5	29.0
Taiwan	31.9	10.6	2	64.5	29.3	1	6.5	2.5
Hong Kong	11.4	4.4	5	60.6	21.9	2	28.0	—
Thailand	9.6	15.5	1	28.2	27.3	1	7.1	24.6
Singapore	22.5	9.4	3	52.6	18.3	1	19.3	0.7
Malaysia	27.4	19.4	2	34.0	25.4	1	10.5	12.0
Philippines	9.8	20.0	2	13.4	17.1	2	8.3	26.7
Indonesia	96.8	45.8	1	37.9	23.1	1	80.2	56.2

Source: MITI, *White Paper on International Trade, Japan; White Paper on International Economic Cooperation, Japan;* Ministry of Finance, *Financial Statistics Monthly.*

Notes: Exports and imports: Korea, Jan.–Nov. 1984; Taiwan, 1984; Hong Kong, 1984; Thailand, 1983; Singapore, 1984; Malaysia, 1983; Philippines, 1983; Indonesia, 1983.

Japan's foreign direct investment: cumulated value on the basis of notification and sanction of MOF for 1951–1984.

Japan's official funds cooperation includes gratuitous and onerous economic cooperation on the basis of official funds. Value is cumulated value on the basis of reciprocated official documents until FY 1984.

relied heavily on investment by U.S. and Japanese multinationals, and their access to markets and technology has therefore often been dependent upon the policies of the parent firms. Although many NIC manufactured goods, such as iron and steel, semiconductors, household electrical appliances, and ships, are now strong competitors of Japanese goods, most do not have free access to the Japanese market because of territorial restrictions imposed by Japanese enterprises upon their foreign joint ventures or overseas licensees of technology. Japan has been slow to respond to Southeast Asian demands for greater transfers of technology and for the development of a more horizontal division of labor, though in the future these demands may become increasingly hard to resist.

At present, however, the Japanese government appears to see the concept of Pacific Rim economic cooperation as holding the key to the long-term future of the region.[31] It has been suggested, indeed, that the Pacific Rim—including Japan, Southeast Asia, Australasia, North America, the west coast of Latin America, and probably also the People's Republic of China—will become the core of the world economic, political, and cultural system in the twenty-first century. The concept of a Pacific Rim Economic Community remains extremely vague, but it does suggest a possible framework for future approaches to regional problems. The concept was particularly strongly endorsed by Prime Minister Ohira at the beginning of the 1980s, and his successor, Prime Minister Suzuki, pledged Japanese support for the idea in 1982. Southeast Asian nations, however, are cautious of initiatives by the industrialized nations for such a community, since they fear an institutionalization of existing international economic and political inequalities in the region. Despite statements by Japanese political and business figures on the potential benefits of a Pacific Community from the point of view of economic development and political cooperation, it is unlikely that Japan will be able to act as the catalyst in the formation of the community. Nevertheless, it is of some interest to note that Japanese capitalism has reached the stage at which it sees the community as potentially serving Japan's interests in both the horizontal and the vertical international division of labor.

Japanese Industrial Imperialism

Contemporary Japanese capitalism can be viewed as "industrial imperialism," a subspecies of the neo-imperialism characteristic of the postwar world. In this section I shall seek to analyze the essential features of this industrial imperialism.

The term "imperialism" was originally used to refer to territorial expansionism, including the expansion of a nation's territorial sphere of influence. In modern times such imperialism has been pursued by means of economic monopoly and the export of capital as well as by military might. Neo-imperialism is the term often given to the postwar capitalist order that stands opposed to socialism, nationalism, and liberation struggles in the less developed world. In speaking of industrial imperialism, I refer to the pursuit of these objectives by means of the expansion of industry and trade, rather than by political or military initiatives. Although the neo-imperialism of the United States, France, and Britain retains a substantial political and military element, Japanese neo-imperialism has concentrated almost entirely on economic activity. It can thus be seen as an archetype of industrial imperialism.

In a sense, Japanese industrial imperialism is a product of the IMF-GATT system. In the early postwar period, when Japan lacked adequate capital resources, the free trade system was vital to Japan's economic survival and growth. But as Japan's international competitiveness improved, the IMF-GATT order came to provide the environment for Japan's overseas economic expansion. It was this system that made possible the policies of "export for export's sake" and enabled Japan to establish and strengthen the vertical international division of labor with its trading partners. Free trade, indeed, can become an element in imperialism precisely because of its power to lock nations into a subordinate and underdeveloped position in the international division of labor. Japan's trade relations with Asia in particular are, therefore, viewed as having imperialistic features.

The world role of the United States suggests that one of the most important elements in neo-imperialism is the multinational corporation. However, one of the marked characteristics of Japanese industrial imperialism is the key role played, not by its multinational enterprises, but by trade. According to *Fortune* (August 20, 1984), twenty-three Japanese companies are ranked among the world's one hundred largest industrial corporations. Such companies are now beginning to develop multinational strategies, and some economists and political observers suggest that foreign investment rather than trade will form the core of future Japanese imperialism. This view is open to question, however, particularly in light of increasing international scrutiny of the activities of multinational enterprises.

In the constitution promulgated after World War II, Japan renounced war, and ever since there has been strong domestic opposition to the building of a powerful military force. This is one of the factors that distinguishes Japanese industrial imperialism from neo-imperialism in general. Limitations on military expenditure, and thus on the expansion of armaments industries, may have been a factor in Japan's postwar industrial success and also probably served to reduce other Asian nations' suspicion of Japan. On the other hand, given the existence of the Japan-U.S. Security Treaty, it is clear that Japanese imperialism has developed within the framework of U.S. world strategy. Rather than maintaining its own military power, Japan has provided some degree of cooperation with U.S. military operations in Asia. This situation has also imposed costs on Japan. For example, Japan was obliged to abandon attempts to improve diplomatic relations and foreign trade with China until the dramatic reversal of U.S. policy toward China in 1971. Likewise, even today, Japanese cooperation in the development of Siberia is limited by U.S. constraints on relations with the Soviet Union. It therefore needs to be emphasized that, despite weak military power, Japan exerts a considerable political and diplomatic influence upon other Asian nations through its involvement in U.S. international strategy.

To say that Japan's activities in Asia constitute "industrial imperialism" is by no means to imply that they constitute "peaceful imperialism." The influx of Japanese goods into other Asian countries has attracted widespread criticism. These goods consist not only of consumer durables but also of a whole range of everyday commodities, some of which are imported from Japan and others manufactured locally by joint ventures. The manufactured products displayed in subsidiaries of Japanese supermarket and department store chains inevitably influence local consumption patterns. Even the nature of urban life is becoming "Japanized," as the younger generation adopts styles of music, fashion, leisure, and diet that are highly influenced by Japan. These commercial developments destroy entrepreneurship in the traditional sector and subvert local customs, cultures, family systems, and communities. At the same time, they give added impetus to the rapid urbanization process that in some areas is resulting in rural depopulation and overcrowding of the cities.

Industrial imperialism also has a destructive effect on the natural environment. Japanese timber imports have resulted in wholesale felling of Malaysian and Philippine forests, while the creation of industrial zones to serve the need of foreign investors frequently leads to environmental pollution. (A number of Japanese firms in particular have been criticized for "exporting pollution."[32]) Japanese industrial imperialism should accept responsibility both for social and for environmental disruption because of its predominant role in the development of capitalism in the region. Those who regard the term "industrial imperialism" as excessively ideological or emotive have clearly failed to grasp the enormity of Japan's impact on community and environment in less developed Asian countries. It is economic arrogance to dismiss the destructive effects of foreign trade, investment, and sometimes even aid as "inevitable costs of rapid development." The critique of Japan's role in Asia implied by the phrase "industrial imperialism" leads to the conclusion that such destruction should be avoided, because, once social structures and natural ecosystems have been destroyed, they can never be recreated.

Some Prospects—In Place of a Conclusion

The world capitalist economy, which had enjoyed stability and prosperity in the 1960s, experienced a severe depression in the following decade. Despite some recovery in the early 1980s, by 1984 twenty-five million people remained out of work in OECD countries. It is quite unrealistic to expect the capitalist economy to come up with a comprehensive solution to so massive a problem. High levels of unemployment will undoubtedly continue to fuel international economic friction in the future.

At the same time, a new wave of technological innovation is altering the industrial structure of all advanced industrial nations and widening the technological gap between North and South. New high-tech industries (such as microelectronics equipment, new materials, biotechnology, and information services) are growing rapidly and have been singled out by many political and business leaders as the main fields of industrial competition in the last decade of the twentieth century. The development of these industries is likely to intensify international industrial competition, but simultaneously to promote international cooperation in the development of new technologies, where costs and risks are high.

During the 1970s, the NICs attained a high level of growth through the development of export-oriented manufacturing. At present, however, the technology gap between the older industrialized countries and the NICs is widening sharply. In this sense, economic relations between advanced and less developed countries will become increasingly vertical, whereby high-growth, high-tech industries in the former coexist with lower-growth, low-technology manufacturing in the latter.

Japanese capitalism is currently making great efforts to develop high-technology industries, restructure and rationalize industry, and liberalize the national economy. These efforts will surely bear fruit. It is doubtful, however, whether they will solve the problems of Japan's relationship with the international economy. On the contrary, they are more likely to enhance Japanese competitiveness to such a degree that further damaging international conflicts occur. Japan should be conscious of its great influence on the world economy and find ways to enhance international economic harmony. These may include paying greater attention to the needs of industrializing Asian countries and developing new and different forms of economic aid and cooperation. At the same time, the growing worldwide integration of the activities of Japanese enterprises may create new domestic problems, including reduced investment within Japan and increased unemployment.

Finally, it should be stressed that the survival and growth of Japanese capitalism depends upon the expansion of world peace. It cannot be denied that national political and economic systems are becoming increasingly interdependent. Japan's future prosperity, therefore, can only be assured by determined attempts to promote international peace and eliminate inequalities in international economic relations.

Notes

1. Economic Planning Agency, *White Paper on the Japanese Economy* (Tokyo, 1956), p. 42.

2. Radha Sinha, *Japan's Options for the 1980s* (Tokyo: Charles E. Tuttle, 1982), pp. 4–23.

3. Ministry of International Trade and Industry, *White Paper on International*

Trade, Japan (Tokyo, 1956, 1972).

4. MITI, *White Paper on International Economic Cooperation, Japan* (Tokyo, 1963, 1964), pp. 312–14.

5. See Miyazaki Yoshikazu, *The Economic Structure of Postwar Japan* (Tokyo: Shinhyoronsha, 1966), chap. 2.

6. Yoichi Okita, "Japan's Fiscal Incentives for Exports," in *The Japanese Economy in International Perspective*, ed. Isaiah Frank (Baltimore: Johns Hopkins University Press, 1975), p. 228.

7. JETRO, *A History of Japan's Postwar Export Policy—Japanese Experience* (Tokyo, 1983), p. 14.

8. Customs and Tariff Bureau, *The Hundred Year History of Customs Bureau* (Tokyo: Nippon Kanzei Kyokai, 1972), final vol., p. 322.

9. Ibid., p. 453.

10. Ibid., pp. 361–66.

11. MITI, *White Paper on International Trade, Japan* (1961), chap. 3.

12. Bank of Japan, *Japan and the World: A Comparison by Economic and Financial Statistics*, vol. 16 (1979), vol. 18 (1981).

13. The sixth UN special session in May 1974 adopted the Declaration on the Establishment of a New International Economic Order. This declaration reflected both the urgent requests and increasing power of developing nations, though the declaration itself was a product of compromise between South and North.

14. *Japan and the World*, vol. 18 (1981).

15. OECD, *Statistics of Foreign Trade*, 1969.

16. MITI, *White Paper on International Trade, Japan* (1971).

17. The ratio is calculated as the proportion of total tariff income to total value of imports. Figures are derived from the Japan Tariff Association, *Foreign Trade Yearbook* (1972, 1985).

18. Tokyo Round Study Group, *Full Picture of Tokyo Round* (Tokyo: Japan Tariff Association, 1980).

19. Daily Automobile Newspaper Co., *Automobile Yearbook* (1982).

20. Specialization index (annual average 1971–1980) = the proportion of exports (imports) of the item concerned to total Japanese exports (imports) – the proportion of exports (imports) of the item concerned to total OECD exports (imports).

21. Bank of Japan, *Foreign Countries Economic Statistical Yearbook* (1980).

22. Mitsubishi General Institute, *Analysis of Business Management*.

23. Science and Technology Agency, *White Paper on Science and Technology* (1984), pp. 55–60.

24. MITI, *Foreign Business of Japanese Enterprises*, 10th and 11th Investigation.

25. MOF, *Financial Statistics Monthly* 398 (June 1985).

26. MITI, *White Paper on International Trade, Japan, 1984*, final chap.

27. Subcommittee on Trade, Committee on Ways and Means, U.S. House of Representatives, *Task Force Report on United States–Japan Trade with Additional Views* (Washington, D.C.: Government Printing Office, 1979).

28. Report by the Comptroller General of the United States, *United*

States–Japan Trade: Issues and Problems (Washington, D.C.: U.S. General Accounting Office, 1979).

29. Subcommittee on Trade, Committee on Ways and Means, U.S. House of Representatives, *United States–Japan Trade Report* (Washington, D.C.: Government Printing Office, 1980).

30. For example, Mike Mansfield, U.S. ambassador's lecture during a seminar of the Liberal Democratic Party at Karuizawa, July 1985. U.S. Information Service, American Embassy.

31. See Cabinet Councillor's Office, ed., *The Conception of Circum-Pan Pacific Solidarity*, fourth report of the Policy Study Group for Prime Minister Ohira (Tokyo: MOF Printing Bureau, 1980).

32. MITI, *Foreign Business of Japanese Enterprises, 6th Investigation* (1977).

Bibliography

Administrative Management Agency, Japan. *Tokushu hōjin soran 1984*. Tokyo: Administrative Management Agency, 1984.

Allen, G. C. *A Short Economic History of Modern Japan*. London: Macmillan, 1946.

Armour, A. J. L., ed. *Asia and Japan: The Search for Modernisation and Identity*. London: Athlone Press, 1985.

Bank of Japan. *Gaikoku keizai tōkei nempō 1980*. Tokyo: Bank of Japan, 1980.

Baran, P. A., and P. M. Sweezy. *Monopoly Capital*. New York: Monthly Review Press, 1966.

Barthes, R. *Empire of Signs*, tr. R. Howard. London: Jonathan Cape, 1982.

Bergson, A., and S. Kuznets, eds. *Economic Trends in the Soviet Union*. Cambridge: Harvard University Press, 1963.

Bisson, T. A. *Zaibatsu Dissolution in Japan*. Berkeley: University of California Press, 1954.

Boatwright, B., and J. Sleigh. "New Technology: The Japanese Approach." *Department of Employment Gazette* (July 7, 1979).

Braddon, R. *The Other Hundred Years War: Japan's Bid for Supremacy, 1941–2041*. London: Collins, 1983.

Braverman, H. *Labor and Monopoly Capital*. New York: Monthly Review Press, 1975.

Cabinet Councillor's Office, Japan. *Kan taiheiyō rentai no kōsō: Ōhira sōri no seisaku kenkyūkai hōkoku 4*. Tokyo: Ministry of Finance Printing Bureau, 1980.

Customs and Tariffs Bureau. *Zeikan hyakunenshi*. Tokyo: Japan Tariff Association, 1972.

Deane, P. *The Evolution of Economic Ideas*. Cambridge: Cambridge University Press, 1978.

Destler, I. M., and J. Sato. *Coping with U.S.-Japanese Economic Conflicts*. Washington, D.C.: Brookings Institution, 1982.

Dore, R. P. *Land Reform in Japan*. Oxford: Oxford University Press, 1950.

Dower, J. W. *Origins of the Modern Japanese State: Select Writings of E. H. Norman*. New York: Pantheon Books, 1975.

Drucker, P. "What We Can Learn from Japanese Management." *Harvard Business Review* (March/April 1971).

Economic Planning Agency, Japan. *Keizai hakusho*. Tokyo: Economic Planning Agency, various years.

Engels, F. *Socialism: Utopian and Scientific*. London, 1892.

Fei, J. C., and G. Ranis. *Development of the Labor Surplus Economy: Theory and Policy*. Homewood, Ill.: Richard D. Irwin, 1964.

Fox, J. "Japan's Electronic Lesson." *New Scientist* (November 20, 1980).

Frank, I., ed. *The Japanese Economy in International Perspective*. Baltimore: Johns Hopkins University Press, 1975.

GATT. *Japan's Economic Expansion and Foreign Trade, 1955 to 1970*. Geneva: GATT, 1971.

Gendai teikokushugi taisei to Nihon shihonshugi. Vol. 1 of *Kōza konnichi no shihonshugi*. Tokyo: Otsuki Shoten, 1981.

Halliday, J. *A Political History of Japanese Capitalism*. New York: Monthly Review Press, 1975.

Halliday, J., and G. McCormack. *Japanese Imperialism Today*. Harmondsworth: Penguin Books, 1973.

Hanabusa, M. *Trade Problems Between Japan and Western Europe*. Oxford: Oxford University Press, 1983.

Hane, M. *Peasants, Rebels and Outcasts: The Underside of Modern Japan*. New York: Pantheon Books, 1982.

Heisenberg, W. *Physics and Philosophy*. New York: Harper and Row, 1958.

Herschede, F., and R. Wiltgen. "Japan's Alternative Road to Serfdom: J. M. Clark and the Japanese Experience." *Review of Social Economy* (December 1981).

Holding Company Liquidation Commission. *Nihon zaibatsu to sono kaitai*. Tokyo: Holding Company Liquidation Commission, 1950.

Ichikawa, S. *Nihon kyōsantō tōsō shōshi*. Tokyo, 1945.

Jansen, M. B., ed. *Changing Japanese Attitudes Toward Moderniza-tion*. Princeton: Princeton University Press, 1965.

Japan Tariff Association. *Bōeki nenkan*. Tokyo: Japan Tariff Asso-ciation, various years.

JETRO. *A History of Japan's Postwar Export Policy: Japanese Ex-perience*. Tokyo: JETRO, 1983.

Johnson, C. *MITI and the Japanese Miracle*. Stanford: Stanford University Press, 1982.

Kajinishi, M., et al. *Nihon shihonshugi no daraku*. Vols. 1–8. Tokyo: Tokyo Daigaku Shuppankai, 1960–1969.

Kelly, A. C., J. G. Williamson, and R. J. Cheetham. *Dualistic eco-nomic development: Theory and history*. Chicago: University of Chicago Press, 1972.

Kinoshita, E., ed. *Gendai no sekai keizai*. Tokyo: Yuhikaku, 1983.

Kinugasa, Y. *Nihon kigyō no kokusaika senryaku*. Tokyo: Nihon Keizai Shimbunsha, 1980.

Kitada, Y., ed. *Bōeki masatsu to keizai seisaku*. Tokyo: Ōtsuki Shoten, 1983.

Kitazawa, Y. *Nihon kigyō no kaigai shinshutsu*. Tokyo: Nihon Hyōronsha, 1979.

Klein, L., and K. Ohkawa, eds. *Economic Growth: The Japanese Experience Since the Meiji Era*. Homewood, Ill.: Richard D. Ir-win, 1968.

Kojima, K. *Nihon no kaigai chokusetsu tōshi*. Tokyo: Nihon Hyōronsha, 1982.

Krauss, E. S., T. P. Rohlen, and P. G. Steinhoff, eds. *Conflict in Japan*. Honolulu: University of Hawaii Press, 1984.

Kudrov, V. "Amerika gasshūkoku to Nihon: Teikokushugi kan kyōsō no senei-ka." *Sekai keizai to kokusai kankei 70*.

Kuhn, T. S. *Structure of Scientific Revolutions*. Chicago: University of Chicago Press, 1962.

Kurokawa, T. "Gendai no ME kakumei to Marukusu no rōdō ka-tei ron." *Mita gakkai zasshi 77*, 2 (1984).

———. *Nihon no teichingin kōzō*. Tokyo: Ōtsuki Shoten, 1964.

———, ed. *Gendai Nihon no keizai kōzō*. Tokyo: Hōritsu Bunka Sha, 1982.

Ladejinsky, W. I. "Japan's Land Reform." *Foreign Agriculture 15, 9* (1951).

Lenin, V. I. *Imperialism: The Highest Stage of Capitalism*. Moscow: Progress Publishers, 1964.

Maclean, B. "Kozo Uno's Principles of Poltical Economy." *Science and Society* (Summer 1981).

McCormack, G., and Y. Sugimoto. *Democracy in Contemporary Japan*. Sydney: Hale and Iremonger, 1986. Armonk, N.Y.: M. E. Sharpe.

Maddison, A. *Economic Growth in Japan and the USSR*. London: George Allen and Unwin, 1969.

Mallet, S. *La nouvelle classe ouvriere*. Paris: Editions du Seuil, 1963.

March, P. "Japan's Recipe for Industrial Success." *New Scientist* 20 (November 1980).

Marx, K. *Capital*. Vols. 1–3. London: Penguin Books/New Left Review, 1976–1981.

Matsui, K. *Keizai kyoryoku: Towareru Nihon no keizai gaikō*. Tokyo: Yuhikaku, 1983.

Ministry of International Trade and Industry, Japan. *Keizai kyōryoku no genjō to mondai ten*. Tokyo: Ministry of International Trade and Industry, various years.

———. *Tsūshō hakusho*. Tokyo: Ministry of International Trade and Industry, various years.

———. *Waga kuni kigyō no kaigai jigyo katsudo*. Tokyo: Ministry of International Trade and Industry, 1983.

Ministry of Labor, Japan. *Rōdō hakusho 1984*. Tokyo: Ministry of Labor, 1984.

Miyazaki, Y. *Kasen*. Tokyo: Iwanami Shinsho, 1972.

———. *Sengo Nihon no keizai kikō*. Tokyo: Shin Hyōronsha, 1966.

Morishima, M. *Marx's Economics: A Dual Theory of Value and Growth*. Cambridge: Cambridge University Press, 1973.

Morris-Suzuki, T. "Gyappu ōkii Ō-Bei no Nihon keizai kenkyu—seichō no kyokun-teki apurōchi o kōete." *Ekonomisuto* (April 10, 1984).

Mouer, R., and Y. Sugimoto. *Images of Japanese Society*. London: Kegan Paul International, 1986.

Nagasu, K. *Nanshin suru Nihon shihonshugi*. Tokyo: Mainichi Shimbunsha, 1971.

Najita, T., and J. V. Koschmann, eds. *Conflict in Modern Japanese History: The Neglected Tradition*. Princeton: Princeton University Press, 1982.

Nakamura, T. *The Postwar Japanese Economy—Its Development and Structure*. Tokyo: University of Tokyo Press, 1981.

National Tax Administration Agency, Japan. *Hōjin kigyō no jittai 1982*. Tokyo: National Tax Administration Agency, 1984.

NHK Shuzaihan. *Bōeki: Nani ga Nihon o kōritsu saseru ka*. Vol. 8 of *Nihon no jōken*. Tokyo: NHK Shuppan Kyoku, 1982.

Nihon shigaku ronsō. Vol. 9 of *Kōza Nihon-shi*. Tokyo: Tokyo Daigaku Shuppankai, 1971.

Nihon shihonshugi to kokumin seikatsu. Vol. 9 of *Kōza konnichi no Nihon shihonshugi*. Tokyo: Ōtsuki Shoten, 1982.

Nikkan Jidōsha Shimbunsha. *Jidōsha nenkan 1982*. Tokyo: Nikkan Jidōsha Shimbunsha, 1982.

Norman, E. H. *Japan's Emergence as a Modern State*. New York: Institute of Pacific Relations, 1940.

Ōhashi T. *Nihon no kaikyū kōsei*. Tokyo: Iwanami Shinsho, 1971.

Ohkawa, K., and G. Ranis. *Japan and the Developing Countries: A Comparative Analysis*. Oxford: Basil Blackwell, 1985.

Ohkawa, K., and H. Rosovsky. *Japanese Economic Growth: Trend Acceleration in the Twentieth Century*. Stanford: Stanford University Press, 1973.

———. *Japanese Economic Growth*. Stanford: Stanford University Press, 1973.

Ohkawa, K., and M. Shinohara. *Patterns of Japanese Development: A Quantitative Appraisal*. New Haven: Yale University Press, 1979.

Ono, Y. *Sengo Nihon shihonshugi-ron*. Tokyo: Aoki Shoten, 1963.

Organization of Economic Cooperation and Development. *Statistics of Foreign Trade 1969*. Paris: OECD, 1969.

Ōuchi, T. *Gendai Nihon keizai-ron*. Tokyo: Tokyo Daigaku Shuppankai, 1971.

———. *Kokka dokusen shihonshugi*. Tokyo: Tokyo Daigaku Shuppankai, 1970.

———. *Nihon shihonshugi no nōgyōmondai*. Tokyo: Tokyo Daigaku Shuppankai, 1952.

———. "Sengo kaikaku e no futatsu no apurōchi." *Shakai kagaku kenkyū* 21, 5–6 (1970).

Ouchi, W. G. *Theory Z: How American Business Can Meet the Japanese Challenge*. Manila: Addison-Wesley, 1981.

Ozawa, T. *Multinationalism, Japanese Style—The Political Economy of Outward Dependency*. Princeton: Princeton University Press, 1979.

Panglaykim, J. *Japanese Direct Investment in ASEAN: The Indone-*

sian Experiences. Singapore: Marusen Asia, 1983.

Parsons, K. H., et al. *Land Tenure*. Wisconsin: University of Wisconsin Press, 1956.

Pascale, R. T., and A. G. Athos. *The Art of Japanese Management*. Harmondsworth: Penguin Books, 1981.

Passin, H. *Encounter with Japan*. Tokyo: Kodansha International, 1982.

Patrick, H., ed. *Japanese Industrialization and Its Social Consequences*. Berkeley: University of California Press, 1976.

Patrick, H., and H. Rosovsky, eds. *Asia's New Giant*. Washington, D.C.: Brookings Institution, 1976.

Piggott, R., and R. Robinson, eds. *Southeast Asia: Essays in the Political Economy of Structural Change*. London: Routledge & Kegan Paul, 1985.

Raper, A. F. "Some Effects of Land Reform in Thirteen Japanese Villages." *Journal of Farm Economics* 33 (1951).

Reischauer, E. O. *Japan Past and Present*. London: Duckworth, 1964.

Report by the Comptroller General of the United States: United States-Japan Trade—Issues and Problems. Washington, D.C.: General Accounting Office, 1979.

Rix, A. *Japan's Economic Aid*. London: Croom Helm, 1983.

Rothacher, A. *Economic Diplomacy Between the European Community and Japan, 1959–81*. London: Gower Publishing Co., 1983.

Saeki, N., and K. Shibagaki, eds. *Nihon keizai kenkyū nyūmon*. Tokyo: Tokyo Daigaku Shuppankai, 1972.

Said, E. *Orientalism*. New York: Pantheon Books, 1978.

Science and Technology Agency, Japan. *Kagaku gijutsu hakusho 1984*. Tokyo: Science and Technology Agency, 1984.

Shibagaki, K., ed. *Sekai no naka no Nihon shihonshugi*. Tokyo: Tōyō Keizai Shimposha, 1980.

Sinha, R. *Japan's Options for the 1980s*. Tokyo: Charles E. Tuttle, 1982.

Small and Medium Enterprises Agency, Japan. *Chūshō Kigyō Hakusho 1982*. Tokyo: Small and Medium Enterprises Agency, 1982.

Soedjatmoko, *Kaihatsu to jiyū*. Tokyo: Saimaru Shuppan, 1980.

Subcommittee on Trade, Committee on Ways and Means, U.S. House of Representatives. *United States–Japan Trade Report*.

Washington, D.C.: Government Printing Office, 1980.

Sugimoto, S., ed. *Gendai shihonshugi no sekai kōzō*. Tokyo: Ōtsuki Shoten, 1980.

Sumiya, T. *Nihon keizai to rokudai kigyō shudan: Gendai shihonshugi no shihai kōzō*. Tokyo: Shinhyōron, 1982.

————. *Sengo Nihon no kigyō keiei: "Nihon-teki keiei" to sono tenkai*. Tokyo: Chūō Keizaisha, 1983.

————. *Kokka to kigyō: Kiki no jidai to kagakuteki shakaishugi*. Kyoto: Mineruba Shobō, 1984.

Takahashi, A., et al., eds. *Daisan sekai to keizaigaku*. Tokyo: Tokyo Daigaku Shuppankai, 1982.

Takamiya, S., and K. Thurley, eds. *Japan's Emerging Multinationals: An International Comparison of Policies and Practices*. Tokyo: Tokyo University Press, 1985.

Tasca, D., ed. *U.S.-Japanese Economic Relations: Cooperation, Competition and Confrontation*. New York: Pergamon Press, 1980.

Tokita, Y. *Gendai shihonshugi to rōdōsha kaikyū*. Vol. 5 of *Gendai shihonshugi bunseki*. Tokyo: Iwanami Shoten, 1982.

Tokyo Round Study Group. *Tokyo Round kenkyū: Tokyo Round no zenbō*. Tokyo: Japan Tariff Association, 1980.

Tomioka, T. "Musume-san o hakkyō sareta ZD undō." *Keizai* (February 1966).

Tōyō Keizai Shimpōsha. *Kigyō keiretsu sōran 1984*. Tokyo: Tōyō Keizai Shimposha, 1983.

Tsuru, S., ed. *Growth and Resources: Problems Related to Japan—Proceedings of Session VI of the Fifth Congress of IEA Held in Tokyo, Japan*. London: Macmillan, 1980.

Tsurumi, Y. *The Japanese Are Coming: A Multinational Interaction of Firms and Politics*. Cambridge: Ballinger, 1976.

Uchino, T. *Japan's Postwar Economy: An Insider's View of its History and Future*. Tokyo: Kodansha International, 1978.

U.S. Department of Commerce. *Japan, the Government-Business Relationship: A Guide for American Businessmen*. Washington, D.C.: Department of Commerce.

Uno, K. *Principles of Political Economy: Theory of a Purely Capitalist Society*, tr. T. Sekine. Sussex: Harvester Press, 1980.

Vernon, R. *Two Hungry Giants—the United States and Japan in the Quest for Oil and Ores*. Cambridge: Harvard University Press, 1983.

Vogel, E. F. *Japan as Number One: Lessons for America*. Cambridge: Harvard University Press, 1979.

Watanabe, M. "Shōkō jieigyō fujin no shūrō to seikatsu no jittai." *Meiji daigaku shakaigaku kenkyūsho kiyō* 19.

Watanabe, T., ed. *Ajia kōgyōka no shinjidai*. Tokyo: Nihon Bōeki Shinkōkai, 1979.

Weiss, A. "Simple Truths of Japanese Manufacturing." *Harvard Business Review* (July/August 1984).

Wolf, M. J. *The Japanese Conspiracy*. Sevenoaks: New English Library, 1984.

Woronoff, J. *Japan: The Coming Economic Crisis*. Tokyo: Lotus Press, 1979.

———. *Japan's Commercial Empire*. Tokyo: Lotus Press, 1984. Armonk, N.Y.: M. E. Sharpe.

Yamaguchi, M. *Keizai to kagaku*. Tokyo: Aoki Shoten, 1975.

Yamamura, K., ed. *Policy and Trade Issues of the Japanese Economy, American and Japanese Perspectives*. Tokyo: University of Tokyo Press, 1982.

Yoshihara, K. *Japanese Economic Development: A Short Introduction*. Oxford: Oxford University Press, 1979.

———. *Japanese Investment in Southeast Asia*. Honolulu: University of Hawaii Press, 1978.

———. *Sogo Shosha: The Vanguard of the Japanese Economy*. Oxford: Oxford University Press, 1983.

Young, A. K. *Sogo Shosha: Japan's Multinational Trading Companies*. Boulder: Westview Press, 1979.

Index